ADVANCES IN
C-SPAN
ARCHIVES

ADVANCES IN RESEARCH USING THE
C-SPAN
ARCHIVES

edited by
Robert X. Browning

Purdue University Press, West Lafayette, Indiana

Cataloging-in-Publication data available from the Library of Congress.

Paper ISBN: 978-1-55753-762-1
ePDF ISBN: 978-1-61249-476-0
ePUB ISBN: 978-1-61249-477-7
Knowledge Unlatched ISBN: 978-1-55753-787-4

To Barbara Hinckley
and
Ira Sharkansky

Extraordinary professors and mentors both.

CONTENTS

FOREWORD

I was one of those geeky teenagers who watched C-SPAN. There are probably more of us out there than who will admit to it. Although I enjoyed watching a good congressional debate, what I really enjoyed was C-SPAN's coverage of the campaign trail. I was exhilarated when C-SPAN would clip a microphone to a presidential candidate and let me "ride along" as he (and occasionally she) shook hands with voters in a donut shop in New Hampshire or in a pizza place in Wisconsin. Growing up in Iowa, I especially recall watching residents of my home state gather at middle schools to participate in caucus meetings, and I recall watching the luminaries in the Democratic Party gather in a farm field for Senator Tom Harkin's Steak Fry. My interest in campaigns turned into an academic career, and I now publish extensively in the area of political communication, focusing on how campaigns target their appeals to various types of voters, often times through their political advertising.

When Robert Browning created the C-SPAN Video Library almost 30 years ago, he certainly made the lives of teens who geek out on politics a lot brighter, but he did so much more. First, he provided a vast data resource for those who study American politics. Second, he provided an amazing tool for educators to use. There was one point in my teaching career when I would reach for a VHS tape with a yellowed label (recorded in 2000) in order to show my students what really happened at a presidential nominating caucus; today, of course, I can call up that same video online from Purdue. But most fundamentally, when Browning started the C-SPAN Video Library, he created a video history of American democracy. We can't thank him enough for his foresight.

The chapters in this edited collection are stellar examples of the types of research that can come out of the C-SPAN archive. The research questions posed—and answered—are varied, ranging from whether liberal and conservatives use those ideological labels differently in their speech (most definitely!) to whether men and women use different words in campaigns debates (no!) and how President Bill Clinton avoided blame during the Lewinsky scandal (through the smart use of rhetorical strategies). And the methods employed run the gamut, from content analysis to statistical modeling to rhetorical analysis. As I scholar, I was excited by all of the new insights I gained about American politics. As an educator, I was excited by the potential of assigning this volume to students in a research methods course, as it demonstrates how smart researchers can successfully take multiple approaches even when using the same data.

As we approach the thirtieth anniversary of the C-SPAN Video Library in 2017, it is important to celebrate the successes of the archive, to take stock of its current uses, and to plan for the future. There is no better way to do so than through the publication of this collection of essays. I trust that you, the reader, will enjoy it as much as I did. And now I must get back to the task of searching for some of those videos that so intrigued me in my younger days.

Travis N. Ridout
Thomas S. Foley Distinguished Professor of Government and Public Policy

PREFACE

The chapters in this third edition of the series on research using the C-SPAN Video Library are a diverse set. All these papers were initially presented at a conference at Purdue University in October, 2015. Scholars from communication and political science came together there to present their research and explore ways that the C-SPAN Video Library can be used to advance our understanding of interactions in communication and political science.

This diversity reflects the maturity of research in this third year of the conferences. Scholarship has advanced in that different researchers demonstrate a range of approaches from their disciplines as they grapple with similar underlying questions. Because the conferences are interdisciplinary, we should not be surprised to see such divergent approaches.

In these chapters, we find researchers using experimental research, content analysis, conversational analysis, detailed studies of facial movements, and language in debates. Readers looking to understand what methods can be used to explore the political phenomena will find them in this book. The unity comes from the common interests of the diverse approaches.

While the approaches may be diverse, the basic questions being asked have much in common. From public attitudes toward Congress, to congressional enactment of legislation, to characteristics of debate language, to how politicians react when in informal settings, these questions all deal with issues of our democratic process.

Jonathan Morris and Michael Joy open the volume seeking to understand more about the public perceptions of Congress. This experimental work teases out the underlying causes for these perceptions. Since Congress is televised, they use this opportunity to understand how conflict and partisanship affect public opinion toward Congress. Since our primary democratic institution remains so unpopular, we need to understand more about the basic causes. Morris and Joy provide that in their chapter.

The second chapter, by Theresa Castor, takes a very different approach. The question here is about congressional influence on Great Lakes water policy. Congressional influence on policy is a common theme in other chapters, but each author addresses the question differently. In Theresa Castor's chapter, her approach is based on a social construction perspective. It is a rich approach that looks at the framing of the issue by the participants.

Robert Kerr uses the C-SPAN Video Library to examine the rhetoric of liberals and conservatives. In a thought-provoking piece he searches the Video Library to find ways that liberal and conservative rhetoric surfaces in political debates. He finds that conservatives dominate the rhetoric and the branding, not only for conservatism, but for liberalism also.

In the chapter by Kropf and Grassett, we find an analysis of gender in U.S. Senate candidate debates. They analyze 942 debate statements from senatorial campaign debates in 2012 and 2014. They find no difference between word choice in debates between male and female candidates.

Stewart and Hall build on the previous work published in Volume 2 of this series by Bucy and Gong. They look at nonverbal and emotional expressions in presidential debates. Their work advances our understanding of appropriate and inappropriate facial displays during debates and gives us an understanding of the analysis of emotion.

Garcia's chapter is the first of two conversational analyses in this volume. The second is by Kurtis Miller. In her chapter, Garcia looks at President Bill Clinton's grand jury testimony. She uses a number of techniques to identify ways that the president evaded or redirected the question. According to Garcia, "These include evasive answering, reframing, reformulating, and extending or deviating from the answering role." She speculates that President Clinton's success in evading blame and his high approval rating may be a result of these techniques.

The chapter by Brown and Gershon is another insightful analysis of congressional behavior in the passage of an important piece of legislation. They analyze the Violence Against Women Act in the 112th Congress. They find that congresswomen dominated the debate, providing an opportunity to compare the statements of Democratic and Republican women. One important conclusion that they reach is that "by examining the content of the bill and lawmakers' articulation of the policy, we soon learn that descriptive representation does not necessarily lead to substantive representation."

Kurtis Miller uses conversational analysis to look at candidate "meet-and-greet" appearances. These "How are you?" sessions are made possible by C-SPAN putting wireless microphones on candidates as they work their way through political crowds. Miller captures the essence of these exchanges by political candidates. These introductions we learn are different from other kinds of introductions. He observes also that "candidates engaging in working the crowd will often have to shift between interactions with general crowd members and interactions with key persons and donors."

Collectively these chapters show the power of the C-SPAN Video Library to drive research on democratic processes. Whether it is congressional debates or candidate debates or formal and informal appearances before a grand jury or a crowd or even the use of liberal and conservative rhetoric, the authors in this volume have found data for their research questions in the Video Library. Each has taken a slightly different research strategy. Perhaps some may think the volume covers an eclectic set of questions, but historically that is what the Video Library reveals. Each scholar can cull data from the collection and together help us advance a diverse research agenda, as the title of this volume suggests.

ACKNOWLEDGMENTS

No book like this comes together without a great deal of help. Of course, it all starts with the C-SPAN Video Library, which is now approaching 30 years of existence and 230,000 hours of indexed, transcribed digital content. It grew out of a conversation with C-SPAN founder and Purdue University graduate Brian Lamb about how C-SPAN could be used in teaching and research. I created the C-SPAN Archives with the help of my colleague and dean David A. Caputo. With this publication of the third volume in the Purdue University Press C-SPAN Series, we continue to demonstrate how we have achieved that goal.

The C-SPAN Board of Directors made a commitment to ensure that the C-SPAN Video Library was digital, free, and accessible to the public.

This book contains the proceedings of our third research conference, this one held at Purdue University in October, 2015. Nita Stickrod of my staff and Stephanie Botkin of Purdue University ably coordinated the details of that conference in which the contributors of this book first came together to discuss their research using C-SPAN video. Alan Cloutier and Steve Strother, both managers of the Archives, helped with all the behind-the-scenes details such as the database management and the recording and archiving. They were assisted by Kevin Ingle, Matt Long, Josh Tamlin, and Gary Daugherty along with Archives catalogers Karen Adams, Martha Lempke, and Martin Swoverland.

Purdue University colleagues Dean David Reingold, Professor Rosie Clawson, Professor Marifran Mattson, Fara Stalker, and Katie Pechin also assisted. Purdue President Mitch Daniels provided sponsorship funds to help with the conference. In addition, he hosted an interview with former Congressman Lee Hamilton and a dinner honoring Hamilton at the conference.

Peter Froehlich, the director of Purdue University Press and Scholarly Publishing, has been an enthusiastic supporter of this series, as is series coeditor Patrice Buzzanell, an encouraging behind-the-scenes advocate. Managers Katherine Purple and Bryan Shaffer make the book reality. Michael Topping provided skillful copyediting.

Finally, this book is dedicated to my two graduate school professors at the University of Wisconsin who mentored me in my studies, helped me learn to research and write, and were always available for advice, counsel, and friendship. Thanks, Barbara and Ira.

Robert X. Browning, Editor
Summer 2016

CHAPTER **1**

CONGRESSIONAL PROCESS AND PUBLIC OPINION TOWARD CONGRESS: AN EXPERIMENTAL ANALYSIS USING THE C-SPAN VIDEO LIBRARY

Jonathan S. Morris and Michael W. Joy

Congress is consistently the least popular branch of government. Nearly a half century ago Ralph Nader called Congress "the broken branch," and that perception has held firm among the public and the media. Even individual members of Congress take care to distance themselves from the chronically disliked institution by running against the Congress. Scholars have examined a number of factors that have been linked to low mass approval of Congress, including negative reactions to congressional policies (Davidson & Parker, 1972; Fenno, 1975; Parker, 1981; Ramirez, 2013), the state of the president's popularity (Patterson & Caldeira, 1990), and public perceptions of the current state of the economy (Durr, Gilmour, & Wolbrecht, 1997; Ramirez, 2013).

Research has also tied low public approval of Congress to the inability of the membership to live up to the public's overall expectations (Kimball & Patterson, 1997) and the institution's tendency to engage in largely unpopular—although democratic—political processes, such as extensive debate, excessive partisanship, conflict, and compromise (Binder, 2003, 2015; Doherty, 2015; Durr, Gilmour, & Wolbrecht, 1997; Hibbing & Theiss-Morse, 1995, 2002; Mann & Ornstein, 2006, 2012; Ramirez, 2009; Sinclair, 2011). Also, recent computerized sentiment analysis has linked the decline of prosocial language on the floor to the erosion of congressional approval over time (Frimer, Aquino, Gerbauer, Zhu, & Oakes, 2015).

Outside the arena of policy and process, researchers have pointed at congressional scandals, involving one or more members of Congress, as a major factor in damaging the institution's reputation (Bowler & Karp, 2004; McDermott, Schwartz, & Valleho, 2015; Rozell, 1994; Sabato, Stencel, & Lichter, 2000).

The televised images of Congress in the media are of particular importance in understanding opinion regarding the institution's actions and behavior. While some Americans have experience dealing with their own congressional representatives (see Cain, Ferejohn, & Fiorina, 1987; Fenno, 1978; Mayhew, 1974), their impressions of the performance of the membership as a whole as well as the institution are grounded primarily in what they have seen on television (Arnold, 2004).

Since 1979, the Cable Satellite Public Affairs Network (C-SPAN) has provided gavel-to-gavel coverage of floor proceedings as well as coverage of congressional committee hearings and press events on television. The C-SPAN Video Library has captured all of this coverage and made it available for public use. The archive, along with its sophisticated online cataloging and indexing system, provides an unprecedented view into the institution of Congress (Browning, 2014; Frantzich & Sullivan, 1996). From a research perspective, C-SPAN's 30 years of archived congressional proceedings constitutes the most complete and publicly accessible accounting of government activity to date. While these data have been used to examine congressional activity and public opinion toward the institution (Morris, 2001; Morris & Witting, 2001), there is still much knowledge that can be gained from the valuable resources provided by the C-SPAN Video Library.

The intent of this project is to use the valuable resource of the C-SPAN Video Library to improve our understanding of how Americans react to Congress on television. Using the C-SPAN Video Library, we construct an experimental analysis that examines how subjects respond to congressional floor process in the House and Senate. The valuable search and editing tools provided by the C-SPAN Video Library provide a unique opportunity to investigate Congress experimentally—an approach which is seldom employed in congressional research.

Overall, our study is an exploration into the public's reaction to floor activity. Our exploration is grounded in the notion that not all floor activity is the same. Specifically, we focus on two different aspects of the legislative process on the floor: partisanship and legislative maneuvering. Our findings show that subjects react negatively to both types of processes, but the degree of these reactions differs. We discuss our findings in the context of how congressional actors can influence how the institution is perceived by the masses.

THE LEGISLATIVE PROCESS AND PUBLIC OPINION TOWARD CONGRESS

Unlike the presidency, the courts, and even nongovernmental institutions where the deliberative process takes place largely away from public view, the U.S. Congress and its proceedings are relatively wide-open for public display. On any given day on Capitol Hill, committee hearings are open to the public, hours of floor debate are captured on C-SPAN, and dozens of press conferences are held. All of these events work to make the congressional process a virtual open book.

From a public-opinion standpoint, however, this openness has consequences. Past research has claimed that the average American does not respond positively to the sight of gridlock, legislative red tape, or seemingly endless political debate (Binder, 2003, 2015; Hibbing & Theiss-Morse, 1995). On the contrary, many Americans often take delight at the thought of benevolent political leaders who take quick, decisive action for the public good (Altemeyer, 1988; Adorno, 1950; Hetherington & Weiler, 2009). Congress, however, was designed precisely to thwart such action. Thus, when Congress performs its constitutional role of meticulously debating political issues and events, the American public tends to respond negatively (Durr, Gilmour, & Wolbrecht, 1997). The institution was designed to promote extensive deliberation and factional conflict. This design makes Congress the most democratic institution in the national government. The research has found that Americans love the idea of democracy in theory, but do not like to see the process play out in action.

In short, the public has a lack of appreciation for the legislature's highly deliberative role in the American democratic process. Instead, Americans would prefer a *stealth democracy* where the political process is accessible yet hidden from the public's sight and left to trustworthy leaders (Hibbing & Theiss-Morse, 2002). Hibbing and Theiss-Morse (1995) sum up this popular perception:

> [Americans] dislike compromise and bargaining, they dislike committees and bureaucracy, they dislike political parties and interest groups, they dislike big salaries and big staffs, they dislike slowness and multiple stages, and they dislike debate and publicly hashing things out, referring to such actions as haggling or bickering. (18)

The degree to which the masses respond negatively to process has been debated. Many scholars argue that policy outcomes are the primary indicator of views toward Congress (Easton, 1965; Jones, 2013; Jones & McDermott, 2009; Wlezien & Carman, 2001). For instance, a recent study by Harbridge and Malhotra (2011) finds that public disdain for a bipartisan process is outweighed by individual-level partisan policy preferences. This reflects the larger notion that elite behavior does not have much influence on the views of the mass public (Fiorina, Abrams, & Pope, 2005).

On the other side of the argument, researchers contend that public reactions to legislative process can actually supersede the policy issues and the outcomes (Durr, Gilmour, & Wolbrecht, 1997; Hibbing & Theiss-Morse, 1995). Ramirez (2009) concluded that the public's desire to mitigate procedural partisan conflict among legislators is more important than the substance of policy actions. Harbridge and Malhotra (2011) find partisan conflict reduces public support for Congress, but also note that the partisan public responds favorably to their own representatives who act in a partisan manner.

Regardless of the degree to which public disdain for legislative process plays a role in shaping mass opinion of Congress, the evidence supports the notion that it is significant. However, what exactly is the legislative process, and how is it measured? While the definitions of the legislative process varies slightly, almost all contain the same core concepts. These concepts include open disagreement of competing interests, compromise, inefficiency, and some degree of adherence to procedural norms (Crick, 1992; Durr, Gilmour, & Wolbrecht, 1997; Hibbing & Theiss-Morse, 1995; Ramirez, 2009).

There is, however, a shortcoming in the current understanding of how legislative process is conceptualized and measured. Specifically, the existing studies have not fully examined the notion that legislative process on the floor of Congress can vary dramatically. Hibbing and Theiss-Morse (1995, 2002) relied primarily on focus groups and cross-sectional survey data to show a general disdain for the process-related issues that are commonplace in Congress. Durr, Gilmour, and Wolbrecht (1997) used time-series analysis to show that mass support for Congress tends to drop when major legislation is under consideration on Capitol Hill. Their measurement of process, however, was dependent on the number of major bills under consideration in Congress, as well as the number of presidential vetoes and subsequent veto overrides. The assumption was that process issues are visible to the American public during times of action on major legislation. When there is no major legislation under consideration, the assumption was that process issues are off the American public's radar screen. Ramirez (2009) relied strictly on the number of partisan-oriented votes in Congress to determine the visibility of process to the masses.

However, the legislative process in not monolithic, and thus should not be conceptualized or measured as such. Legislative conflict on the floor is not the same as the procedural wrangling that is discussion of committee hearings, markups, and amendments. Who is to say the public's response would be uniform? The most significant shortcoming of earlier studies on public reactions to process is that the nature of the legislative process had been somewhat oversimplified. Likewise, generalizations regarding the public's reaction to process may have been oversimplified as well. A more detailed examination of the specific elements of legislative process in Congress may provide greater understanding of how the American public reacts. Because the research into this topic has mostly examined aggregate opinion of the legislative process, we lack more detailed analysis at the individual level.

We thus propose to examine two unique aspects of the legislative process on the floor of the United States Congress: conflict between parties and legislative maneuvering. While it is clear that conventional wisdom suggests both of these process elements prompt negative responses from the public, they deserve to be examined separately. Likewise, a comparison is warranted. While conflict and legislative maneuvering have been conflated, some content-analysis research suggests that the media cover these process

elements differently (Morris & Clawson, 2005). Specifically, legislative maneuvering is more prevalent in mainstream media coverage (70%) than partisan conflict (33%, categories not mutually exclusive). These elements certainly overlap with frequency, but they are often presented to the masses in
different contexts.

Based on the preceding discussion, our intent is to explore the effect of
exposure to congressional partisan conflict as well the effect of exposure to
legislative maneuvering. We will investigate how individuals respond to these
process elements singularly, and we will examine responses to both elements
simultaneously. In the section below, we discuss how we collected samples of
congressional partisan conflict and legislative maneuvering from C-SPAN.
We will then discuss how these samples were used in a controlled online experiment.

CAPTURING PARTISAN CONFLICT AND LEGISLATIVE MANEUVERING ON C-SPAN

The public availability of video from the C-SPAN Video Library allows the
ability to search through congressional floor debate. The indexing tool within
each day of coverage allows the ability to search for specific types of floor action, including amendments, motions, and references to committee reports.
The same tool also allows the ability to locate usage of unconstrained floor
time, which includes one-minute speeches, five-minute speeches, and special
orders. Using these tools, we were able to locate an array of floor behavior that
exemplified both partisan conflict and legislative maneuvering. The C-SPAN
Video Library clipping feature also allows selected video to be captured and
downloaded for editing. This gave us the opportunity to peruse a wide array of
coverage that typifies both partisan conflict and legislative maneuvering. The
sophistication of these online search and editing tools provides researchers
a unique ability to acquire footage of the congressional institution in many
forms. Certainly, this is ideal for experimental analysis of Congress—an area
of research that borders on nonexistent.

From these scores of selected clips, we first settled on six partisan speeches
from unconstrained floor time in the U.S. House of Representatives—three
from the Republicans and three from the Democrats. These speeches constituted the conflict element of legislative process. Combined, these clips

were 6 minutes and 34 seconds long. In order to control for variations in the demographics of the speakers, we chose to use only clips of White males. Additionally, we chose speeches delivered from the well of the House floor, thus allowing for similar camera angles. Finally, we controlled for substance by including speeches that only spoke of pending budget legislation offered by the House Republicans and Democrats. Below is a transcript of a sample partisan conflict video:

> Mr. Speaker, today Americans are working more and earning less. The cost of college is rising, young people are in debt and America's infrastructure is in decay. Mr. Speaker, the Republican budget does nothing to help struggling Americans, it gives tax breaks to the wealthy, ends the Medicare guarantee, makes it harder for Americans to buy a home, and cuts funding for education. Our military leaders even testified that the Republican budget will put the lives of our men and woman in uniform at risk. Mr. Speaker, this is outrageous, the American people elected us, we owe them to pass a budget that addresses their needs, keeps them safe, and gives them the best opportunity possible to live the American dream. Let's focus on creating good-paying jobs, providing universal pre-K, and restoring food stamps programs that have helped many American families through these tough times, and let's ensure that our military has the resources they need to make sure they can fight the fight that America wants. Democrats will keep standing with the American people and do the job they were elected to do on behalf of the American people.

Second, we selected three separate clips of members of Congress discussing legislative maneuvering. These clips made little reference to substantive policy issues. Instead, these were discussions from both the House and Senate floor that were procedural in nature. There was no mention of partisanship, either. The only evidence of partisanship was in the "R" or "D" attached to the name of the speaker on the bottom of the screen. Similarly, policy was only mentioned in the title of the bills and reports discussed. As was the case with the partisan-conflict video, this video contained only White male speakers. In total, the video was 5 minutes and 18 seconds in length. See the following excerpt:

Mr. Speaker, for the purpose of debate only I yield the customary thirty minutes to the gentlewoman from New York, Ms. Slaughter. I yield myself such time as I may consume, and ask unanimous consent to revise and extend my remarks and insert extraneous material in the record.

Speaker: Without objection, so ordered.

During consideration of the resolution, all time is yielded for the purpose of debate only. Last night the Rules Committee met and granted a modified closed rule for H.R. 10, the Comprehensive Retirement Security and Pension Reform Act of 2001. The rule provides for ninety minutes of general debate, with sixty minutes equally divided and controlled by the chairman and the ranking member of the Committee on Ways and Means, and thirty minutes equally divided and controlled by the Chairman and Ranking Member of the Committee on Education and the Work Force. Additionally, the rule waives all points of order against consideration of the bill, and against consideration of the amendment printed in the report. The rule provides that in lieu of the amendments recommended by the Committee on Ways and Means and the Committee on Education of the Work Force, the amendment in the nature of a substitute printed in the *Congressional Record* and numbered one shall be considered as adopted. The rule also provides for consideration of the amendment in the nature of a substitute printed in the rules committee report. If offered by Representative Rangel or his designee, which shall be considered as read and separately debatable for one hour equally divided and controlled by a proponent and an opponent. Finally the rule provides for one motion to recommit with or without instructions.

A third video was constructed as an abbreviated compilation of the preceding videos. This contained four of the six partisan videos (two Democrats, two Republicans) and half of the process-element videos. This clip was 8 minutes long. Each of the three videos can be viewed as edited at the following web locations: http://www.politicalresearchlab.org/clip1.html; http://www.political researchlab.org/clip2.html; and http://www.politicalresearchlab.org/clip3.html

RESEARCH DESIGN AND METHODS

We used the three videos discussed above to create posttest-only control group experimental analysis, in which subjects watched a video and took a brief on-line posttest questionnaire. Condition One was partisan conflict, Condition Two was legislative maneuvering, and Condition Three was a combination of partisanship and maneuvering. The fourth condition is a control group.

Subjects were recruited into the experimental pool via Amazon.com's Mechanical Turk, which allows requesters (in this case the researchers) to hire workers (in this case the subjects) to complete short tasks, typically for minimal fees. This service has become popular among experimental social scientists for the purpose of subject recruitment beyond the typical usage of voluntary student subjects. While this subject pool lacks the generalizability of randomly selected participants, research has suggested that Mechanical Turk's samples "will often be more diverse than [other] convenience samples and will always be more diverse than student samples" (Berinsky, Huber, & Lenz, 2012, p. 361; see also Paolacci, Chandler, & Ipeirotis, 2010).

Our subjects were paid $0.50 each for participation in the experiment, and randomly assigned to one of the four conditions. To control for validity, subjects were only permitted to participate a single time in a single condition. Additionally, in order to ensure that subjects assigned to Conditions One through Three actually did experience the experimental stimuli (the video in full), we included two filter questions on the posttest questionnaire. The first question asked, "Where was the video you just watched taking place?" Response options included a sporting event, a music concert, Congress, or a farm equipment convention. Subjects who answered incorrectly were excluded from participation. The second filter question was tied to the content of the videos. Specifically, the last few seconds of the video showed a screen shot that said, "Remember this number: 12." In the survey, subjects were asked, "Which number was shown at the end of the video you just watched?" Subjects who answered incorrectly had the option to go back and watch the video again, and were allowed to continue if they got the question correct on the next chance. In order to prevent subjects from skipping to the end of each video, the videos were posted using technology that prevented subjects from simply skipping to the end and observing the number. In short, we did all we could in order to make certain the subjects did indeed watch the videos they were assigned to watch.

The primary independent variable was the experimental condition to which the subjects were exposed. Additional independent variables were collected from the posttest survey as well. These variables included age, race, gender, education, income, and partisan identification. See the Appendix to this chapter for measurement details.

Multiple dependent variables were collected as well. The first was a general question that assessed the subjects' perception of Congress as a whole: "On a scale of 1–10, how do you feel about the U.S. Congress? The higher the number, the more favorably you feel toward the U.S. Congress. The lower the number, the less favorably you feel toward the U.S. Congress. An answer of 5 would indicate you feel neither favorably nor unfavorably toward the U.S. Congress. Click the number that best corresponds to your feelings." The second set of dependent variables was collected by asking respondents to agree or disagree with a number of statements about Congress, congressional parties, and the ability of the parties and factions in Congress to work together (1 = strongly disagree; 2 = somewhat disagree; 3 = neither agree nor disagree; 4 = somewhat agree; 5 = strongly agree). These statements are listed in the Appendix to this chapter. In the following section, we outline the findings from our experiment and discuss the results.

FINDINGS

Table 1.1 displays a set of ordinary least squares regressions in which the dependent variables are thermometer scores toward Congress, President Obama, the Democratic Party, and the Republican Party (1 to 10 scale). These models were run only on the control group, and use the following basic predictors of approval: party identification, gender, education, income, ideology, race and age. Unlike feelings toward the president, the Democrats, and the Republicans, it is clear that feelings toward Congress are much less predictable. None of the standard predictors are statistically significant, not even partisan identification or ideology—even though Republicans control both chambers. The low adjusted R-squared (.07) compared to the others illustrates this point.

In order to examine the effect of the experimental stimuli on feelings toward Congress, variables for Condition 1, 2, and 3 were added into the model for Congress. Each condition was generated as a dummy variable in which 1 =

Table 1.1 Thermometer Scores (1–10) Control Group Only

Variable	Congress	President Obama	Democratic Party	Republican Party
Party ID	-.22 (.17)	-.83 (.17)**	-.98 (.16)**	.57 (.15)**
Male	-1.14 (.33)**	-.15 (.33)	-.73 (.31)*	-.57 (.29)
Education	.07 (.14)	.06 (.14)	-.09 (.13)	.12 (.13)
Income	.08 (.07)	.22 (.07)**	.16 (.07)*	.04 (.06)
Conservative/Liberal	-.44 (.26)	.72 (.25)**	.29 (.24)	-.79 (.22)**
White	.10 (.47)	-.71 (.46)	.35 (.43)	.08 (.41)
Age	-.02 (.01)	-.00 (.01)	-.00 (.01)	-.03 (.01)
Constant	6.67 (1.59)**	5.60 (1.56)**	7.73 (1.46)**	4.60 (1.39)**
N	172	172	172	172
Adj. *R*-Squared	.07	.53	.51	.48

Note: Cell entries are ordinary least squares coefficients with standard errors in parentheses. *p ≤ .05, **p ≤ .01 (two-tailed)

Table 1.2 Thermometer Scores Toward Congress by Experimental Condition

Variable	Thermometer Score (1–10)
Partisan Condition	-.01(.23)
Legislative Maneuvering	.17(.23)
Combination	.07(.23)
Party ID	-.10(.08)
Male	-.64(.16)**
Education	-.07(.07)
Income	.02(.04)
Conservative/Liberal	-.31(.13)*
White	-.38(.21)
Age	-.02(.01)*
Constant	6.54(.82)*
N	694
Adj. *R*-Squared	.04

Note: Cell entries are ordinary least squares coefficients with standard errors in parentheses. *p ≤ .05, **p ≤ .01 (two-tailed)

exposure to that condition and 0 = no exposure to that condition. The control condition is the excluded category in the regression. Table 1.2 displays the results. These results show conclusively that neither exposure to partisan conflict nor legislative maneuvering significantly influenced the dependent variable of feelings toward Congress. Table 1.3 confirms these null results in an ordered logistic regression model in which overall approval for Congress was the dependent variable (1 = strongly disapprove; 2 = somewhat disapprove; 3 = neither approve nor disapprove; 4 = somewhat approve; 5 = strongly approve).

Table 1.3 Overall Approval for Congress by Experimental Condition

Variable	Approval
Partisan Condition	-.12(.20)
Legislative Maneuvering	.06(.20)
Combination	-11(.21)
Party ID	.02(.07)
Male	-.59(.15)**
Education	-.01(.06)
Income	.00(.03)
Conserv./Liberal	-.17(.11)
White	-.45(.19)*
age	-.02(.01)***
N	694
Constant 1	-2.60
Constant 2	-.88
Constant 3	.16
Constant 4	2.39
Chi-Squared	47.11
Log Likelihood	-853.61

Note: Cell entries are ordered logit coefficients with standard errors in parentheses. *$p \leq .05$, ** $p \leq .01$ (two-tailed)

What about perceptions of the ability of congressional factions to work together in Washington? Did the experimental stimuli have an influence? We address this question by asking respondents in the posttest to disagree or agree with the following statements: (1) "I believe that the liberals and conservatives in Congress can put aside their differences to do what is best for

America," (2) "The liberals in Congress don't seem willing to work with the conservatives," and (3) "The conservatives in Congress don't seem willing to work with liberals" (1 = strongly disagree; 2 = somewhat disagree; 3 = neither agree nor disagree; 4 = somewhat agree; 5 = strongly agree). These items were regressed against exposure to experimental condition and the control variables in an ordered logit analysis. The results are presented in Table 1.4. As it can be seen, the experimental stimuli did not significantly influence perceptions of the two sides of Congress to work together.

Table 1.4 Perceptions of Cooperation and Government

Variable	Agree With Statement (1 = strongly disagree . . . 5 = strongly agree)		
	Liberals and conservatives can put disagreements aside	Liberals in Congress don't seem willing to work with conservatives	Conservatives in Congress don't seem willing to work with liberals
Conflict	.04(.19)	-.08(.20)	.02(.20)
Legislative Maneuvering	.24(.20)	.08(.20)	-.09(.21)
Both	.17(.20)	-.21(.20)	-.11(.21)
Knowledge	-.08(.05)	.02(.04)	.16(.05)**
Party ID	-.06(.07)	.30(.07)**	-.06(.08)
Male	-.41(.14)**	-.14(.15)	-.05(.15)
Education	-.08(.06)	-.06(.07)	.00(.07)
Income	.02(.03)	-.02(.04)	.03(.04)
Conservative/Liberal	-.01(.11)	-.62(.12)**	.45(.12)**
White	-.45(.18)*	.22(.18)	.60(.19)**
Age	.01(.01)	.00(.01)	.00(.01)
N	694	694	694
Constant 1	-2.59	-3.96	-1.38
Constant 2	-1.28	-2.48	.21
Constant 3	-.56	-1.68	1.25
Constant 4	.85	.00	2.77
Chi-Squared	29.18**	235.12**	81.49**
Log Likelihood	-1,080.45	-952.58	-854.84

Note: Cell entries are logit coefficients with standard errors in parentheses. *p ≤ .05, **p ≤ .01 (two-tailed)

Overall, the results from the first set of analyses reported in Tables 1.1 through 1.4 indicate that exposure to congressional partisan conflict and legislative maneuvering do not significantly impact perceptions of Congress as a whole or the perception of the ability of the membership to work together. But were there other reactions that shed light on the differential reactions to congressional partisanship versus legislative maneuvering? The findings from Table 1.5 demonstrate how exposure to the experimental stimuli influenced individuals' perception of their own understanding of politics and government, also referred to as internal political efficacy (Niemi, Craig, & Mattei, 1991). The results clearly show that partisan conflict has no effect on internal efficacy, but the legislative-maneuvering condition has a significant negative impact. That is, individuals who witnessed legislative maneuvering were much more likely to agree that "sometimes politics and government seem so complicated that a person like me can't really understand what's happening." Also, the combination of legislative maneuvering and partisan conflict has the same effect, but to a lesser extent.

While internal political efficacy is an individual's perception of the individual's ability to comprehend politics, external political efficacy is the perception of how political figures react to them (Craig, Niemi, & Silver, 1990). In other words, how responsive does an individual feel governmental figures are to the individual's own wishes? In order to measure this concept, we included two items in the posttest that asked subjects to agree or disagree with statements about members of Congress. The first statement read, "I don't think members of Congress care much what people like me think," and the second read, "People like me don't have any say about what Congress does" (1 = strongly disagree; 2 = somewhat disagree; 3 = neither agree nor disagree; 4 = somewhat agree; and 5 = strongly agree). We combined these two responses to create an additive index ranging from 2 to 10. Due to the nature of the measurement, higher values reflected lower levels of external efficacy toward Congress. For ease of interpretation, we reversed the coding so that 2 = lowest external efficacy and 10 = highest external efficacy.

Table 1.6 illustrates the effect of our experimental stimuli on external efficacy toward Congress. If we relax our expectation of statistical significance to $p \leq .10$, it can be seen that there appears to be a positive effect when it comes to exposure to partisan conflict and the combination of partisan conflict and legislative maneuvering. In other words, individuals who witnessed partisan

Table 1.5 Internal Political Efficacy

Variable	Agree That Politics and Government Seem Complicated (1 = strongly disagree . . . 5 = strongly agree)
Conflict	.09(.19)
Legislative Maneuvering	1.13(.20)**
Both	.49(.20)*
Knowledge	-.32(.05)**
Party ID	-.01(.07)
Male	-.54(.14)**
Education	-.08(.06)
Income	.07(.03)*
Conservative/Liberal	-.07(.11)
White	-.21(.19)
Age	.01(.01)*
N	694
Constant 1	-2.79
Constant 2	-1.36
Constant 3	-.80
Constant 4	.97
Chi-Squared	117.89**
Log Likelihood	-1,015.77

Note: Cell entries are ordered logit coefficients with standard errors in parentheses.
*$p \leq .05$, **$p \leq .01$ (two-tailed)

conflict were less cynical about the responsiveness of Congress than those in the control group. The legislative-maneuvering condition, however, failed to reach statistical significance, again illustrating a differential impact across different elements of legislative process.

Were there other differential emotional responses to the experimental stimuli? The findings from Table 1.7 strongly suggest that there is a significant difference. Each participant in Conditions 1 through 3 was asked to report how the videos of Congress made them feel. The response options were (a) interested, (b) uninterested, (c) frustrated, (d) angry, (e) happy, and (f) none of the above. Subjects were permitted to click as many feelings that applied. Table 1.7 shows the effects of the partisan conflict on emotions relative to legislative maneuvering,

Table 1.6 External Political Efficacy

Variable	External Efficacy (2 = lowest . . . 10 = highest)
Conflict	.39(.22)*
Legislative Maneuvering	.36(.22)
Both	.41(.22)*
Knowledge	-.02(.05)
Party ID	-.14(.08)*
Male	-.22(.16)
Education	.01(.07)
Income	.06(.04)
Conservative/Liberal	-.26(.12)**
White	-.38(.21)*
Age	-.00(.01)
Constant	5.72(.79)**
N	694
Adj. R-Squared	.01

Note: Cell entries are ordinary least squares regression coefficients with standard errors in parentheses. $*p \leq .10$, $**p \leq .01$ (two-tailed)

Table 1.7 Emotional Responses to Clips (Partisan-Conflict and Legislative-Maneuvering Groups Only)

Variable	Interested	Uninterested	Frustrated	Angry
Conflict	1.14(.26)**	-2.14(.28)**	1.41(.25)**	1.45(.37)**
Party ID	-.22(.14)	.50(.14)**	-.04(.13)	-.10(.18)
Male	.23(.25)	-.25(.26)	-.29(.24)	.83(.33)*
Education	-.04(.11)	.04(.11)	.16(.11)	.06(.15)
Income	-.10(.06)	.01(.07)	.02(.06)	-.05(.08)
Conservative/Liberal	-.05(.21)	.45(.22)*	.07(.19)	.14(.14)
White	-.45(.30)	.11(.33)	.43(.31)	.42(.42)
Age	-.00(.01)	-.05(.01)	.03(.01)	-.00(.01)
Constant	.57(1.42)	-.94(1.46)	-3.46(1.34)**	-3.64(1.89)
N	349	349	349	349
Chi-Squared	39.40**	99.36**	46.23**	33.61**
Log Likelihood	-199.32	-187.55	-215.88	-131.84

Note: Cell entries are logit coefficients with standard errors in parentheses. $*p \leq .05$, $**p \leq .01$ (two-tailed)

which is the excluded category. The combination condition and the control group were dropped from this analysis. Note that "happy" and "none of the above" are not included due to the extreme rarity of that response (only three respondents reported feeling happy or none of the above). They demonstrate starkly different emotional reactions. In short, partisan conflict drew much more interest from the subjects than legislative maneuvering. At the same time, partisan conflict was significantly more likely to arouse frustration and anger among viewers.

CONCLUSION

Our study contributes to the current understanding of public responses to Congress by exploring reactions to unique elements of the legislative process on the floor. Although perceptions of Congress as a whole are fairly stable in the face of exposure to congressional partisan conflict and legislative maneuvering on the floor of Congress, we discovered unique emotional responses. While it is not generally thought that exposure to Congress in action on C-SPAN would provoke emotion among viewers, our results suggest otherwise. Legislative maneuvering is associated with decreased external efficacy, but not internal efficacy. Exposure to partisan conflict, on the other hand, generates more interest among viewers and is tied to higher levels of external efficacy toward Congress. This is a compelling result in the context of our findings that exposure to the partisan-conflict condition of our experiment is also associated with much higher levels of anger and frustration.

The idea that exposure to partisanship on the House floor is tied to more positive views toward any aspect of Congress is in contrast to conventional wisdom on the topic (Durr, Gilmour, & Wolbrecht, 1997; Hibbing & Theiss-Morse, 1995; Ramirez, 2009). Why may this be the case? Perhaps the public is not entirely sure what it wants from government (Ladd, 1983, 1990). This, Everett Ladd argues, sets the stage for a "cognitive Madisonianism" among the masses, where conflict between tenacious actors with divergent views on the role of government is welcomed (1990). Individually, most Americans would decry the perils of a Congress mired in gridlock, but the public as a whole may have a more accommodating view on the matter. David Mayhew (1996) follows this logic and cautiously proposes the notion that Americans as a collective find partisan tension at the federal level comforting.

From this perspective, policy outcomes may not be as important to the public as the image that congressional actors are fulfilling their representative function by engaging in conflict. When conflict is less apparent to the public, larger stereotypes of a do-nothing Congress are more likely to take hold on the masses. As Hibbing and Theiss-Morse (2001) note, "People want decision making to be a balance between elected officials and ordinary people, but they think they are getting a process dominated by officeholders" (p. 152). In other words, a Congress devoid of conflict is a Congress in collusion with itself and the special interests. While it is unconventional to suggest that Congress may improve its image by conducting more vigorous partisan debate over the issues, our exploration warrants further study. We urge future researchers to at least take this possibility under consideration.

Furthermore, we wish to encourage greater usage of the C-SPAN Video Library as a resource. Experimental research is the key to gaining a more nuanced understanding of how the public feels about the United States Congress. The vast majority of work on public opinion toward Congress has relied on survey data. If we wish to understand the affective responses individuals have to Congress, further experimental studies should be employed. The C-SPAN Video Library is the most valuable resource available to researchers in this regard.

REFERENCES

Adorno, T. W. (1950). *The authoritarian personality*. New York, NY: Harper.

Altemeyer, B. (1988). *Enemies of freedom: Understanding right-wing authoritarianism*. San Francisco, CA: Jossey-Bass.

Arnold, R. D. (2004). *Congress, the press, and political accountability*. Princeton, NJ: Princeton University Press.

Binder, S. A. (2003). *Stalemate: Causes and consequences of legislative gridlock*. Washington, DC: Brookings.

Binder, S. A. (2015). The dysfunctional Congress. *Annual Review of Political Science, 18*, 85–101.

Bowler, S., & Karp, J. A. (2004). Politicians, scandals, and trust in government. *Political Behavior, 26*(3), 271–284.

Browning, R. X. (2014). The C-SPAN Video Archives: A case study. *The American Archivist, 77*, 425–443.

Cain, B., Ferejohn, J., & Fiorina, M. (1987). *The personal vote: Constituency service and electoral independence.* Cambridge, MA: Harvard University Press.

Craig, S. C., Niemi, R. G., & Silver, G. E. (1990). Political efficacy and trust: A report on the NES Pilot Study items. *Political Behavior, 12*(3), 289–314.

Crick, B. R. (1992). *In defense of politics* (4th ed.). Baltimore, MD: University of Chicago Press.

Davidson, R., & Parker, G. (1972). Positive support for political institutions: The Case of Congress. *Western Political Quarterly, 25*, 600–612.

Doherty, D. (2015). How policy and procedure shape citizens' evaluations of senators. *Legislative Quarterly, 40*(2), 241–272.

Durr, R. H., Gilmour, J. B., & Wolbrecht, C. (1997). Explaining congressional approval. *American Journal of Political Science, 41*, 175–207.

Easton, D. (1965). *A framework for political analysis.* Englewood Cliffs, NJ: Prentice-Hall.

Fenno, R. F., Jr. (1975). If, as Ralph Nader says, Congress is "the broken branch," How come we love our congressmen so much? In N. J. Ornstein (Ed.), *Congress in change: Evolution and reform.* New York, NY: Praeger.

Fenno, R. F., Jr. (1978). *Home style: House members in their districts.* Boston, MA: Little, Brown.

Fiorina, M. P., Abrams, S. J., & Pope, J. C. (2005). *Culture war? The myth of a polarized America.* New York, NY: Pearson Longman.

Frantzich, S. E., & Sullivan, J. (1996). *The C-SPAN revolution.* Norman: University of Oklahoma Press.

Frimer, J. A., Aquino, K., Gerbauer, J. E., Zhu, L., & Oakes, H. (2015). A decline in prosocial language helps explain public disapproval of the US Congress. *Proceedings of the National Academy of Sciences, 112*(21), 6591–6594.

Harbridge, L., & Malhotra, N. (2011). Electoral incentives and partisan conflict in Congress: Evidence from survey experiments. *American Journal of Political Science, 55*, 494–510.

Hetherington, M. J., & Weiler, J. D. (2009). *Authoritarianism and polarization in American politics.* New York, NY: Cambridge University Press.

Hibbing, J. R., & Theiss-Morse, E. (1995). *Congress as public enemy.* New York, NY: Cambridge University Press.

Hibbing, J. R., & Theiss-Morse, E. (2001). Process preferences and American politics: What the people want government to be. *American Political Science Review, 95*, 145–153.

Hibbing, J. R., & Theiss-Morse, E. (2002). *Stealth democracy: Americans' beliefs about how government should work*. New York, NY: Cambridge University Press.

Jones, D. R. (2013). Do major policy enactments affect public evaluations of Congress? The case of health care reform. *Legislative Studies Quarterly, 38*(2), 185–204.

Jones, D. R., & McDermott, M. L. (2009). *Americans, Congress, and democratic responsiveness: Public evaluations of Congress and electoral consequences*. Ann Arbor: University of Michigan Press.

Kimball, D. C., & Patterson, S. C. (1997). Living up to expectation: Public attitudes toward Congress. *Journal of Politics, 59*, 701–728.

Ladd, E. C. (1983, December/January). Politics in the '80s: An electorate at odds with itself. *Public Opinion, 5*, 4–6.

Ladd, E. C. (1990, Summer). Public opinion and the "Congress problem." *Public Interest, 100*, 57–67.

Mann, T. E., & Ornstein, N. J. (2006). *The broken branch: How Congress is failing America and how to get it back on track*. New York, NY: Oxford University Press.

Mann, T. E., & Ornstein, N. J. (2012). *It's even worse than it looks*. New York, NY: Basic Books.

Mayhew, D. (1974). *Congress: The electoral connection*. New Haven, CT: Yale University Press.

Mayhew, D. (1991). *Divided we govern: Party control, lawmaking, and investigations 1946–1990*. New Haven, CT: Yale University Press.

McDermott, M. L., Schwartz, D., & Vallejo, S. (2015). Talking the talk but not walking the walk: Public reactions to hypocrisy in political scandal. *American Politics Research, 43*(6), 952–974.

Morris, J. S. (2001). Reexamining the politics of talk: Partisan rhetoric in the 104th House. *Legislative Studies Quarterly, 26*, 101–122.

Morris, J. S., & Clawson, R. A. (2005). Media coverage of Congress in the 1990s: Scandals, personalities, and the prevalence of process. *Political Communication, 22*, 297–313.

Morris, J. S., & Witting, M. (2001). Congressional partisanship, bipartisanship and public opinion: An experimental analysis. *Politics & Policy, 29*(1), 47–67.

Niemi, R. G., Craig, S. C., & Mattei, F. (1991). Measuring internal political efficacy in the 1988 National Election Study. *American Political Science Review, 85*, 1407–1413.

Parker, G. (1981). Can Congress ever be a popular institution? In J. Cooper & G. C. Mackenzie (Eds.), *The House at work*. Austin: University of Texas Press.

Patterson, S. C., & Caldeira, G. A. (1990). Standing up for Congress: Variations in public esteem since the 1960s. *Legislative Studies Quarterly, 15*, 25–47.

Ramirez, M. D. (2009). The dynamics of partisan conflict on congressional approval. *American Journal of Political Science, 53*, 681–694.

Ramirez, M. D. (2013). The policy origins of congressional approval. *The Journal of Politics, 75*, 189–209.

Rozell, M. (1994). Press coverage of Congress, 1946–1992. In T. E. Mann & N. J. Ornstein (Eds.), *Congress, the press, and the public*. Washington, DC: American Enterprise Institute and the Brookings Institution.

Sabato, L. J., Stencel, M., & Lichter, S. R. (2000). *Peep show: Media and politics in an age of scandal*. Lanham, MD: Rowman & Littlefield.

Sinclair, B. (2011). *Unorthodox lawmaking: New legislative processes in the U.S. Congress* (4th ed.). Washington, DC: CQ Press.

Wlezien, C., & Carman, C. (2001). Ideological placements and political judgments of government institutions. *Public Opinion Quarterly, 65*, 550-561.

APPENDIX

Survey of Political Attitudes

As a part of a research project we are conducting a brief survey about political attitudes. We ask that you answer the following questions, which should take approximately 3–4 minutes. It is designed to be completely anonymous and confidential. Your participation is greatly appreciated.

1. Where was the video you just watched taking place?
    Sporting event
    Music concert
    The United States Congress (Correct)
    Farm equipment convention

2. How did the video you just watched make you feel?
Check as many feelings as you want.
    Interested
    Uninterested
    Frustrated
    Angry
    Happy
    None of the above

3. Which number was at the end of the video you just watched?
    57
    100
    25
    12 (Correct)

Please answer the following questions:

4. On a scale of 1–10, how do you feel about Barack Obama? The higher the number, the more favorably you feel toward Barack Obama. The lower the number, the less favorably you feel toward Barack Obama. An answer of 5 would indicate you feel neither favorably nor unfavorably toward Barack Obama. Click the number that best corresponds to your feelings.

	1	2	3	4	5	6	7	8	9	10	
Cold	O	O	O	O	O	O	O	O	O	O	Warm

5. On a scale of 1–10, how do you feel about the U.S. Congress? The higher the number, the more favorably you feel toward the U.S. Congress. The lower the number, the less favorably you feel toward the U.S. Congress. An answer of 5 would indicate you feel neither favorably nor unfavorably toward the U.S. Congress. Click the number that best corresponds to your feelings.

	1	2	3	4	5	6	7	8	9	10	
Cold	O	O	O	O	O	O	O	O	O	O	Warm

6. On a scale of 1–10, how do you feel about the Democratic Party? The higher the number, the more favorably you feel toward the Democratic Party. The lower the number, the less favorably you feel toward the Democratic Party. An answer of 5 would indicate you feel neither favorably nor unfavorably toward the Democratic Party. Click the number that best corresponds to your feelings.

	1	2	3	4	5	6	7	8	9	10	
Cold	O	O	O	O	O	O	O	O	O	O	Warm

7. On a scale of 1–10, how do you feel about the Republican Party? The higher the number, the more favorably you feel toward the Republican Party. The lower the number, the less favorably you feel toward the Republican Party. An answer of 5 would indicate you feel neither favorably nor unfavorably toward the Republican Party. Click the number that best corresponds to your feelings.

	1	2	3	4	5	6	7	8	9	10	
Cold	O	O	O	O	O	O	O	O	O	O	Warm

8. Generally speaking, do you consider yourself a Republican, a Democrat, an independent, or what?

    1 = Strong Democrat
    2 = Democrat
    3 = Independent leaning Democrat
    4 = Independent/Don't know/Apolitical
    5 = Independent leaning Republican
    6 = Republican
    7 = Strong Republican

9. Did you vote in the 2012 presidential election?

    1 = Yes
    2 = No
    3 = Don't remember

Please indicate whether you agree or disagree with the following statements. Check only one response for each statement.

10. I don't think members of Congress care much what people like me think.

    1 = Strongly Disagree
    2 = Somewhat Disagree
    3 = Neither Agree nor Disagree
    4 = Somewhat Agree
    5 = Strongly Agree

11. People like me don't have any say about what Congress does.

    1 = Strongly Disagree
    2 = Somewhat Disagree
    3 = Neither Agree nor Disagree
    4 = Somewhat Agree
    5 = Strongly Agree

12. Sometimes politics and government seem so complicated that a person like me can't really understand what's happening.
- 1 = Strongly Disagree
- 2 = Somewhat Disagree
- 3 = Neither Agree nor Disagree
- 4 = Somewhat Agree
- 5 = Strongly Agree

13. I believe that the liberals and conservatives in Congress can put aside their differences to do what is best for America.
- 1 = Strongly Disagree
- 2 = Somewhat Disagree
- 3 = Neither Agree nor Disagree
- 4 = Somewhat Agree
- 5 = Strongly Agree

14. The liberals in Congress don't seem willing to work with the conservatives.
- 1 = Strongly Disagree
- 2 = Somewhat Disagree
- 3 = Neither Agree nor Disagree
- 4 = Somewhat Agree
- 5 = Strongly Agree

15. The conservatives in Congress don't seem willing to work with the liberals.
- 1 = Strongly Disagree
- 2 = Somewhat Disagree
- 3 = Neither Agree nor Disagree
- 4 = Somewhat Agree
- 5 = Strongly Agree

16. The Democratic Party is too liberal.
- 1 = Strongly Disagree
- 2 = Somewhat Disagree
- 3 = Neither Agree nor Disagree
- 4 = Somewhat Agree
- 5 = Strongly Agree

17. The Republican Party is too conservative.
     1 = Strongly Disagree
     2 = Somewhat Disagree
     3 = Neither Agree nor Disagree
     4 = Somewhat Agree
     5 = Strongly Agree

Please indicate whether you agree or disagree with the following statements. Check only one response for each statement.

18. Liberals want to raise taxes on hard-working Americans and give it to lazy people who can't keep a job.
     1 = Strongly Disagree
     2 = Somewhat Disagree
     3 = Neither Agree nor Disagree
     4 = Somewhat Agree
     5 = Strongly Agree

19. Conservatives only care about the rich.
     1 = Strongly Disagree
     2 = Somewhat Disagree
     3 = Neither Agree nor Disagree
     4 = Somewhat Agree
     5 = Strongly Agree

20. I trust the media to cover political events fairly and accurately
     1 = Strongly Disagree
     2 = Somewhat Disagree
     3 = Neither Agree nor Disagree
     4 = Somewhat Agree
     5 = Strongly Agree

21. It is possible that I would vote for a presidential candidate from a political party different than my own.
    1 = Strongly Disagree
    2 = Somewhat Disagree
    3 = Neither Agree nor Disagree
    4 = Somewhat Agree
    5 = Strongly Agree

22. Congress is too heavily influenced by interest groups when making decisions.
    1 = Strongly Disagree
    2 = Somewhat Disagree
    3 = Neither Agree nor Disagree
    4 = Somewhat Agree
    5 = Strongly Agree

23. Members of Congress should do what their district wants them to even if they think it's a bad idea.
    1 = Strongly Disagree
    2 = Somewhat Disagree
    3 = Neither Agree nor Disagree
    4 = Somewhat Agree
    5 = Strongly Agree

For each of the following please indicate if you watch it, listen to it, or read it regularly, sometimes, hardly ever, or never.

24. Watch MSNBC?
    4 = Regularly
    3 = Sometimes
    2 = Hardly Ever
    1 = Never

25. Watch the Cable News Network (CNN)?
    4 = Regularly
    3 = Sometimes
    2 = Hardly Ever
    1 = Never

26. Watch the Fox News Channel?
    4 = Regularly
    3 = Sometimes
    2 = Hardly Ever
    1 = Never

27. Watch C-SPAN?
    4 = Regularly
    3 = Sometimes
    2 = Hardly Ever
    1 = Never

28. Read a daily newspaper?
    4 = Regularly
    3 = Sometimes
    2 = Hardly Ever
    1 = Never

Please answer the following questions:

29. Overall, do you approve or disapprove of the way Congress is handling its job?
    1 = Strongly Disapprove
    2 = Somewhat Disapprove
    3 = Neither Approve nor Disapprove
    4 = Somewhat Approve
    5 = Strongly Approve

30. Overall, how would you rate the ability of Congress to work with the president of the United States in passing laws?

    1 = Poor
    2 = Only Fair
    3 = Good
    4 = Excellent

31. Overall, how would you rate the job the federal government as a whole is doing?

    1 = Poor
    2 = Only Fair
    3 = Good
    4 = Excellent

Answer each of the following to the best of your ability:

32. Who is the Speaker of the U.S. House of Representatives?

    John Boehner (Correct)
    Steve Scalise
    Paul Ryan
    Barack Obama
    Nancy Pelosi
    Don't know

33. Do you know which party has a majority in the House and Senate of the U.S. Congress?

    Republicans (Correct)
    Democrats
    The Democrats control the House and the Republicans control the Senate
    The Republicans control the House and the Democrats control the Senate
    Don't know

34. Who is the Chairperson of the Federal Reserve Board?
    Joe Biden
    Richard Cheney
    Carly Fiorina
    John Kerry
    Janet Yellen (Correct)
    Don't know

35. Which of the following individuals is a Justice on the U.S. Supreme Court?
    John Roberts (Correct)
    Ben Carson
    Newt Gingrich
    Steny Hoyer
    John Kerry
    Don't know

36. Who is the Secretary of State?
    Joe Biden
    Ben Carson
    Ashton Carter
    Nancy Pelosi
    John Kerry (Correct)
    Don't know

37. What is your gender?
    0 = Female
    1 = Male

38. What is the last grade or class that you completed in school?
    1 = None, or grades 1–8
    2 = High school incomplete (grades 9–11)
    3 = High school graduate (grade 12 or GED certificate)
    4 = Technical, trade, or vocational school AFTER high school

5 = Some college, no 4-year degree (including associate degree)

6 = College graduate (B.S., B.A., or other 4-year degree)

7 = Postgraduate training or professional schooling after college (e.g., toward a master's degree or Ph.D.; law or medical school)

Missing = Don't know

39. Last year, that is in 2014, what was your total family income from all sources, before taxes?

1 = Less than $10,000

2 = $10,000 to under $20,000

3 = $20,000 to under $30,000

4 = $30,000 to under $40,000

5 = $40,000 to under $50,000

6 = $50,000 to under $75,000

7 = $75,000 to under $100,000

8 = $100,000 to under $150,000

9 = $150,000 or more

Missing = Don't know

40. In general, would you describe your political views as . . .

1 = Very Conservative

2 = Conservative

3 = Moderate/Don't know

4 = Liberal

5 = Very Liberal

41. How old are you?

42. What is your race?

1 = Caucasian

2 = African American

3 = Non-White Hispanic

4 = Asian

5 = Other

CHAPTER **2**

DISCURSIVELY CONSTRUCTING THE GREAT LAKES FRESHWATER

Theresa R. Castor

Freshwater resources and the protection of freshwater are becoming recognized as increasingly important as various parts of the world, including the U.S. Southwest, are experiencing drought conditions. The Great Lakes area of the United States provides an alternative picture given the abundance of freshwater in this area. The aforementioned drought conditions illustrate the significance of freshwater, and have called public attention to the delicate environmental and human-usage issues involved with the sustainable management of water resources (see Annin, 2009).

The Great Lakes of North America (hereafter, Great Lakes) consist of five lakes that are bordered by eight U.S. states and one Canadian province (Ontario). The Great Lakes Basin has an impressive set of freshwater statistics as the largest surface area of freshwater in the world, containing 90% of the U.S. supply and 18% of the world's supply of freshwater by volume, providing drinking water for 40 million people (National Oceanic and Atmospheric Administration, n.d.). To manage Great Lakes freshwater and to protect it from water diversions, in 2008 the U.S. Congress passed a piece of legislation known as the Great Lakes–St. Lawrence River Basin Water Resources Compact or, more informally, the Great Lakes Compact.[1] The Compact is an interstate, federally approved agreement that outlines regulations to prevent the diversion of water from the Great Lakes Basin area. The Compact is significant for protecting the Great Lakes, especially in light of current global concerns regarding freshwater availability and access.

Given the importance of the Compact as federally sanctioned law for Great Lakes freshwater management, the purpose of this project is to analyze congressional discourse related to the approval of the Compact. In doing so, I seek to analyze how, within this significant context, Great Lakes freshwater was discursively constructed as an exigency. In some ways, the approval of the Great Lakes Compact can be viewed as an example of *prospective sensemaking*, or making sense of a problem before it has actually occurred. In examining the Compact, I seek to provide insight into the proactive construction of or anticipation of a problem. In taking this lens, this analysis can aid in the understanding of how social actors may "see" (i.e., anticipate) a problem before it has occurred in order to take actions to avert rather than react to the problem.

The data for this project consist of transcripts from C-SPAN on the congressional discussions related to the Great Lakes and water diversion. This project utilizes a discourse analytic approach to examine how particular accounts discursively construct the Great Lakes and protection of their waters (see Buttny, 2004). This project is also based generally on a social construction perspective (see Bartesaghi & Castor, 2009; Galanes & Leeds-Hurwitz, 2009), and builds on the following assumptions:

1. Problems are discursively and socially constructed.
2. When speakers account for their choices, those accounts present particular constructions of problems, causes, and/or solutions.
3. Sensemaking about problems occurs in the process of accounting for a decision.

In the following sections, contextual information will be provided on the Great Lakes Compact and related legislation. Then, the aforementioned assumptions will be expanded upon and the specific research questions for this project presented. This will be followed by a description of the research methods and then presentation of the results of the project analysis.

CONTEXTUAL BACKGROUND

The five Great Lakes of North America are Lakes Michigan, Superior, Erie, Huron, and Ontario, and are bordered by eight U.S. states and one Canadian province. Containing approximately 21% of the world's surface freshwater and 84% of North America's surface freshwater (United States Environmental Protection Agency, 2015), they are an important source of water and an economic engine for the Great Lakes area. The Great Lakes are so vast that they are technically considered seas. The example of the Aral Sea disaster has been used as a cautionary tale to show what could happen if a water resource such as an inland sea is not carefully managed (Annin, 2009). Due to the diversion of water from the rivers that fed the Aral Sea, parts of this inland sea have been permanently transformed into desert.

The history of water management policy in North America is long, dating back to the 1909 Boundary Waters Treaty and the creation of the International Joint Commission to manage water disputes between the U.S. and Canada (Annin, 2009). Throughout the 20th century, a number of proposals were developed that involved diverting water from the Great Lakes; most of these were not successful, but nonetheless, were of significant concern for governors and residents in the Great Lakes area. While various water management policies were proposed to prevent diversion, "most of those measures have proven awkward and dysfunctional" (Annin, 2009, p. 19). Some functioned as agreements among the Great Lakes states and provinces with no ramifications for violation; others were rejected because they were viewed to not go far enough in protecting the Great Lakes (Annin, 2009).

The Great Lakes Compact, approved in 2008, is a legally binding interstate compact with regulations and guidelines on water management and water diversions from the Great Lakes. As an interstate compact, it is an agreement across specific states that allows for implementation and management at the state and regional levels rather than through a federal agency. However, it is enforced as federal law. The Compact was spurred in part in 1998 when a Canada-based company proposed to divert water from Lake Superior by bottling and shipping it to Asia (Schaper, 2008). The Compact prohibits diversions of Great Lakes water from the Great Lakes Basin.[2] As a compact, this policy document was initially approved by the state governments of each of the eight Great Lakes states and then introduced into Congress, where it went through relatively swiftly for final approval as public law by President George W. Bush on October 3, 2008.

DISCURSIVE CONSTRUCTION OF PROBLEMS

Rittel and Webber (1973) described two general types of problems: tame and wicked. A tame problem is one that can be easily analyzed and whose solution is easy to determine and implement. In contrast, a wicked problem is messy: it is difficult to analyze and the solution or solutions are not easy to determine and implement. Grint (2005) expanded on Rittel and Webber's typology by adding critical problems that appear as self-evident and call for quick decision making, such as a train crash or a fire emergency. Grint's key point was that problems are socially constructed in that the nature of a problem can shift. For example, a tame problem could become a wicked problem and vice versa. The Hurricane Katrina disaster illustrates this latter point: what initially was defined as a problem of a hurricane transformed into a wicked problem in the days, weeks, and months afterward as Hurricane Katrina exposed socioeconomic disparities and flaws in governmental coordination and municipal planning. In making this point, Grint highlighted the nature of problems as social constructions.

Focusing on a range of problems that include interpersonal as well as institutional interactions, Buttny (2004) illustrated how problems are interactively defined and discursively negotiated. Similarly, Scott and Trethewey (2008) analyzed discourse related to risk management and occupational hazards in a firefighting department. They found that risks, rather than being external, were discursively constructed.

Describing problems as socially constructed is not meant to imply that they are disconnected from material circumstances. For example, as Grint (2005) noted in considering the role of the environment in problem construction:

> As to the role of the environment in determining what leaders should do, we only have to consider the differing positions taken by leaders on the issue of global warming to know that, once again, the environment is not some objective variable that determines a response but rather an "issue" to be constituted into a whole variety of "problems" or "irrelevances." (p. 1470)

Grint's description of problem construction and the environment can be related to the Great Lakes. For example, water usage may be intended to solve one problem such as providing freshwater, but can cause other problems such as biosystem damage. How an event or situation is defined as a problem or not is part of a dynamic interplay of social, material, and discursive circumstances (see Murphy, 2004; Tracy & Muller, 2001).

ACCOUNTS AND PROBLEM CONSTRUCTION

Scott and Lyman (1968) defined an account as a linguistic device used by speakers when they are accused of wrongdoing. Other descriptions of accounts describe them more generally in terms of making actions intelligible to others (see Buttny & Morris, 2001). Common across these conceptualizations is the notion that accounts are utilized when an action, event, or situation is called into, or anticipated to be called into, question. The response to that questioning is an account. Within a congressional debate, speakers provide explanations for their choices and positions, and in this process, they provide accounts for their stance on a particular issue.

Accounts implicate agency in that they function to craft particular notions of who or what was responsible for an action; accounts also implicate social accountability in shaping notions of wrongdoing or morality (see Buttny, 1993; Shotter, 1984). Accounts are related to problem construction in that in the process of identifying a problem, one is essentially asking "what is going on here that should not be going on here?" The response to that inquiry is an account where a speaker could, among many possibilities, accept responsibility for the action, blame someone or something else, or deny that the event in question is problematic (Scott & Lyman, 1968).

Mills (1940) presented the concept of vocabulary of motives as relevant for understanding notions of causality and accounts. Mills recognized the significance of examining accounts beyond structure identification and in describing the content or substance of the account and how this mattered for a given group. Hence, he identified these as vocabulary of motives or key terms or phrases that interlocutors may invoke in the course of providing an account.

Accounts and social accountability are interrelated in that for an account to be accepted by a given community, the speaker must present the account in a way that appeals to the values and ideals of a given group (Buttny, 1993; Shotter, 1984). Shotter (1993) also highlighted how speakers must be rhetorically responsive to a given situation. Accounts are not a sole matter of logic, but of tapping into a community's sense of ethics as well as into the expectations of how to act and interact within a specific circumstance.

In a project that ties together these various themes of problem construction, accounts, and social accountability, Castor and Cooren (2006) described problem formulation as the process of selecting an agent in a chain of agencies, within the context of a university faculty governance meeting on a past crisis. They described how a problem is defined will depend on which agent is emphasized by interlocutors as more acting/active rather than acted upon. In other words, for a given problem, a matrix of influencing and influenced agents may be identified that act upon each other.

In applying an accounts analysis perspective to a discussion of Great Lakes water policy, I seek to examine how speakers present their stances on Great Lakes water. Speaker accounts can provide insight into issues such as how speakers define problems to be solved in association with Great Lakes water, who or what was responsible for these problems, who or what has the capacity to solve such problems. In addition, as noted above, accounts implicate social accountability and the ethics of a given community. Speaker accounts on the Great Lakes can provide insight regarding what actions are considered to be ethical in human actions toward the Great Lakes.

PROSPECTIVE SENSEMAKING AND ACCOUNTING

Sensemaking in its most basic definition refers to giving or making meaning of experience. This concept has been studied in many different areas such as organizational sensemaking (e.g., Weick, 1995), communication and information processing (e.g., Dervin, 1999), and sociology (e.g., Garfinkel, 1967). This project draws primarily from Weick's work on sensemaking given the close intersection of Weick's sensemaking approach with crisis sensemaking.

Weick (1995) described sensemaking as occurring through a three-stage process: enactment, selection, and retention. In the enactment phase, organizational members attend to particular cues in the environment as a means of making sense of and understanding what is occurring in the environment. Weick emphasized that the environment is not something that is necessarily premade, but rather, it is enacted or constructed through the process of sensemaking. In the selection phase, organizational members attend to specific cues that were identified through the enactment phase. These cues are made sense of in ways that in turn prompt specific actions. Those actions may be selected to be used in future circumstances in the phase of retention.

Research on organizational sensemaking has been robust (see Maitlis & Christianson, 2014), with a strong focus on crisis sensemaking (Maitlis & Sonenshein, 2010). Weick and others have described how sensemaking occurs during crisis situations, with attention to how people have made sense of crises and possibly may even create a crisis in overlooking certain cues as a crisis was emerging.

Weick (1995) emphasized that sensemaking is retrospective, and the concept of sensemaking has been conceptualized and described by other scholars as retrospective, thereby confining sensemaking to looking toward the past. In addition, Weick even argued that making sense of the future is not possible because it has not yet happened. He did allow for an exception to this in what he termed "future perfect" thinking, where one imagines that the future has already occurred and reflects back on what has occurred (Weick, 1979).

However, other scholars, notably, Gioia, Corley, and Fabbri (2002) have put forth the notion of prospective sensemaking where the process of looking ahead and making sense of the future, although still challenging, is not as problematic as Weick explained it to be. Indeed, in thinking of organizational actions from a metapragmatic sense, there are several terms that are readily available that point toward prospective sensemaking: strategic planning, foresight, and forecasting.

In developing a model of prospective sensemaking, Stigliani and Ravasi (2012) relate future-oriented sensemaking with accounts:

> Our model describes prospective collective sensemaking as based on three interrelated cycles of retrospective cognitive work occurring as members of groups go back and forth between the tentative organization of selected material cues and the refinement of corresponding categories, embody provisional interpretations in material form, and engage in retrospective reflection to establish the plausibility of emerging accounts. (p. 1233)

Of note in Stigliani and Ravasi's model and of significance for this project is the relevance of materiality in the development of accounts and future-oriented sense-making. The Great Lakes have a material form, and human activity in relation to the Great Lakes can have a material impact in affecting water levels and biosystems.

Policy development can be considered a form of prospective sensemaking in that one function of policies is to affect the future and to avert potential problems. The discussion of the Great Lakes Compact can be viewed as a prospective-sensemaking activity in that the Compact addresses future actions towards the Great Lakes.

RESEARCH QUESTIONS

Based on the preceding literature review, the following research questions (RQs) are addressed through this project:

RQ1: What account vocabularies were prominent in the congressional discourse associated with the Great Lakes Compact?

RQ2: How were the problems associated with Great Lakes discursively constructed?

RQ3: How does the discourse associated with the Great Lakes Compact reflect prospective sensemaking?

DATA GATHERING AND METHOD OF ANALYSIS

The C-SPAN Video Library was used as the primary source of data. This was supplemented by the use of Congress.gov and the Library of Congress THOMAS website to locate transcripts and bill background not available through the C-SPAN Video Library. The C-SPAN Video Library provided the timelines for the courses of action on the House and Senate bills on the Compact and video recordings of the introductions, congressional actions, and House debate on the Compact. The THOMAS website[3] provided committee reports on the bills. Hearing statements and video recordings from the Senate Committee on the Judiciary website were also obtained.

The initial design of the project was intended to focus on the discourse related to two bills (the Great Lakes Compact and H.R. 2973); however, there was not a debate associated with H.R. 2973. While I would like to have presented a methodological approach that progressed in a linear fashion that was carried out as initially conceptualized, that narrative would not have been appropriate for the actual track of the research process, which shifted as data was gathered and more information learned from the C-SPAN Video Library on the course of approval for the Compact.[4] I acknowledge this unexpected turn of my research plan as it is also a key finding related to what can be learned from using the C-SPAN Video Library and in documenting the legislative approval process.

For the data analysis procedures, I read through the available transcripts and viewed video recordings at the floor level and committee level. Across these, I identified account vocabularies, approximately following guidelines described in Buttny (1993) for conducting a conversation analytic constructionist perspective on accounts. Buttny's description emphasized the importance of paying attention to specific utterances, including words used, actions performed, and interactional structuring, in order to understand how accounts and social accountability are constructed by interlocutors. A key issue that Buttny noted is to identify "what accounts make relevant": "the *nature, magnitude,* and *consequences* of the problematic event are themselves interactional constructions* [emphasis in original] which are made relevant by the actor in the course of the accounts talk" (p. 61). Through this process, a goal of the researcher in interpreting the discourse is to "make the implicit explicit" (p. 63) by using contextual information to aid in the analysis and in developing interpretations of the data.

ANALYSIS

The Great Lakes Compact

Before being considered in Congress, the Compact went through an eight-state approval process such that it already had the status of an interstate agreement, with the wording and language worked out over a 4-year period among the Great Lakes states and the Canadian province of Ontario, resulting in a

19-page document (Council of Great Lakes Governors, n.d.). The main task for Congress was to enact (or not) the Compact into public law in order to make the agreement legally binding.

In the House of Representatives, the Compact was introduced as H.R. 6577, with lead sponsor James Oberstar (D-MN) and 47 cosponsors that constituted bipartisan support from representatives of the Great Lakes states. It was introduced to the House on July 23, 2008, referred to the House Committee on the Judiciary, reported and approved by that committee; it received no further action in the House. Although H.R. 6577 did not pass the House, it is nearly identical to Senate Joint Resolution 45 (S.J. Res. 45), which was eventually approved by both the House and Senate as the Great Lakes Compact.

In the Senate, the Compact was introduced as S.J. Res. 45, with lead sponsor Carl Levin (D-MI), and 15 cosponsors that constituted bipartisan support from all senators from the Great Lakes states and included well-known names such as then-Senators Barack Obama and Hillary Rodham Clinton. The Compact was classified within the C-SPAN Video Library as dealing with water resources development. It was introduced on July 23, 2008, read twice, and referred to the Committee on the Judiciary, where hearings were held on July 30, and it was discharged and laid before the Senate on August 1, 2008, where it was amended (S. Amdt. [Amendment] 5263) and passed in the Senate by unanimous consent.

On September 8, it was received in the House as a Senate Joint Resolution. On September 22, Betty Sutton (D-OH) moved to "suspend the rules and pass the resolution." Also on September 22, the first and only congressional debate occurred on the Great Lakes Compact. The C-SPAN Video Library reported that there were 4 speakers in the debate, and that as a suspension of the rules, a debate of 40 minutes was allocated. One speaker made a procedural motion. There were 3 speakers on the substance of the resolution (Betty Sutton, D-OH; Bart Stupak, D-MI; and, Howard Coble, R-NC), plus the Speaker Pro Tempore. The debate lasted for approximately 15 minutes.

In the *Congressional Record*, there were additional "speakers" with comments that were added to the official record (Vernon Ehlers, R-MI; James Oberstar, D-MN; Sander Levin, D-MI). The three additional remarks were all in favor of the Compact. Although written and spoken discourse are different in character, because the comments of the additional speakers are part of official record, they are also included in this analysis. On September 23, the Compact was approved in the House and passed on to the White House, where the President signed it into law on October 3.

The primary analysis includes the Compact-related oral statements and debate made on the congressional floor. Statements by representatives intended for inclusion in the public record are included to provide additional background context. These also contribute to the congressional discourse on the approval of the Compact. Statements that were added after the floor debate are indicated by "(written statement)" following the speaker's name. The closed-captioned transcript was used as the primary transcript. These transcripts were compared with the spoken discourse, and either corrected or modified to reflect what was said, including capturing nonverbal disfluencies and word emphasis (indicated through either ALL CAP for emphasis through increased volume or underlining for stressed words). Bold indicates words and phrases highlighted for analysis purposes.

The following were identified as key account vocabularies: natural resource, economic development, stewardship, and diversion. This analysis is divided into three sections by describing the prodrome, or key triggering event; describing how the account vocabularies were used within the accounts in favor of the Compact; and then discussing how these account vocabularies were also addressed in the opposition to the Compact.

The Prodrome

The main threat to the Great Lakes and key impetus for the passage of the Great Lakes compact was fear of diversion of the freshwater out of the Great Lakes. *Diversion*, *diversions*, or *divert* were mentioned nine times during the debate. Of note isn't just the fact that diversion is mentioned, but how it is discursively built up as a threat.

Background context regarding the threat of diversions can be gleaned from the written record. In written statements, two representatives spoke of how a private Canadian company had made an agreement in 1998 to export 160 million gallons of water from Lake Superior to Asia. This event prompted an immediate response and protest from the eight neighboring U.S. states and was credited with leading to the development of the Great Lakes Compact. This event constituted a prodrome, or early warning of a threat, to the Great Lakes in the form of the diversion of water away from the Great Lakes region:

Mr. Ehlers (written statement): The catalyst for the creation of a Great Lakes Compact came in 1998 when the government of Ontario granted a permit to a private Canadian company to ship up to 160 million gallons of water per year to Asia.

In the above excerpt, Representative Ehlers (R-MI) outlined the sequence of events that led to the development of the Great Lakes Compact. He noted that the catalyst was specifically the possibility of water being shipped out of the Great Lakes to a different part of the globe.

However, what is crucial to examine about this prodrome is how social actors made sense of this event as a threat to the Great Lakes:

Mr. Ehlers (written statement): The Great Lakes comprise the largest source of freshwater in the world—20 percent of the Earth's total and 95 percent of the surface freshwater in the United States—and they provide drinking water, transportation and recreation to tens of millions of people in the United States and Canada. Although the Great Lakes contain copious amounts of fresh water, less than one percent of the water in the Great Lakes is renewed every year through rain, snow melt, and groundwater recharge, with the remaining ninety-nine percent remaining in the lakes each year. In other words, the Great Lakes are a non-renewable resource that is **currently at jeopardy from large-scale water diversions** outside the Great Lakes Basin.

Diversion is a key account-vocabulary term in connection to its relationship to other aspects of Great Lakes ecology. Specifically, the Great Lakes are a large freshwater resource, but that water is nonrenewable due to limitations in the rain, snowmelt, and groundwater recharge cycle. Diversion is discursively worked up as a key concern in relation to ecology, freshwater, and conservation. This is significant in that diversion could have been developed as a threat in other ways such as a lost economic opportunity for the region. However, this would call for a particular crafting of a chain of agencies (Castor & Cooren, 2006) that would link freshwater diversion to economic resource. What trumps the preference of this chain of agencies is an alternative network of agencies that traces back to how Great Lakes freshwater is a resource with a limited cycle of replenishment. Linking diversion as threat to a limited resource establishes the overall framework of the Compact in functioning to protect Great Lakes freshwater as a natural (regional) resource.

House Debate

There were multiple account vocabularies that were used to describe and define the Great Lakes including: natural resource to be protected, freshwater resource of finite quantity, and economic resource. These multiple vocabularies were not treated as being in conflict with each other or contradictory, but rather as different aspects of the Great Lakes. What is notable in the remarks of the speakers who inserted statements and spoke in favor of the Great Lakes Compact is the diversity of account vocabularies that they utilized, which included national interests, impact and scope of Great Lakes, economic impact, and local control.

The Great Lakes as a natural resource was highlighted with *natural* being mentioned 3 times during the debate and 22 times in written statements. However, when *natural* was mentioned, it was usually as a part of a phrase: *natural resources*, *natural resource*, or *natural asset*. As a natural resource, it is something that should be protected:

> Ms. Sutton: The Great Lakes Compact will help preserve and improve this important natural resource, our Great Lakes, for years to come. The Great Lakes are one of our greatest treasures, an important **natural asset** that we must never take for granted and that we must always **protect**.

Representative Sutton's comment highlights the nature of the Great Lakes as a natural resource—it must be preserved, and its preservation is vital when projecting into the future and considering the needs of future generations. In this respect, the vocabulary of Great Lakes as natural resource is a prospective-sensemaking tool in anticipating a specific need in the future.

The value of the Great Lakes as a natural resource however is in relation to its uses:

> Ms. Sutton: Mr. Speaker, the Great Lakes are not only a source of drinking water, but they are also essential for **recreation, jobs, and the overall health of our economy**. Lake Erie alone supports 240,000

jobs and \$5.8 billion in wages. The Great Lakes **are also highways, moving goods, people and services** throughout the region. In addition, the Great Lakes support **a multi-billion dollar a year sport fishing and recreational boating industries** [*sic*], and also support **travel** and **tourism** throughout the region.

The Great Lakes are an economic driver through recreation, transportation, sport fishing, recreational boating, travel, and tourism. Ms. Sutton also invoked what I describe as freshwater statistics, which highlight the scope and impact of Great Lakes freshwater: "With one-fifth of the world's fresh water, the Great Lakes attracted the early settlers to the region, and today nearly 33 million people live and work within the basin, spanning eight States . . ." Coupled with the freshwater statistics were statistics that emphasized the importance of the Great Lakes to the economy of the area. This framing emphasizes the Great Lakes as important because of what they provide to improve human and economic quality of life. In other words, the Great Lakes are important because of their relationship to society.

In addition to building up the importance of the Great Lakes to the area as a freshwater resource and as an economic engine, Ms. Sutton also discursively developed a case for a problem that the Compact would help solve:

However, the Great Lakes are **vulnerable to depletion**. Each year, rainfall- rainfall and snowmelt replenish only about 1 percent of the water in the basin. **Uncontrolled and careless diversions of water** could thus be HIGHLY detrimental to the health of the Great Lakes. This compact will bring an end to **destructive diversions** of water from the basin.

The development of problems or threats to the Great Lakes is twofold: first, focusing on the nonrenewable and therefore, potentially, fleeting nature of Great Lakes water, and second, highlighting the threat of diversions. What is notable in her descriptions of diversions is that whenever water diversion is mentioned, it is accompanied with an adjective (e.g., *uncontrolled, careless, destructive*), which allows for other types of diversions that are not uncontrolled, careless, or destructive.

Another account vocabulary that she utilized to support the Compact dealt with prioritizing local control:

The purpose of this compact is to formalize cooperation among the Great Lakes States, to develop and implement **regional** goals and objectives for water conservation while **preserving the States' flexibility** regarding their water management programs.

In addition, she emphasized how "**the people of the eight States** have worked diligently to craft this compact to preserve this vital resource, and it is urgent that we approve it **now** to ensure that our Great Lakes are here for **future generations**."

In the final comments of her introductory remarks (see the previous paragraph), Ms. Sutton again emphasized two terms related to time and timing: "now" and "future generations." These two terms are key to understanding how prospective sensemaking is framed in terms of future potential problems of the Great Lakes. In other words, the future is viewed in terms of what is happening in the here and now. This point will be elaborated on later, in the Discussion section.

The other speaker who spoke in favor of the Compact was Mr. Howard Coble (R-NC). His comments were brief (lasting approximately 1 minute and 17 seconds), where he expressed agreement with Ms. Sutton's remarks ("Mr. Speaker, the gentlelady from Ohio pretty THOROUGHLY covered this already"). Mr. Coble also highlighted the work involved in the development of the Compact ("the compact we are called upon to approve today caps off years of effort.").

In terms of accounts and agency, Mr. Coble also highlighted the role of "the States, users of these waters in the United States, and Canadian authorities" as agents and stakeholders in the management of Great Lakes waters. Therefore, without highlighting a specific problem per se, Mr. Coble focused on the role of particular agents (individual states, the U.S. and Canadian authorities) in implementing a solution that would prevent problems with the Great Lakes. In terms of how the Great Lakes are discursively constructed, they are treated as a resource to be managed.

The Great Lakes are part of a network not of agents, but of activity (see Czarniawska, 2009). The account vocabularies of natural resource, limited freshwater resource, and economic resource functioned as devices to make sense of the Great Lakes in a definitional way by describing their present relationship with human needs and activities. These vocabularies also were utilized as prospective-sensemaking devices in how they were connected with other activities.

Opposing the Compact to Support the Lakes

There was only one representative (Mr. Stupak, D-MI) who spoke out against the Great Lakes Compact. His opposition ultimately was in favor of measures to protect the Great Lakes, and so he expressed concerns about gaps in the Compact in its ability to effectively protect the Great Lakes in the long term, especially given other unknown contingencies. Mr. Stupak had a total of seven speaking turns. Unlike other segments of the debate where utterances were more akin to minispeeches with no specific responses, the segment of the debate that involved Mr. Stupak's comments were more obviously interactional, with his turns relatively short in duration followed by responses from Ms. Sutton that were explicitly directed toward Mr. Stupak's comments.

Mr. Stupak opened his remarks and opposition by expressing his "deep concern" that "this compact would allow Great Lakes water to be defined as a product." In addition, Mr. Stupak claimed that there was "no language in the compact that recognizes the Great Lakes waters held in trust. The public owns the water of the Great Lakes, and anything we pass should preserve this." Mr. Stupak's comment here can be taken as calling into question how the Compact functions to discursively construct the Great Lakes as a water resource (and by extension, economic resource) rather than as a public resource.

As with the views expressed to support the Compact, Mr. Stupak also expressed a concern about water diversion. However, instead of equating the Compact as a mechanism to prevent diversion, Stupak claimed that the Compact "may have unintentionally have the opposite effect and set a precedent that would open the DOOR to diversions." Another vocabulary that Stupak utilized in his objections to the Compact dealt with process: he cited how Congress did not have enough time to consider the Compact, was "rushing" it through, and that there were several unanswered questions regarding the Compact and its future implications.

Mr. Stupak posed a series of questions based on his concerns. Of note is the use of the common vocabulary of diversion in the pro and con sides to the Compact, and the framing of diversion as undesirable:

> While the original intent of the Great Lakes Compact was to **protect** our water from **diversions**, the compact that the States have sent to Congress may have unintentionally have the opposite effect and set a precedent that would **open the DOOR to diversions**.

What is under dispute with regard to the vocabulary of diversion is how the Great Lakes Compact connects to diversion prevention or diversion facilitation. Mr. Stupak's "action net" (see Czarniawska, 2009) with respect to the Compact and diversion differs from that of the Compact supporters because of the relationship he crafts between the Compact and diversion. Mr. Stupak's comments highlight how the Compact does not ban diversions altogether but rather places a limitation on what kind of diversions may occur, a position that is resonant with Ms. Sutton's earlier description of diversions modified by adjectives such as *uncontrolled, careless,* and *destructive.*

The way Mr. Stupak discursively builds the relationship between the Compact and diversions is by posing questions to be answered. Mr. Stupak stated that he posed several questions to various agencies such as the International Joint Commission, U.S. Trade Representative, and Department of State, but that while the request was acknowledged, "they were unable to provide me with any substantive responses." In the response to the several concerns that Stupak raised, Ms. Sutton addressed some of them in stating:

> We have specifically retained the right to amend and alter the compact. And I would um just also mention that we have worked to effectively address the gentleman's concerns ah in the committee report.

Of note in this response is its brevity, which is accomplished in part by not addressing each of the specific issues raised by Mr. Stupak and by referring to another organizational text ("the committee report") that purportedly addresses each of the concerns raised by Mr. Stupak. The prospective-sensemaking issues raised by Mr. Stupak are not treated as new issues or items, but rather are encompassed as part of an ongoing conversation. Thus, future possible problems associated with the Great Lakes or possibly caused by the Compact itself, are intertwined with other organizational conversations and an organizational text ("the committee report"). Mr. Stupak's comments are oriented toward the future and projected into a future chain of agencies. His projections into the future are resisted through invoking an alternative, competing chain of agencies vis-à-vis prior organizational conversations and texts.

Ms. Sutton addressed Mr. Stupak's concerns and questions in turn. In her last set of comments in response to Mr. Stupak, she explicitly addressed the problem that the Compact was intended to solve:

Our Great Lakes' water is **CURRENTLY, at PRESENT, at risk to
be carelessly diverted** from our basin, and that is why action is so
important here today. If we allow that to happen, this water will
never return.

The problem as Ms. Sutton has defined it is "present." Therefore, from a
sensemaking perspective, the Compact addresses a present or current problem, rather than a future problem.

The debate ended after approximately 15 minutes, 25 minutes short of the
40 minutes allocated for the debate. Ms. Sutton moved to suspend the rules
and pass the resolution, effectively ending Mr. Stupak's floor questions and
challenges to the resolution. This move can be viewed as a negative sanction-
ing of Mr. Stupak's objections.

As the Speaker Pro Tempore was initiating the voting process, Mr. Stupak
objected based on the grounds that a quorum was not present. The vote was
subsequently postponed until September 23. When it was taken up as unfin-
ished business, there was immediately a motion to suspend the rules and pass
the resolution. After a 5-minute period where electronic votes were being cast
and much conversation and activity was observed on the House floor, the bill
was approved with 390 yeas and 25 nays. Two days later, it was presented to
the president, who subsequently signed the Great Lakes Compact into Public
Law No. 110-342 on October 3, 2008.

DISCUSSION

By the time that the Great Lakes Compact was introduced in Congress, it
had undergone a great deal of discussion and debate at the state level such
that it already had the status of state authorization and, by extension, support of the constituents who in turn supported the politicians at the federal
level. Therefore, in many ways the Compact seemed destined for approval
prior to its introduction in Congress. The limited number of speakers also
illustrates the noncontroversial nature of the Compact. This project's research
questions address how this lack of controversy can be understood in terms
of political discourse.

RQ1: What account vocabularies were prominent in the congressional discourse associated with the Great Lakes Compact?

Despite the limited amount of actual talk associated with the Great Lakes Compact, there were actually quite a few account vocabularies that were utilized within the debate: national interests, natural resource of freshwater, economic resource, water diversions, and local/state control of Great Lakes water. As I noted elsewhere (Castor, 2005), in governance debates similar account vocabularies may be used by opposing sides, but differences may occur in how they relate those vocabularies to the issue at hand. In addition, this project highlights how, while there may be similar account vocabularies being utilized, they may be emphasized in different ways. For example, the arguments in favor of the Compact tended to focus on the economic relevance of the Great Lakes, whereas the arguments against the Compact were expressly critical of an economic perspective. The opposition arguments instead emphasized the Great Lakes as a public trust.

RQ2: How were the problems associated with Great Lakes discursively constructed?

The key issue that speakers in favor of and against the proposal acknowledged was the problem of water diversions from the Great Lakes. This was viewed as a problem in part because of the limitations on how Great Lakes water is replenished. However, why this is a problem can be construed in a variety of ways. For instance, without Great Lakes water, the region is without an important source of freshwater. However, also without Great Lakes water, the region is without an important economic engine that supports jobs, tourism, fishing, sporting, and transportation. It is this latter set of framings that were emphasized.

Grint (2005) and Castor and Cooren (2006) noted that the framing of a problem can be shifted. Rather than casting it as a solution to a problem, the opposition attempted to frame the Compact as a potential cause of problems by opening the door to future diversions. Part of this framing relates to defining the Great Lakes as economic resource rather than natural resource.

RQ3: How does the discourse associated with the Great Lakes Compact reflect prospective sensemaking?

The Compact was intended to deal with the issue or potential problems associated with water diversions. As noted in the supplemental written statements, the supporters of the Compact focused on water diversions as a current threat as exemplified by a Canadian company attempting to divert water from the Great Lakes. In this respect, the sensemaking that occurred regarding the need for the Compact was retrospective in orientation by focusing on a past incident as the basis for future actions.

The opposition to the Compact also engaged in sensemaking regarding problems and the Compact, but in this case, the sensemaking was future oriented in attempting to project ahead to potential problems that in turn are not tangible and therefore are relegated to vague and ambiguous risks. Indeed, the only way to determine if the concerns of the opposition are valid would be to approve the Compact and see what happens.

A key implication of this project regarding prospective sensemaking involves the challenges involved in attempting to make sense of possible, projected future problems. In some ways, Weick's caution about prospective sensemaking can be seen in that it is hard to make sense of the future without reference to the past. In addition, this project illustrates some factors that enable prospective sensemaking, such as when a threat is specific, tangible, and grounded in a concrete past action.

CONCLUSION

This particular dataset addresses the congressional approval process for the Great Lakes Compact. The video record is valuable for analysis of public discourse related to approval of the Compact. There was an emphasis on discourse that was in favor of the Compact, as indicated through the number of speakers and written statements in support of the Compact in comparison to the one speaker against the Compact. What this also shows is that the Compact was already at least informally approved and any further discussion could be considered ceremonial rather than critical.

From a political perspective, this project is relevant in highlighting some of the circumstances related to approval. Perhaps because of the diverse vocabularies, there was something for everyone in terms of bipartisan approval. Plus, there was the support of the states that would be most affected by the Great Lakes Compact.

The goal of this project was to bring together several important areas of study and research: using the unique and valuable resource of the C-SPAN Video Library; addressing freshwater policy issues; problem construction, and making sense of future, projected problems. The focal points for bringing together these areas were the Great Lakes and Great Lakes Compact. In analyzing discourse associated with the discussions of the Great Lakes, this project identified how there were varying account vocabularies that were used to describe the Great Lakes, with an economic resource vocabulary being prevalent.

Because so little documented congressional discussion exists regarding the similar water bills that did not pass, it's difficult to tell from a discursive analysis what was different about the Compact as compared to the other ones. However, this analysis was able to identify and analyze explicit public discourse relating to the Great Lakes Compact. In doing so, several account vocabularies for discussing support of the Great Lakes were identified.

One purpose in analyzing the Compact was to examine the debate and discourse to determine what factors may have contributed to the success of this piece of freshwater protection legislation. Some key aspects related to its success were its response to a past circumstance (the threat of foreign water diversion), economic connections, and local/regional support from the Great Lakes states. While in some ways the Compact was approved swiftly by Congress, in other ways it was slow moving in that the initial water diversion threat that prompted the Compact occurred in 1999 (nearly a decade before the actual congressional approval of the Compact). However, the Compact went through approval in each of the eight Great Lakes states before arriving in Washington, D.C.

Reflections on the Use of C-SPAN Library

An important backdrop has been the availability of the C-SPAN Video Library as a tool for analysis. In this section, I wish to reflect on the use of the C-SPAN Video Library in order to highlight its utilities and to provide some caveats. First, in many ways the C-SPAN Video Library provided a remarkably accurate picture of what actually occurred on the House floor, as opposed to the official record which also includes comments and remarks that have been added after the fact. In addition, written records may not be accurate in capturing what occurred. However, congressionally controlled cameras are also limited in what they capture. So, for example, in the final House vote on the Compact, there was much talk and movement occurring on the House floor, but specific conversations could not be captured on camera, thus losing out on some of the interactional dynamics involved with the approval of the Compact.

Second, in focusing on what was available through the C-SPAN video, there were other aspects of the Compact that I did not explore in this particular chapter, including factors external to the congressional discourse. For example, some unanswered questions are: How did the overall political dynamics of the House and Senate contribute to how the Compact was received and voted upon? What occurred at the state level leading up to the introduction of the Compact? How did the external societal awareness of the importance of freshwater and dangers of water diversions, as exemplified in Peter Annin's 2009 book, *The Great Lakes Water Wars*, contribute to the reception of the Compact as compared to other water legislation proposed at different points in time?

NOTES

1. For brevity, *the Compact* will be used interchangeably with the Great Lakes Compact.

2. Exceptions may be granted in the case of communities in "straddling counties." Such requests for exceptions must go through a rigorous review process.

3. The THOMAS website is now retired. The same content can be found at congress.gov.

4. See Tracy, Eger, Huffman, Redden, and Scarduzio (2014) for a discussion of how qualitative research can take unexpected turns.

REFERENCES

Annin, P. (2009). *The Great Lakes water wars*. Washington, DC: Island Press.

Bartesaghi, M., & Castor, T. (2009). Tracing our steps through communication social construction: Six propositions for how to go on. In W. Leeds-Hurwitz & G. Galanes (Eds.), *Socially Constructing Communication* (pp. 225–243). Mahwah, NJ: Hampton Press.

Buttny, R. (1993). *Social accountability in communication*. London, England: Sage.

Buttny, R. (2004). T*alking problems: Studies of discursive construction*. Albany: State University of New York.

Buttny, R., & Morris, G. H. (2001). Accounts. In W. P. Robinson & H. Giles (Eds.), *The new handbook of language and social psychology* (pp. 285–301). London, England: Wiley.

Castor, T. R. (2005). Constructing social reality in organizational decision making: Account vocabularies in a diversity discussion. *Management Communication Quarterly, 18*(4), 479–508.

Castor, T. R., & Cooren, F. (2006). Organizations as hybrid forms of life. *Management Communication Quarterly, 19*(4), 570–600.

Council of Great Lakes Governors. (n.d.). Great Lakes–St. Lawrence river basin water resources compact: Project background, organization and road to development. Retrieved from http://www.cglslgp.org/media/1311/project_background_organization_and_road_to_development.pdf

Czarniawska, B. (2009). Introduction: Action nets. In B. Czarniawska (Ed.), *Organizing in the face of risk and threat* (pp. 1–8). Glasgow, Scotland: Edward Elgar.

Dervin, B. (1999). Chaos, order and sense-making: A proposed theory for information design. In R. Jacobson (Ed.), *Information design* (pp. 35–57). Cambridge, MA: MIT Press.

Galanes, G. J., & Leeds-Hurwitz, W. (Eds.). (2009). *Socially constructing communication*. Creskill, NJ: Hampton Press.

Garfinkel, H. (1967). *Studies in ethnomethodology*. Cambridge, United Kingdom: Polity Press.

Gioia, D. A., Corley, K. G., & Fabbri, T. (2002). Revising the past (while thinking in the future perfect tense). *Journal of Organizational Change Management, 15*(6), 622–634.

Grint, K. (2005). Problems, problems, problems: The social construction of "leadership." *Human Relations, 58*(11), 1467–1494. http://dx.doi.org/10.1177/0018726705061314

Maitlis, S., & Christianson, M. (2014). Sensemaking in organizations: Taking stock and moving forward. *Academy of Management Annals, 8*(1), 57–125. http://dx .doi.org/10.1080/19416520.2014.873177

Maitlis, S., & Sonenshein, S. (2010). Sensemaking in crisis and change: Inspiration and insights from Weick (1988). *Journal of Management Studies, 47*(3), 551–580. http://dx.doi.org/10.1111/j.1467-6486.2010.00908.x

Mills, C. W. (1940). Situated actions and vocabularies of motive. *American Sociological Review, 5*(6), 904–913.

Murphy, R. (2004). Disaster or sustainability: The dance of human agents with nature's actants. *Canadian Review of Sociology/Revue canadienne de sociologie, 41*(3), 249–266.

National Oceanic and Atmospheric Administration. (n.d.). *About our Great Lakes: Great Lakes Basin facts.* Retrieved from http://www.glerl.noaa.gov/pr/ourlakes/facts.html

Rittel, H. W. J., & Webber, M. M. (1973). Dilemmas in a general theory of planning. *Policy Sciences, 4,* 155–169.

Schaper, D. (2008, July 8). States approve Compact to protect Great Lakes. *National Public Radio.* Retrieved from http://www.npr.org/templates/story/story.php ?storyId=92297955

Scott, C. W., & Trethewey, A. (2008). Organizational discourse and the appraisal of occupational hazards: Interpretive repertoires, heedful interrelating, and identity at work. *Journal of Applied Communication Research, 36*(3), 298–317. http:// dx.doi.org/10.1080/00909880802172137

Scott, M. B., & Lyman, S. M. (1968). Accounts. *American Sociological Review, 33,* 46–62.

Shotter, J. (1984). *Social accountability and selfhood.* Oxford, England: Basil Blackwell.

Shotter, J. (1993). *Conversational realities: The construction of life through language.* London, England: Sage.

Stigliani, I., & Ravasi, D. (2012). Organizing thoughts and connecting brains: Material practices and the transition from individual to group-level prospective sensemaking. *Academy of Management Journal, 55*(5), 1232–1259. http://dx.doi .org/10.5465/amj.2010.0890

Tracy, K., & Muller, H. (2001). Diagnosing a school board's interactional trouble: Theorizing problem formulating. *Communication Theory, 11,* 84–104.

Tracy, S. J., Eger, E. K., Huffman, T. P., Redden, S. M., & Scarduzio, J. A. (2014). Narrating the backstage of qualitative research in organizational communication: A synthesis. *Management Communication Quarterly, 28*(3), 422–431. http:// dx.doi.org/10.1177/0893318914536964

United States Environmental Protection Agency. (2015). *Great Lakes: Basic information*. Retrieved from http://www.epa.gov/glnpo/basicinfo.html

Weick, K. E. (1979). *The social psychology of organizing* (2nd ed.). New York, NY: McGraw-Hill.

Weick, K. E. (1995). *Sensemaking in organizations*. Thousand Oaks, CA: Sage.

CHAPTER 3

CONSIDERING CONSTRUCTION OF CONSERVATIVE/LIBERAL MEANING: WHAT AN EXTRATERRESTRIAL MIGHT DISCOVER ABOUT BRANDING STRATEGY IN THE C-SPAN VIDEO LIBRARY

Robert L. Kerr

In this study of what constructed meaning in media discourse reveals about recent changes in political semantics, the power of political branding strategy is demonstrated through a remarkable lesson in not missing the forest for the trees. That's not to suggest the trees in this case don't also provide some useful lessons, however, as we shall see.

Quite arguably, the terms *conservative* and *liberal* have come to form the cornerstones for the dominant themes that have played out in American political discourse over the past three or four decades. Mainstream media accounts now, almost rotely, dichotomize the manner in which they construct virtually all discourse involving almost any sort of political activity. The respective positions, players, interests, etc., are ubiquitously and almost offhandedly labeled as either *conservative* or *liberal*—as if the terms had finite and universally understood meanings, within which all life can be categorized as one or the other. Rarely do such accounts provide definitional guidance as to specifically what they mean by this categorization. The terms tend to be used more as ordinary qualifiers, as if they were as objective in their meaning as terms more clearly dichotomous—such as *tall/short* or *black/white*—regardless of the historical, geographical, or cultural context.

And yet *conservative* and *liberal* have in reality been almost anything but terms with constant meaning regardless of time or place. Just a few generations ago, for example, Americans held very different understandings of both. As historian Laura Jane Gifford's 2009 work notes, referencing someone as a liberal in the 19th and early 20th centuries "generally indicated an individual who adhered to the principles of classical liberalism—laissez-faire capitalism. Even mid-century figures such as Herbert Hoover and Ohio Senator Robert Taft insisted on being called liberals, despite being two of the more right-wing figures of their day" (Gifford, 2009, p. 10). The term *conservative* in particular has undergone a dramatic evolution in usage, particularly in recent decades. Historically, Jerry Muller has noted in his 1997 anthology on conservatism, "The institutions which conservatives have sought to conserve have varied, the major targets of conservative criticism have changed over time, and conservatism differs from one national context to another" (Muller, 1997, p. xiii). For historians, even writing about conservatism over much historical time creates organizational and semantic challenges because until relatively recently, "it was unusual for Americans to refer to themselves politically as *conservatives* [emphasis in original], though many used the term as an adjective," observed Patrick Allitt in his 2009 study of the history of conservatism. Even with figures in earlier American history who can be understood as conservatives, "this was not a noun most of them used about themselves," and indeed, "before the 1950s there was no such thing as a conservative *movement* [emphasis in original] in the United States" (Allitt, 2009, p. 2).

And yet, a few decades later, in mainstream media the terms *conservative* and *liberal* are used as commonly and regularly in accounts involving political activity as are references to rain and sunshine in the weather reports. In both cases, the clear assumption is that the terminology references phenomena so much a part of the long-fixed everyday landscape for audiences that understanding of their meaning will automatically be received and processed in the same way by all. But as political historians attest, such meanings more typically shift from one generation to another and from one geographical or cultural locale to another.

The reasons behind the changes in political culture over this period in American history can be considered from a number of perspectives. This study approaches the subject in the context of the argument that one powerful dynamic in the changes has been the establishment of conservatism as one of the most successfully entrenched brands of the late 20th and early 21st centuries. "The brand strategy is the tool that Conservatives have used to build their movement from 1964 until the present," declared political scientist Kenneth Cosgrove in his 2007 study of how "conservatives have employed brands to sell their candidates in much the same way that many businesses use brands to sell products to consumers. Both use brands because they are powerful tools with which a marketer can cut through the noise of a crowded marketplace" (Cosgrove, 2007, pp. 1–2). In Cosgrove's analysis, the timing for such a strategy was perfect: "The brand strategy has become a key part of the Conservative movement's success because the movement was developing at exactly the same time that consumer marketing techniques were improving and as an ethos of consumerism was taking hold across the country. For a new movement to present its candidates, using the same techniques to that being used to sell other kind of products, was an entirely logical occurrence" (Cosgrove, 2007, p. 8).

And that assertion is hardly limited to scholarly analysis. Longtime political activist Richard Viguerie, who is widely credited with pioneering direct-marketing techniques that proved highly influential in the success of conservative political causes in the latter 20th century, has spoken very clearly of how central the branding strategy was. He detailed in 2004 how his early efforts, decades before, at promoting conservatism failed until he grasped the power of branding. "There's nothing more important than being the first to lock in a brand identification," he wrote. "I had not understood branding, and the importance of the image that your potential customers or donors have of you. But I never again made that mistake" (Viguerie & Franke, 2004, pp. 94–96, 223). At the same time, in Cosgrove's analysis, liberalism has failed to advance a successful branding strategy "in the same long-term way that Conservatives have," while conservatives "have not only branded themselves, but their opponents as well" (Cosgrove, 2007, pp. 2, 11).

Although branding cannot be argued as the sole factor, the rise of conservatism in relation to liberalism as a dominant political force in American democracy, especially since the late 1970s, is undeniable. Although many developments played a role in that, the rise of Ronald Reagan over the course of the seventies to the White House in 1980 is most widely accepted as marking the beginning of that dominance (Edwards, 1999, p. 224; Micklethwait & Wooldridge, 2004, p. 91; Shirley, 2005, p. 340). "From the late 1970s to the early twenty-first century, American conservatism was constantly in the news. Conservative intellectuals challenged nearly all the liberal verities of the 1950s and 1960s," Allitt summarized the period. "Powerful conservative think tanks served up a steady stream of policy proposals, and politicians from both major parties took notice. New media outlets . . . began to approach the news from an openly conservative vantage point, and by the 1990s some politicians were disavowing liberalism because even use of the 'L word' appeared to cost them popular support." In time, "government began to dismantle decades-long welfare and busing programs. A succession of appointments under President Reagan and the two Bush presidents changed the character of the Supreme Court. In foreign-policy, conservatives theorized exhaustion of the Soviet Union, then celebrated the end of the Cold War, before looking ahead to new geopolitical challenges" (Allitt, 2009, p. 1). In its rise, conservatism focused squarely on displacing the influence of liberalism. First, "in their struggle against the dominant liberal state, conservatives gained control of the Republican Party by defeating its liberal eastern wing," as historian Donald Critchlow (2007) has documented the process. "Modern liberalism proved to be a formidable opponent, politically and institutionally. The administrative state established in the New Deal and later expanded in the 1960s by Lyndon Johnson's Great Society institutionalized a liberal regime that was not easily overturned by conservative opponents" (Critchlow, 2007, pp. 1–2).

However, liberalism faced its own challenges as it struggled to respond to an economy shifting from an industrial manufacturing base to a postindustrial era with a workforce more white collar and less unionized. Traditional family structure also began to be transformed dramatically, with far more women developing careers, family size decreasing, and the divorce rate increasing. "In this changing cultural environment, social issues such as gender equality, abortion, and gay rights took on new urgency and political salience,"

Critchlow (2007) wrote. The major political parties "responded to constituents' anxieties and interest in their own ways. Whereas Democrats held fast to their New Deal liberal and internationalist vision, Republicans represented the fears of white middle-class and religious voters through a political platform of low taxes, national defense, preservation of family values, regulation of social morality, and opposition to policies that affirmed racial, gender, or sexual preferences in the public sphere." Over the span of the tumultuous, late-20th-century decades, the latter strategy boosted the political fortunes of conservatives. "Although the course of the conservative movement was neither preordained nor inevitable, it did ultimately triumph over its foes," Critchlow concluded. "Republicans battled Republicans for control of their party, and conservatives battled liberals for control of government. But ultimately, the Right did ascend to political power against all odds" in a period when the "tensions and contradictions of modern American conservatism" can be seen to "have a parallel in the limitations of liberalism in the postwar period" (Critchlow, 2007, pp. 3–5).

Those trends have established conservative political influence as solidly locked in, if not quite fully in control of the national government. "Although the Republican Party has dominated American politics over the past 40 years, it has not achieved a political realignment. Instead, the GOP has developed the capacity to eke out victory by slim margins in a majority of closely contested elections, losing intermittently but winning more than half the time," declared political journalist Thomas Edsall in 2006. "It is likely to continue this pattern for the foreseeable future. Conservatives have, furthermore, created a political arena in which winning Democrats are likely to find themselves forced to move to the right" (Edsall, 2006, p. x). Such indications of conservatism's power to rein in liberal impulses beyond its own ranks further suggest the success of the conservative branding process asserted by Cosgrove and others. It has also likely played a factor in increasing polarization of the major political parties. "The traditional American party was almost defined by its peculiarly nonideological character," wrote political scientist Nicole Rae (1989), observing that as early as 1989, the parties had entered a "new world of American politics" in which, "the Democratic Party has become a more consistently liberal party, and the Republican Party more consistently conservative, than has been the case in any previous period of American history" (Rae, 1989, p. 3).

In order to more clearly articulate the impact of that dramatic evolution of the conservative/liberal relationship in political influence and power on media discourse, the study discussed in this chapter sought to examine the nature of meaning constructed in related media representations in the C-SPAN Video Library. The times have relatively rapidly gone from an era when *conservative* was scarcely used as a noun in reference to an individual's political orientation to one in which "the label 'conservative' is promiscuously applied to fundamentalists, populists, libertarians, fascists, and the advocates of one or another orthodoxy," as Muller characterized it (Muller, 1997, p. xiii). Common labeling of liberals is similarly amorphous in the varied range of positionings to which it is casually and loosely applied.

This study utilized the search function of the vast database of the C-SPAN Video Library to spawn an algorithmically generated data pattern for guiding a qualitative framing analysis focused on identifying media frames and the dominant understandings they reflect, or what Gitlin characterized as "persistent patterns of cognition, interpretation, and presentation, of selection, emphasis, and exclusion" (Gitlin, 1980, p. 7). The C-SPAN Video Library database offered an ideal means to systematically identify and assess bodies of relevant representations of the objects of this study that are extremely rich in revelatory discourse. For the C-SPAN Video Library not only represents a vast database of the sort of media-discourse artifacts from recent political events, it offers a research interface that allows scholars to search its archives systematically and objectively.

In short, framing is a well-established method of content analysis, deeply grounded in theoretical concepts discussed more fully below in the section Methodological and Theoretical Context. Utilizing framing methodologically provided the means of analysis for identifying the degree of effectiveness of the branding effort discussed above—branding being a marketing strategy to develop stronger relationships between products and audiences. The search engine of the C-SPAN Video Library was utilized in this study to algorithmically retrieve information stored in the video database—retrieve it in a systematic manner determined by the search-algorithm function of the C-SPAN Video Library search engine, rather than the subjective selection process of a human retrieval effort. (While a search algorithm can potentially reflect biases of its programmer, in the context of this study, the scholar is utilizing a research tool independent of the scholar's own biases—any scholar entering the same search terms will obtain the same results.)

Perhaps a more narratively illustrative way to consider the conceptual basis for this study and the significance of its findings could be to consider it in terms of a sort of thought experiment. If we imagine, let us say, the effort of an extraterrestrial who had recently arrived here to develop a greater understanding of early 21st-century American culture, and if such a being were to begin tuning into random discourse, quite possibly among the terms that would soon begin to suggest salience by the frequency of their usage would be the terms *conservative* and *liberal*. It plausibly could suggest to our extraterrestrial the need for a more systematic examination of the terms and what greater meaning they held in the culture of this unfamiliar landscape. And then let us imagine that the extraterrestrial were to come upon the C-SPAN Video Library and recognize the potential it offered to quickly advance the effort to learn more about the nature of meaning constructed through a sampling of its massive body of media discourse, with its emphasis on political culture. What might that process suggest to a fresh consciousness unmarked by the longer-term mediated conditioning that has influenced the understanding of American audiences over the course of recent decades?

To provide a short summary of the findings discussed in more detail below in the sections Searching for Conservatism and Searching for Liberalism, our extraterrestrial would find significant evidence to support the argument that in terms of branding strategy, conservatism is indeed now a brand quite compellingly established—and that liberalism conversely seems to have scarcely any branding presence of its own provenance. For he would discover that searching the database with a simple focus on the term *conservatism* would produce, almost exclusively, video recordings of individuals who represent themselves as conservatives discussing conservatism. And he would discover that searching the database with the term *liberalism* would produce, almost exclusively, video recordings of individuals who represent themselves as conservatives discussing liberalism. In both cases, conducting such searches via the purest and most direct of search strategies indicates first of all that it is conservatives who are engaging in far more public discourse on both conservatism and liberalism. Thus it is also conservatives who are dominant in the overall construction of meaning for the audiences of this programming. Those findings will be elaborated upon following the discussion of the methodological and theoretical grounding of this analysis, in the sections Searching for Conservatism and Searching for Liberalism.

METHODOLOGICAL AND THEORETICAL CONTEXT

The concept of framing can be particularly useful in studies of the ways that media producers construct representations of reality. Framing theory holds that the ways in which ideas and issues are framed become powerful factors in media discourse. The construction of symbolic meaning that contributes to promotion of themes vital to communicators is a particularly important element of the framing process. The degree of effectiveness with which framing is employed offers insights into why the content of discourse may hold meaning for audiences. Carey proposed that analysis of such themes or narratives can reflect efforts to utilize cultural ideals of an era to create "systems of meaning, and standards of reality shared by writer and audience" (Carey, 1974, p. 5). Societies negotiate the greater meaning of events in many ways, and the media and legal discourse focused upon in this study offers intriguing evidence for considering the manner in which audiences may develop understandings of the terms *conservative* and *liberal.*

Framing theory asserts that successful framing can be the most powerful feature of discourse and in fact as powerful as language itself. Framing was originally discussed in the early 1970s as a psychological concept that described the ways that individuals include, exclude, and organize experience. Bateson compared the influence of a psychological frame to the way that a "picture frame tells the viewer that he is not to use the same sort of thinking in interpreting the picture that he might use in interpreting the wallpaper" (Bateson, 1972, pp. 172–193). Goffman described the psychology of framing as a process by which humans define a situation according to the organizing principles of social events and our subjective involvement in those events. Thus, human beings frame reality in order to order, negotiate, and manage it (Goffman, 1974, pp. 10–11).

From that conceptual perspective, framing analysis was utilized as a means of structuring this qualitative study. Such analysis can be particularly useful in studies of the ways that media producers construct representations of reality. Gamson conceptualized the media frame as "a central organizing idea used for making sense of relevant events," which can provide a basis for exploring how readers may "understand and remember a problem" (Gamson, 1989, p. 157). In this study of understandings of the terms *conservative* and *liberal* advanced in bodies of political discourse from the C-SPAN Video Library, framing analysis provided methodological discipline for guiding the critical evaluation of representations of those terms. Those representations were evaluated in terms of the way they utilized narrative elements in a manner that contributed to recurring themes and dominant frames. Such analysis seeks to identify "the specific properties of the . . . narrative that encourage those perceiving and thinking about events to develop particular understandings of them . . . and [that] convey thematically consonant meanings across media and time," as Entman has discussed it (Entman, 1991, p. 7). This approach to analysis does not eliminate all inconsistent or incongruent information from texts, but on balance serves to "render one basic interpretation more readily discernible, comprehensible, and memorable than others" (Entman, 1991, p. 7). That occurs through a process Entman has detailed in which "framing essentially involves selection and salience. To frame is to select some aspects of a perceived reality and make them more salient in a communicating text, in such a way as to promote a particular problem definition, causal interpretation, moral evaluation, and/or treatment recommendation for the item described" (Entman, 1993, pp. 52–53).

Specifically, this study utilized Altheide's "document analysis" process to connect the media representations that are the focus of the study to broader ideas in discourse and ideology (Altheide, 1996, pp. 23–44). Altheide's approach defines the conceptual relationship of discourse, themes, and frames in this manner: "The actual words and direct messages of documents carry the discourse that reflects certain themes, which in turn are held together and given meaning by a broad frame. . . . Frames are a kind of 'super theme'" (Altheide, 1996, p. 31). This method relies less on counting than on qualitative identification of prominent themes through a multistep process (Altheide, 1996, pp. 23–44).[1]

This methodological approach is not without bias, but it does provide a systematic framework to guide the critical evaluation of relevant media discourse. As Gamson and Modigliani have discussed, "Media discourse is part of the process by which individuals construct meaning" (Gamson & Modigliani, 1989, p. 2). Considering framing in this context suggests that texts potentially represent symbolic meaning relevant to both communicators and receivers, both of which influence and are influenced by the times and culture in which they live. Therefore, the analysis in this research focuses most directly on the texts involved, embracing Entman's assertion that "whatever its specific use, the concept of framing consistently offers a way to describe the power of a communicating text" (Entman, 1993, pp. 52–53). While it cannot ultimately tell us definitively how audiences understood the media representations of political ideas or terminology such as are the subject of this study, it offers insight into symbolic meaning through prominent ideas recently disseminated in the media universe in which those audiences live.

The study drew upon these basic research questions to guide the analysis:

- What understandings are most evident in representations of prominent political discourse centered substantially upon the term *conservative* in relevant media content from the C-SPAN Video Library?

- What understandings are most evident in representations of prominent political discourse centered substantially upon the term *liberal* in relevant media content from the C-SPAN Video Library?

- Are there significant commonalities and/or contrasts among understandings identified in the respective bodies of prominent political discourse from the C-SPAN Video Library?

- What does this analysis suggest regarding how examination of understandings identified in this study of relevant bodies of prominent political discourse from the C-SPAN Video Library can help place in historical and social context recent media representations related to the terms *conservative* and *liberal*?

SEARCHING FOR CONSERVATISM

When searching the C-SPAN Video Library database with a focus on the term *conservatism*, the first consistent understanding that is most evident is the fact that, as could probably be expected, one's results produce, almost exclusively, video recordings of individuals who represent themselves as conservatives discussing conservatism. In that body of discourse, one does find the framing reflected in those conservatives' representations of conservatism to some extent advanced through the contrasts asserted regarding liberalism.[2]

Liberals are commonly represented, for example, as removed from mainstream life: "Most liberals live in pretty cloistered communities" (Brooks, 2015). And liberalism has "an impulse toward centralization and technocratic expertise that . . . is problematic" (Wehner, 2014). However, that sort of framing even more frequently involves representations of conservatism that advance understandings that contrast conservatives with one identified liberal in particular: Barack Obama. Not only is he said to make "no . . . effort to stand on the side of freedom" and to be "quick to deal with the oppressors but slow to deal with the oppressed," he uses "shameful, derogatory rhetoric" that "should have no place in our democracy" (Rubio, 2015). Thus that sort of framing advances understandings of conservatism as antithetical to such behavior.

That is represented as why "with President Obama, you are looking at a failed presidency," because conservative "ideas are still more with the grain of the American character" (Lowry, 2015). President Obama does not know that "people built the farms, the ranches, the schools, the churches, the not-for-profit associations," rather than government (Sasse, 2015). Instead, he is a president who "loves the word 'collective'" and uses it more often than can be counted (Kengor, 2014).

So one of the clearest understandings framed as vital definitionally to conservatism in this body of discourse is one that represents it as distinct from actions taken or thoughts held by Barack Obama. Indeed the assertion is made that a problem with the candidates seeking the Republican nomination midway through 2015 is that "they are not talking about . . . the way the Obama Presidency has gone" (Graham, 2015). Thus, they are not clearly enough advancing a message of true conservatism.

Beyond that, however, this body of political discourse reflects a considerable range of understandings that are sought to be advanced as essential meanings of conservatism:

- Conservatism places "a very high premium on what sociologists call mediating institutions—family, churches, schools, civic associations and so forth" because "between the state and the individual there is a large area of human life that needs to be respected and supported" (Wehner, 2014).

- Conservatism "opposes an echo of the same old politics, the same old policy" (Martin, 2015).

- Conservatism "features an inherent distrust of government, an adherence to the rule of law, not of men, a constitutional system that gives an outside place for deliberative assemblies, a belief in certain unchanging truths about human nature and our God-given rights, and finally a concrete expression of what was once called a free-labor ideology, which rests on a belief in the dignity of all labor and a right to the proceeds of our own labor" (Lowry, 2015).

- Conservatism "empowers me to be whatever kind of woman I want to be" (Wright, 2014).

- Conservatism has "often had an agenda that focuses on an effort to bring down the top marginal tax rate" (Ponnuru, 2014).

- Conservatism has "the best ideas for lifting people out of poverty, . . . not saying how can we get a better capital-gains tax for billionaires. It doesn't come up. We think about what can we do to create greater opportunity for people who have been left behind" (Brooks, 2015).

- "The seed idea of" conservatism "is the idea upon which this nation was founded. Divine ownership, natural rights, that men are born free and independent, as such they own their bodies, they own their minds, they own their labor and the fruits thereof" (Phillips, 2014).

- Conservatism is the "ideal . . . that allows people to live the lives they want to live, that we choose to live, that best suit us as individuals. We are all going to make different kinds of choices, and it is only the conservative ideal that allows that" (Wright, 2014).

That highlighting of the variety of understandings as to the meaning of conservatism is useful not because it brings together a coherent whole but precisely because it suggests how misleading it is for mainstream media to so often routinely label broad collections of positions, players, interests, and so forth. That is what this sampling generated via the C-SPAN Video Library search function helps illuminate—that mainstream media could contribute more meaningful representations by avoiding rigidly dichotomized labeling and utilizing more nuanced characterizations. While there is some commonality in the understandings advanced by individuals representing themselves as conservatives, there is on balance far more contrast.

SEARCHING FOR LIBERALISM

When searching this database with the term *liberalism* and going back the previous 2 years, this is where one realizes it is time in the analysis to step back from the trees and considerable what a remarkable pattern of "forest" this algorithmically generated data pattern indicates. And that is, quite simply, that conservatives appear to be engaging in much more discourse at the sort of events where C-SPAN cameras are present than liberals are—so much so that the systematically objective search function of the C-SPAN video library identifies far more videos from events at which conservatives are talking about the meaning of liberalism than at which liberals are talking about liberalism. And that suggests that the conservative branding effort is markedly more robust than any similar effort by liberals—because that conservative branding effort, in effect, serves to brand liberalism in such a manner as to contribute even more to its own objectives.

This body of political discourse does not exactly advance understandings of liberalism that have clear commonality, except that by and large those understandings frame liberalism as a negative societal influence and inferior to conservatism:

- Liberalism has "no set, fixed values. . . . They are constantly looking up, finding new sins, new laws, new ways to offend. . . . You disagree with one, you aren't just wrong, you're not just unenlightened, you're immoral. You're sinful. And you're deserving of punishment in the here and now, not in the afterlife" (Cashill, 2015).

- Liberalism treats Jean-Jacques Rousseau (and his *The Social Contract*) "as some great guru in the conventional history lesson, and yet, if you read what he actually said, it's appalling. . . . Well, what he says basically is that government can just do anything it wants to and that the social contract . . . is that we allocate all of our rights to the general will, to the community with no reservation of freedom whatsoever. . . . That's the premise of all the totalitarian movements of the modern era, and it's totally destructive of freedom" (Evans, 2015).

- Liberalism "lost faith with the American project" in the 1960s and 1970s, and "when middle America feels that its values are being attacked by liberal elites, meaning educated, higher-income liberals who took over the Democratic Party in the late Sixties, there is some truth to it. So middle American voters, who had heretofore been the rank and file of the Democratic Party, turn against their own party and leave their own party because their party took on a different tone towards their country and towards them" (Bloodworth, 2013).

- Liberalism "like communism, Fabianism, and fascism, . . . was a vanguard movement born of a new class of politically self-conscious intellectuals. . . . Critical of mass democracy and middle-class capitalism, liberals despise the individual businessman's pursuit of profit as well as individuals' self-interested pursuit of success. . . . A sense of alienation from American life, a sense that America was the worst of all places was essential to liberalism in its inception" (Siegel, 2014).

- Liberalism's "political dream is a dream of justice without virtue. Its moral dream is a dream of virtue without discipline or censure. And spiritually, it's a dream of self-realization as salvation" (Reno, 2014).

- Liberalism "sees liberty and individualism as somehow an impediment to radical egalitarianism" (Hanson, 2013).

- Liberalism is "wrong on just about every issue," and if given a choice between Saddam Hussein and the United States, "will not only side with Saddam Hussein, . . . will viciously slander good and decent Americans in order to do so. . . . Vulgarizing society is part of the modern liberal agenda" (Sayet, 2014).

- Liberalism "is in fact a religion, or at least functions like a religion, . . . [and] Christians and other opponents of the agenda of liberalism . . .

can turn the tables on liberal secularism by actively bringing cases to dis-establish it as a state-imposed worldview in education, in federal agencies, and even in the courts" (Wiker, 2013).

One must search back farther than the 2-year period of this study to begin to find even a small number of videos of events at which individuals identifying themselves as liberals discuss substantially the meaning of liberalism. Even then, there are still more videos from the sorts of events highlighted in this section, in which individuals identifying themselves as conservatives discuss the meaning of liberalism.

CONCLUSION

This approach to considering what constructed meaning in media discourse reveals about how effective the asserted branding of conservatism has been in recent decades suggests it has been quite effective—and that liberalism cannot be seen to have established any significant branding presence of its own provenance. Certainly, the question can be considered via other approaches than the one utilized here. But utilizing the C-SPAN Video Library in this manner does provide a systematically neutral mechanism for sampling a considerable body of recent political discourse—and the results were unambiguous: Searching the database for *conservatism* produced, almost exclusively, videos of individuals who represent themselves as conservatives discussing conservatism, while conversely searching the database for *liberalism* produced, almost exclusively, video recordings of individuals who represent themselves as conservatives discussing liberalism.

Although the search strategy involved in the overall research design of this study was not a particularly complex one, the results that strategy yielded suggest quite significant, almost startling, implications. By locating and operating video cameras at an incomparably broad range of public-affairs events, including far more types of events than just congressional proceedings and hearings, the three C-SPAN networks transmit a staggering quantity and diversity of unedited or minimally edited political discourse. With all of that being recorded and indexed in the C-SPAN Video Library, a collection totaling more than 223,000 hours of programming since 1987 has been amassed and made available online—"one of the most comprehensive video archives of governmental and political content," as the Video Library site characterizes it.

So it could hardly be expected that utilizing broad, neutral search strategies of that vast archive of media discourse for the term *conservatism* would produce, almost exclusively, videos of individuals who represent themselves as conservatives discussing conservatism, while searching the database for *liberalism* would also produce, almost exclusively, video recordings of individuals who represent themselves as conservatives—not liberals—discussing liberalism. This study does not attempt to explain all that that finding represents. But it strongly suggests that conservatives are engaging in far more public discourse on not only conservatism, but also on liberalism. And that suggests conservatives are dominant in contributing to the overall construction of related meaning for audiences of a broad and massive body of television programming.

With conservatives apparently engaging in far more public discourse on both conservatism and liberalism, it can only enhance conservative branding efforts to maintain such domination of the overall construction of meaning for audiences of such a considerable quantity of video programming. Whatever the dominant societal understandings may be of conservatism and liberalism today, the findings of this study of media content suggest they are both being determined more by avowed proponents of the former than of the latter.

NOTES

1. Altheide's method utilizes a 12-step process that involves devising research questions, developing context for the sources of documents to be analyzed, examining a small number of the documents to begin developing categories to guide data collection, testing the categories on more documents, revising the categories, implementing "progressive theoretical sampling" (which refers to "the selection of materials based on emerging understanding of the topic under investigation"), collecting data, performing data analysis (which "consists of extensive reading, sorting, and searching through" the documents), comparing and contrasting extremes and key differences, summarizing findings, and integrating findings with interpretation.

2. The discourse highlighted was drawn from videos of events over the 2 years preceding the summer 2015 research period, all of which were identified through the search strategies discussed. In order to minimize researcher search biases, none of the search filters offered for the "Search the Video Library" search box of the C-SPAN Video Library were employed. All searches were conducted by entering the terms noted with the default "All" option selected (rather than, for example, filtering the search with any of the offered filters, which include "Videos," "Clips," "People," "Mentions," and "Bills"). The priority was on utilizing the basic C-SPAN Video Library search function with as little intentional or unintentional researcher bias as possible, so as to obtain whatever selections of video events that search function determined to be most relevant—and then to apply to those selections the framing analysis discussed.

REFERENCES

Allitt, P. (2009). *The conservatives: Ideas and personalities throughout American history*. New Haven, CT: Yale University Press.

Altheide, D. L. (1996). *Qualitative media analysis*. Thousand Oaks, CA: Sage, 1996.

Bateson, G. (1972). A theory of play and fantasy. In G. Bateson. *Steps to an ecology of mind: Collected essays in anthropology, psychiatry, evolution, and epistemology* (pp. 177–193). New York, NY: Ballantine.

Bloodworth, J. (2013). *Book discussion on* Losing the Center [online video]. Available from http://www.c-span.org/video/?315191-1/book-discussion-losing-center

Brooks, A. (2015, July 20). *After Words with Arthur Brooks* [online video]. Available from http://www.c-span.org/video/?327223-1/words-arthur-brooks

Carey, J. W. (1974). The problem of journalism history. *Journalism History, 1*(1), 3–5, 27.

Cashill, J. (2015). *Book discussion on* Scarlet Letters [online video]. Available from http://www.c-span.org/video/?327452-1/jack-cashill-scarlet-letters

Cosgrove, K. M. (2007). *Branded conservatives: How the brand brought the right from the fringes to the center of American politics*. New York, NY: Peter Lang.

Critchlow, D. T. (2007). *The conservative ascendancy: How the GOP right made political history*. Cambridge, MA: Harvard University Press.

Edsall, T. B. (2006). *Building red America: The new conservative coalition and the drive for permanent power*. New York, NY: Basic Books.

Edwards, L. (1999). *The conservative revolution: The movement that remade America*. New York, NY: Free Press.

Entman, R. M. (1991). Framing U.S. coverage of international news. *Journal of Communication, 41*(4), 6–27.

Entman, R. M. (1993). Framing: Toward clarification of a fractured paradigm. *Journal of Communication, 43*(4), 51–58.

Evans, M. S. (2015). *Book discussion on* The theme is freedom [online video]. Available from http://www.c-span.org/video/?62252-1/book-discussion-theme-freedom

Gamson, W. A. (1989). News as framing. *American Behavioral Scientist, 33*(2), 157–161.

Gamson, W. A., & Modigliani, A. (1989). Media discourse and public opinion on nuclear power: A constructionist approach. *American Journal of Sociology, 95*(1), 1–37.

Gifford, L. J. (2009). *The center cannot hold: The 1960 presidential election and the rise of modern conservatism*. DeKalb: Northern Illinois University Press.

Gitlin, T. (1980). *The whole world is watching: Mass media in the making and unmaking of the left*. Berkeley: University of California.

Goffman, E. (1974). *Frame analysis: An essay on the organization of experience*. New York, NY: Harper and Row.

Graham, T. (2015). *Tim Graham on 2016 presidential campaign media coverage* [online video]. Available from http://www.c-span.org/video/?327490-3/washington -journal-tim-graham-2016-campaign-media-coverage

Hanson, V. D. (2013). *Victor Davis Hanson on liberalism* [online video]. Available from http://www.c-span.org/video/?314245-3/victor-davis-hanson-liberalism/

Kengor, P. (2014, March 2). *Book discussion on* 11 principles of a Reagan conservative [online video]. Available from http://www.c-span.org/video/?318009-1/paul-kengor -11-principles-reagan-conservative

Lowry, R. (2015). *Conservative panel at* National Review *Ideas Summit* [online video]. Available from http://www.c-span.org/video/?325690-3/former-governor-jeb -bush-rfl-remarks-national-review-ideas-summit

Martin, E. (2015). *Ed Martin on the conservative agenda* [online video]. Available from http://www.c-span.org/video/?327724-3/washington-journal-ed-martin -conservative-agenda/

Micklethwait, J., & Wooldridge, A. (2004). *The right nation: Conservative power in America*. New York, NY: Penguin.

Muller, J. Z. (1997). *Conservatism: An anthology of social and political thought from David Hume to the present*. Princeton, NJ: Princeton University Press.

Phillips, J. (2014). *Communicating conservatism* [online video]. Available from http:// www.c-span.org/video/?317944-1/communicating-conservatism

Ponnuru, R. (2014). *Future of conservatism* [online video]. Available from http://www .c-span.org/video/?323049-1/discussion-future-conservatism/

Rae, N. C. (1989). *The decline and fall of the liberal Republicans from 1952 to the present*. New York, NY: Oxford University Press.

Reno, R. R. (2014). *Liberalism at home* [online video]. Available from http://www .c-span.org/video/?322871-4/discussion-liberalism-west

Rubio, M. (2015). *Senator Marco Rubio on foreign policy* [online video]. Available from http://www.c-span.org/video/?327636-1/senator-marco-rubio-rfl-remarks -foreign-policy

Sasse, B. (2015). *Conservatism and young people* [online video]. Available from http://www.c-span.org/video/?324557-3/cpac-2015-discussion-conservatism -young-people

Sayet, E. (2014). *Liberals and the media* [online video]. Available from http://www .c-span.org/video/?317048-1/liberals-media

Shirley, C. (2005). *Reagan's revolution: The untold story of the campaign that started it all*. Nashville, TN: Nelson Current.

Siegel, F. (2014). *Book discussion on* The revolt against the masses [online video]. Available from http://www.c-span.org/video/?317203-1/book-discussion-revolt-masses

Viguerie, R. A., & Franke, D. (2004). *America's right turn: How conservatives used new and alternative media to take power*. Chicago, IL: Bonus Books.

Wehner, P. (2014). *The conservative movement* [online video]. Available from http:// www.c-span.org/video/?316998-3/conservative-movement

Wiker, B. (2013). *Book discussion on* Worshipping the state [online video]. Available from http://www.c-span.org/video/?314071-4/book-discussion-worshipping-state

Wright, C. (2014). *Conservative Political Action Conference 2014 Women's Issues Panel* [online video]. Available from http://www.c-span.org/video/?318148-13 /conservative-political-action-conference-2014-womens-issues-panel

CHAPTER **4**

WHAT CAN THE PUBLIC LEARN BY WATCHING CONGRESS?

Tim Groeling

When I was a student in graduate school, I remember arguing with a professor about how scholars and the public should go about studying Congress. My professor (who shall remain nameless here) firmly believed that studying anything other than actual votes in Congress was a waste of time, while I believed that there was value in studying both the deeds *and* the words of members of Congress.

The preceding chapters of the book help validate that more expansive view, as they provide a variety of ways in which scholars and the public can use the coverage provided by C-SPAN to learn about Congress and American politics in general. In other words, all three studies presented here examine the reasoning that underlies public discourse, using C-SPAN as their key tool for analysis, employing strikingly diverse empirical and theoretical approaches:

- In the first chapter, Jonathan Morris and Michael Joy examine how that the congressional deliberative process shapes the public's perceptions of Congress.

- Next, Theresa Castor analyzes congressional discourse to examine how politicians can understand and address policy concerns before they become a crisis.

- Finally, Robert Kerr uses C-SPAN to examine how political actors work to shape their brands and representations in the media.

CONGRESSIONAL DELIBERATIONS

Otto von Bismarck is often credited with the observation that "laws, like sausages, cease to inspire respect in proportion as we know how they are made." While this observation is apparently apocryphal (Shapiro, 2008), it does link our first two chapters here, in that they are trying to help us better understand whether the public decreases their respect for Congress when shown congressional deliberations (Chapter 1) and how policy is made in Congress in a particular case (Chapter 2).

In Chapter 1, Morris and Joy empirically test whether viewing the legislative process actually alienates viewers, and experimentally test whether such alienation might stem from partisan bickering, or from the complexity and tedium of the legislative process (or both). Their findings indicate that legislators wishing to manage their image with the public face a trade-off wherein the same partisan rhetoric that cements their bond with fellow partisans can engage the public, but also angers and frustrates citizens.

In Chapter 2, Castor's analysis of congressional discourse related to the passage of the Great Lakes–St. Lawrence River Basin Water Resources Compact (or, the Great Lakes Compact) is an interesting study of a somewhat puzzling occurrence: Congress anticipating and addressing a potential problem *before* it became a crisis. In conducting her analysis, Castor also identifies a secondary puzzle: the relatively limited amount of congressional discussion and debate that occurred prior to the law's passage. Indeed, although her research found a substantial amount of policy effort preceded congressional involvement, it is surprising—and potentially worrisome for democratic theory—that such a major change in policy could be enacted with so little public debate. Of course, minimal public debate might be a sensible reaction for members of Congress if the public reacts negatively to their "sausage-making" deliberations.

CONSERVATIVE AND LIBERAL BRAND MANAGEMENT

Members of parties face numerous challenges when they try to define themselves and communicate their brand to the public (Cox & McCubbins, 1993; Green, 2015; Groeling, 2010; Sellers, 2010)—particularly when other actors convey their messages to the public. In Chapter 3, Robert Kerr examines how political actors work to shape their brands and representations in the media. In so doing, Kerr identifies two interesting paradoxes in how they work to define their ideological labels to the public:

- First, he argues that conservatives apparently work to define and add value to the conservative brand, but liberals apparently concede the playing field and let conservatives negatively define liberal labeling.

- Second, he concludes that both the public and media still use the liberal and conservative labeling for the major blocs in American politics, even though conservatives apparently define both brands in this study.

The preceding three studies thus illuminate how the public reacts when it observes Congress, how Congress deliberates, and how political actors of opposite ideological persuasions are pitted against one another. Each shows how the C-SPAN Video Library can be used to advance research in these areas. They provide a starting point on which other scholars can build further research.

REFERENCES

Cox, G. W., & M. D. McCubbins. (1993). *Legislative Leviathan*. Berkeley: University of California Press.

Green, M. N. (2015). *Underdog politics: The minority party in the U.S. House of Representatives*. New Haven, CT: Yale University Press.

Groeling, T. (2010). *When politicians attack! Party cohesion in the media*. New York, NY: Cambridge University Press.

Sellers, P. (2010). *Cycles of spin: Strategic communication in the US Congress*. New York, NY: Cambridge University Press.

Shapiro, F. R. (2008, July 21). "Quote . . . misquote." *New York Times Magazine*. Retrieved from http://www.nytimes.com/2008/07/21/magazine/27wwwl-guestsafire-t.html

CHAPTER 5

GENDERED LINGUISTICS: A LARGE-SCALE TEXT ANALYSIS OF U.S. SENATE CANDIDATE DEBATES

Martha E. Kropf and Emily Grassett

Even as United States voters consider former Senator and Secretary of State Hillary Clinton for the highest office in the land, no one can deny that women are underrepresented in political office. According the Center for American Women and Politics (CAWP), as of 2015 only about 20% of the House and Senate are women (Center for American Women and Politics, 2016). Such uneven representation has motivated scholars such as Evans and Clark (2015) to theorize that this out-group status causes "women candidates [to] adopt a different style of communication during their campaign to both combat stereotypes and to distinguish themselves from male candidates" (Evans & Clark, 2015, p. 2). Indeed, in examining tweets in 2012, they found women did tweet more attacks and more women's issues when there were fewer women in the race.

Yet this finding about communication style is not consistent. For example, Banwart and McKinney (2005) examined differences in style between men and women by examining four different mixed-gender debates (two guber-natorial debates and two United States Senate debates). They examined use of attacks, types of appeals, issues discussed, candidate traits, and messaging strategies. Statistically speaking, the authors found very little difference in the styles of females and males. The scholars argued that candidates adapt their communication styles so that neither masculine nor feminine communication styles dominate.

Yet, we wonder if debate style is more than types of attacks, appeals, issues discussed, or more accurately, other big-picture elements of communication. An ever-growing body of research suggests that the type of words that a person uses in speaking and writing can provide information about the underlying personality of the person, including motives and thoughts (e.g., Pennebaker, Mehl, & Niederhoffer, 2003). Newman, Groom, Handelman, and Pennebaker (2008, p. 216) argue that "this approach to language suggests that differences in how individuals communicate can sometimes be as meaningful as what they communicate." Psychologist James W. Pennebaker and his colleagues have developed software that enables large-scale analysis of word choice in other political contexts. The software, called Linguistic Inquiry and Word Count (LIWC), has been utilized in studying political content, for example, in congressional speeches (e.g., Pearson & Dancey, 2011; Yu, Kaufmann, & Diermeier, 2008) and analysis of messages tweeted during local mayoral and city council races (Kropf, 2014). The software counts the use of different parts of speech, particularly connector words and pronouns (*I*, *we*, *he*), but also categorizes the types of words communicated. That is, given text of a speech, the software indicates the percentage of the words used in one piece of writing/speaking that classifies not only parts of speech used, but also measures emotional tone and cognitive processes. For example, the software categorizes the words *maddening* and *suffering* as indicative of negative emotions. It classifies *folks*, *family*, and *forgave* as social words, indicating a person who interacts more with other people. Pennebaker, Chung, Ireland, Gonzales, and Booth (2007) have developed and validated dictionaries of indicator words that measure "various emotional, cognitive, and structural components present in individuals' verbal and written speech samples" (Pennebaker et al., 2007, p. 3).

This allows us to take a different approach here and ask the research question: What are the differences in word usage between male and female U.S.

Senate candidates in their responses to debate questions and in rebuttals? Using 16 U.S. Senate debates spanning the years 2010–2014, we analyze candidate statements in this context. Our results indicate that women and men candidates have very few differences in language use.

WORD CHOICE IN DEBATE STYLE

Thousands of articles have been written about various aspects of political candidate debates, but the vast majority of the research examines presidential debates (McKinney & Carlin, 2004). Even fewer report on gendered differences in candidate debates (but see Banwart & McKinney, 2005). Banwart and McKinney (2005) use literature examining differences in campaign advertisements to build a theoretical framework for their empirical analyses of *debatestyle*. Banwart and McKinney (p. 357) invoked the idea of *videostyle*, particularly utilizing the gendered framework in the work of Bystrom, Banwart, Kaid, and Robertson (2004). The framework focused on types of appeals, issue discussion, and qualifications/traits in a variety of communication formats. Banwart and McKinney note that political advertisements are far more controlled in message than debates; but the framework provides a useful coding scheme in examining candidate statements. Banwart and McKinney find no statistical difference between male and female candidates. They argue that women seemed to be adopting a more masculine debate style, and suggest women candidates might be aware of gender stereotypes and are attempting to adapt accordingly.

While current research does not indicate a distinctive debatestyle that differentiates men and women, much vote-choice research indicates that potential voters do sometimes see candidates through the lens of gender—even when voters profess not to possess gender stereotypes. For example, early work by Alexander and Andersen (1993) gave a detailed description about how a candidate's gender is not typically considered by voters but stereotypes and gender roles do influence voters. The results of their survey found that voters do not agree with outward gender stereotypes, but when asked about specific issues, the respondents said women would be better at traditionally women's issues (health care, education, and poverty) and men would be better at male issues (foreign policy, military, and the economy).

More recent research indicates that these stereotypes persist, but the effects are potentially more subtle than a simple belief that women should have a certain role (e.g., a leader or not). There are many examples of such research. Dolan and Lynch (2014) argue that stereotypes help the average person create shortcuts to evaluate candidates. However, they also found that the party of the candidate, for females, plays a role in the stereotypes about that candidate. For instance, Dolan and Lynch argue that "people who hold traditional stereotypes about female traits are more likely to vote for Republican women" (Dolan & Lynch, 2014, p. 669). They conclude that while the candidate's gender plays a role in deciding whether a candidate is qualified or not, there are many other factors that contribute to that decision as well. Dolan (2014) builds upon Dolan and Lynch and found that while gender plays an abstract role in evaluating women candidates, party affiliation plays more of a role. Both analyses come from a survey of 3,000 adults regarding the 2010 U.S. House races across 29 states. This does not take away from our study, but reminds us that our control variables will need to include political party and incumbency to be sure that we are isolating the proper effects.

Further building on the idea that the effects of gender are subtle, but persistent, other research indicates that female candidates believe they must be more prepared than male candidates when they run. Fulton (2012) studied the quality of candidates and concluded that "relative to men, women have to work harder at developing greater political quality to be equally competitive" (Fulton, 2012, p. 310). Because women tend to be challenged within their party as well as outside of it, the candidates who continue their campaigns tend to be more qualified than their male counterparts.

Combining the literature about voter stereotypes and gender differences in communication, we wonder why research results in gender differences in communication style should ever vary. Perhaps the issue is measurement. Specifically, coding involves big-picture issues rather than the smaller, more likely unconscious word choice—for example, something so unconscious as using the word *I* versus using the word *we*. The issue may also be sample size. With manual coding, naturally, case studies or smaller sample sizes dominate the research because coding is so intensive and reliability checks demand multiple coders. With a smaller sample size, scholars lose leverage that might allow them to observe the relationship between gender, party affiliation, candidate experience, and gendered style.

In examining studies of rhetoric and communication that analyze word choice, studies with larger sample sizes are beginning to establish that there are differences between how women and men use particular words and that word choice is meaningful. Newman, Groom, Handelman, and Pennebaker (2008) compiled 14,000 samples from all types of writing and spoken language to evaluate whether there was a difference in the way that men and women use particular words. Computerized text analysis has opened new areas of exploration, providing much more analytic leverage than in communication studies where language is coded by hand, according to the authors:

> Unfortunately, many previous studies have had fewer than 50 participants per cell. Larger samples are often difficult to collect when each sample must be hand coded. The need to conserve coder time also reduces the number of features that can be coded in a single study. This reality has focused attention toward features of language that can be easily related to gender stereotypes (e.g., hedges), potentially missing differences in less obvious language categories (e.g., pronouns). Thus, a strategy that allowed for the efficient analysis of large samples of text could help to create a more complete picture of gender differences in language use. (Newman, Groom, Handelman, & Pennebaker, 2008, p. 215)

Newman and his colleagues utilize LIWC, developed by Pennebaker, Francis, and Booth (2001; Pennebaker et al., 2007). Scholars such as Pearson and Dancey (2011) also use LIWC to analyze congressional speeches, and show that women members of Congress are more likely to mention women, which the scholars argue shows that the members of Congress are representing women's issues.[1]

LIWC software categorizes specific words or word stems (more than 2,300 of them) based on the trait or quality attributed to the word:

> These dimensions include standard language categories (e.g., articles, prepositions, pronouns—including first person singular, first person plural, etc.), psychological processes (e.g., positive and negative emotion categories, cognitive processes such as use of causation words, self-discrepancies), relativity-related words (e.g., time, verb tense, motion, space), and traditional content dimensions (e.g., sex, death, home, occupation). (Pennebaker et al., 2003, p. 571)

Pennebaker and his colleagues[2] (2007) continue by noting that "independent judges" categorized words as measures of concepts in the software dictionary; then the researchers used extensive procedures to ensure the reliability of the categorizations across the judges.[3] It is important to note these scholars all acknowledge that one possible flaw in this software is that it is unable to identify expressions such as sarcasm. For instance, if a candidate were to say "I am going mad," LIWC would categorize the term *mad* as a negative emotion, rather than a term signifying a mental state.

Thus, Newman and his colleagues (2008) utilize the software to analyze the gendered differences in word choice in the 14,000 files. They did not hypothesize a direction of relationship in the differences between female and male word choice because of so many conflicting findings among previous studies. However, the scholars did note that previous work finds that women are more likely to use the word *I* than men; even though this seems contrary to the conventional wisdom that men might be more selfish.[4] To the extent the authors did hypothesize, they

> expected the largest differences to be found on function words because these words appear to be particularly good markers of how individuals relate to the world. However, we also examined a range of social and psychological process words, including references to friends, family, and emotions, to better understand how men and women differ in their language use. (Newman et al., 2008, p. 218)

Indeed, over all the word-choice categories considered together, the authors found statistically significant differences between male's and female's language use. In particular, men swore more than women, and women were more likely to say "I" than men. Female language was more likely to reference emotions and "social processes." Male language was more likely to emphasize current concerns such as job or money. Men and women were just as likely to use "tentative" words; women were more likely to be "certain." The authors argue that their findings are consistent with the idea that females and males use language in order to accomplish different things.

What does that mean in the realm of a political campaign? Analyzing the word choice of political candidates may give scholars insight not only into communication style (debatestyle more specifically) but also may very well provide some insight into whether a certain debatestyle contributes to a winning campaign. Of course, if the major interest is gender differences (which, given the underrepresentation of women in Congress and other political offices, is a key scholarly interest), the first step to a successful analysis is to examine the debates using LIWC (or similar software wherein the categorized words have been similarly vetted for measurement validity and reliability) to see if there are gender differences at all. Indeed, Jones (2015) used LIWC to analyze Hillary Clinton's word choice over time. She found that Clinton used more and more masculine words over time. Jones argues that her analysis "support[s] the notion that females may sub-consciously conform to a masculine style when engaging in politics" (Jones, 2015, p. 13).

In the present research, we analyze U.S. Senate debates. We are not the first scholars to conclude that debates are a good source of information concerning sex differences in candidates. Edelsky and Adams (1990) argue that debates are a good medium to evaluate candidates because the environment is seemingly equal. Through their study, they concluded that when the rules are not followed and the debate becomes unequal, gender qualities are more likely to show with an impact on the overall debate. This study also argued that the moderator within the debate mattered regarding the tempo of the debate. The moderator could enforce rules when needed and could give candidates extra time to speak when they felt it was necessary. The study did not take into account how a moderator might affect the word choice used by the candidates; it could be an area where further research could be done. Benoit, Brazeal, and Airne (2007) studied the political debate environment as a medium for political communication. They found that debates might be able to provide a relatively candid view of the candidates because of the unanticipated questions and discussions that arise throughout the debate.

Analyzing the word choices in debates may give us another realm in which to examine gender roles. As politics has largely been controlled by men, analyzing how women are presenting themselves in this traditionally masculine field can give us insight about gender roles, their changes over time, and then, possibly, how they are different in politics than in other fields. Further research can be done, as well, on the differences in presentation of self when comparing candidates of both genders.

HYPOTHESES

Our research question is: What are the differences in word usage between male and female U.S. Senate candidates in their responses to debate questions? Our hypothesis is that a female candidate's word usage will be different from a male candidate's word usage, even when controlling for incumbency, political party, and whether a candidate was vying for an open seat. The particular types of words where we expect to see differences are the following, which serve as dependent variables in a series of hypotheses: Inclusiveness, Exclusiveness, Family, Social, Tentativeness, Certainty, Pronouns, Use of *I*, and Use of *We*.

We chose these categories to analyze in the present research because previous literature highlighted women's use of the LIWC category labeled social (Newman et al., 2008; see also Schwartz et al., 2013). Given the family and social findings, we expected that female candidates might use more inclusive and fewer exclusive words than male candidates. Newman and his colleagues (2008, p. 215) cite research that indicates females may be more likely to hedge than men. Even though Newman et al. found no difference in certainty versus tentativeness, we nevertheless examine that difference on the analysis. Finally, women are more likely to use pronouns, particularly *I*.

METHODS

For our study, we will be using a regression model[5] and the LIWC text analysis software to test our hypotheses. The debate data were gathered from the C-SPAN Video Library, where video and closed captioning (CC) of most U.S. Senate debates are located. As a part of the network's campaign coverage, C-SPAN cooperated with local stations to provide the debates, which it has been airing since 2002.[6] Thus, we were able to transcribe each of 16 different debates over the time period of 2010–2014 (covering a full electoral cycle of U.S. Senate candidates). We started with CC transcripts and then checked for typographical and other errors by listening to each debate, the video of which was also located on the Video Library (see Figure 5.1 for a screen shot of the New York U.S. Senate debate in 2012).[7] Then, each debate is divided into *statements*, similar to the work of Banwart and McKinney (2005). In one case, for example, in the 2012 Wisconsin dmade 18 different statements.

Figure 5.1 Screen shot of the 2012 New York U.S. Senate debate.

We use multiple methods to select the sample of debates for the analysis. First, we stratified the debates according to what type of candidates and contests are represented (incumbent in office, open seat).[8] Then, we took into account incumbency and partisanship. Finally, we looked at gender: Was a woman debating another woman? Was a woman debating a man? Was a man debating a man? Then, we randomly selected state/years within each category. If there was more than one debate for each state and each year, we randomly selected debates. Then, we checked the availability of each transcript.[9] These debates were analyzed:

- Alaska, 2014
- California, 2010
- Hawaii, 2012
- Iowa, 2014
- Kansas, 2014
- Maine, 2014
- Nebraska, 2014
- Nevada, 2010
- New Hampshire, 2014
- New Mexico, 2012
- New York, 2012

- North Carolina, 2014
- South Dakota, 2014
- Vermont, 2012
- West Virginia, 2014
- Wisconsin, 2012

For this analysis, we watched debates available in the C-SPAN Video Library to verify that the CC transcript was edited to include all words used by each candidate when responding to questioning. The opening and closing statements of each debate were not included in the data as they are likely to be prepared beforehand and do not exhibit the qualities sought in our analysis.

We then coded each statement for whether it was made by a woman, a Democrat, a Republican, or an independent;[10] for incumbency status; and for whether the contest was an open seat or not. We also coded for the year in which the statement was made; 2012 was a presidential election year, so we consider 2012 versus 2010 and 2014. Our focal independent variable is candidate gender, but we are also able to control for the other factors mentioned in this paragraph.

As noted before, the dependent variable is word use. Word choice is the decision by an individual to use a specific word as opposed to other words. Note that the LIWC program provides the number of words in each statement and the percentage of the words that are of each of the qualities. The software codes candidate statements based on the established categories given by LIWC. The data on candidate gender, the candidate's partisanship, the candidate's incumbency, and the year of the debate constituted the independent variables.

RESULTS

We analyzed a total of 942 candidate statements from the 16 debates. Table 5.1 indicates how many statements each candidate made and the percentage that each individual contributed to the total number of statements that were analyzed. There is variation in the number of statements each candidate made because some debates were longer than others.

Table 5.1 The Candidates and Number of Statements Each Made

Candidate, State, Year	Number of Statements	Percentage of Total
Angle, Nevada, 2010	26	2.76
Baldwin-Wisconsin, 2012	18	1.91
Begich, Alaska, 2014	21	2.23
Bellows, Maine, 2014	31	3.29
Bossi, South Carolina, 2014	13	1.38
Boxer, California, 2010	50	5.31
Braley, Iowa, 2014	31	3.29
Brown, New Hampshire, 2014	33	3.50
Capito, West Virginia, 2014	18	1.91
Collins, Maine, 2014	31	3.29
Diamondstone, Vermont, 2012	11	1.17
Dickerson, South Carolina, 2014	13	1.38
Domina, Nebraska, 2014	11	1.17
Ericson, Vermont, 2012	11	1.17
Ernst, Iowa, 2014	32	3.40
Fiorina, California, 2010	49	5.20
Gillibrand, New York, 2012	28	2.97
Hagan, North Carolina, 2014	29	3.08
Heinrich, New Mexico, 2012	26	2.76
Herono, Hawaii, 2012	25	2.65
Howie, South Dakota, 2014	9	0.96
Jenkins, Nebraska, 2014	11	1.17
Laframboise, Vermont, 2012	9	0.96
Lingle, Hawaii, 2012	24	2.55
Long, New York, 2012	32	3.40
MacGovern, Vermont, 2012	21	2.23
Moss, Vermont, 2012	9	0.96
Orman, Kansas, 2014	27	2.87
Pressler, South Dakota, 2014	8	0.85
Reid, Nevada, 2010	29	3.08
Roberts, Kansas, 2014	25	2.65
Rounds, South Dakota, 2014	8	0.85

Continued

Table 5.1 Continued

Candidate, State, Year	Number of Statements	Percentage of Total
Sanders, Vermont, 2012	19	2.02
Sasse, Nebraska, 2014	16	1.70
Scott, SouthCarolina, 2014	12	1.27
Shaheen, New Hampshire, 2014	33	3.50
Sullivan, Alaska, 2014	31	3.29
Tennant, West Virginia, 2014	20	2.12
Thompson, Wisconsin, 2012	17	1.80
Tillis, North Carolina, 2014	29	3.08
Watson, Nebraska, 2014	13	1.38
Weiland, South Dakota, 2014	8	0.85
Wilson, New Mexico, 2012	25	2.65
Total	942 statements	100%

Second, we present a bivariate analysis simply comparing female candidates to male candidates on the dimensions of interest. We use difference-of-means tests in order to compare the percentages of each type of words used in each statement. Figure 5.2 shows the percentages of words and indicates there are very few differences between male and female candidates in terms of word use; the darker bars indicate male candidates (left); the lighter represent the female candidates (right). Other than the use of *I*, where there are differences, they are contrary to what we expect: male candidates are more likely to use inclusive words and use the word *we*. On all other dimensions, there are no statistically significant differences.

Do these results continue to hold when controlling for the other political factors? Table 5.2 includes a series of Generalized Linear Model (GLM) regressions with a logit link function in order to analyze this question.

Table 5.2 indicates very few differences between male and female candidates. Concerning gender, the only difference in the use of word is the use of the word *I*, a finding that is marginally significant at best at $p < 0.1$ for a two-tailed test.

Note the use of the dummy variables affects the interpretation of the findings; when there are a series of dummy variables such as whether the candidate is vying for an open seat or whether the candidate is an incumbent or

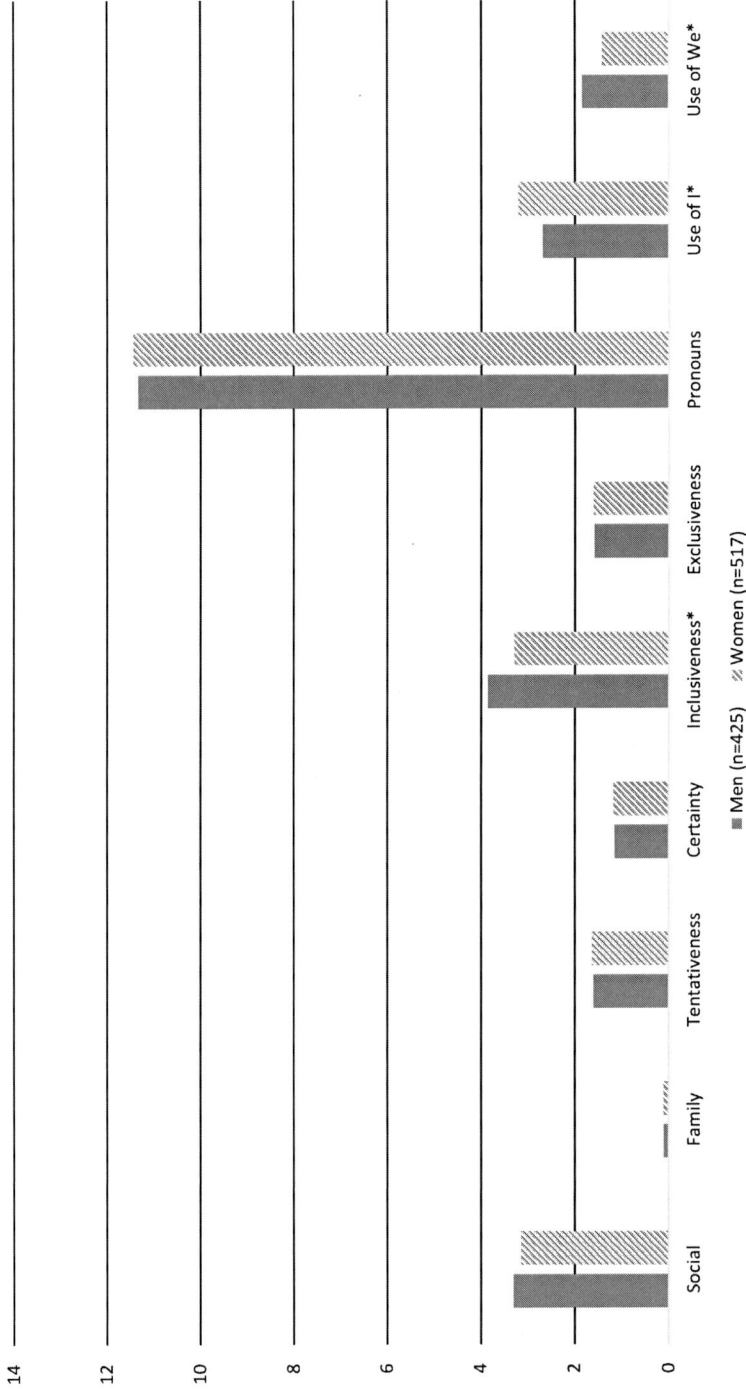

*The differences between male and female candidates are statistically significant at the 0.0001 level.

Figure 5.2 Word-use comparisons between male and female candidates for U.S. Senate.

Table 5.2 Results of GLM Regression on Various Types of Words

VARIABLES	(1) Social	(2) Family	(3) Tentativeness	(4) Certainty	(5) Inclusiveness	(6) Exclusiveness	(7) Pronouns	(8) Use of I	(9) Use of We
Woman	0.222	0.214	0.0692	0.0359	-0.0204	0.104	0.0535	0.233*	-0.196
	(0.397)	(0.294)	(0.121)	(0.121)	(0.158)	(0.136)	(0.0990)	(0.120)	(0.171)
Democrat	-0.346	-0.156	-0.111	-0.0542	-0.235	-0.216	-0.0498	-0.0198	-0.0584
	(0.498)	(0.313)	(0.111)	(0.135)	(0.220)	(0.172)	(0.141)	(0.150)	(0.178)
Independent	0.571	0.376	0.103	-0.000378	0.417**	0.246	0.112	0.118	0.246
	(0.454)	(0.426)	(0.102)	(0.149)	(0.192)	(0.151)	(0.151)	(0.141)	(0.205)
Incumbent	0.409	0.590	-0.0289	-0.0197	0.403	0.117	0.0899	0.0765	0.314
	(0.824)	(0.418)	(0.139)	(0.207)	(0.297)	(0.213)	(0.173)	(0.176)	(0.253)
Open	1.427**	1.092***	-0.0548	0.264*	0.715***	0.308*	0.302**	0.0946	0.563***
	(0.574)	(0.345)	(0.115)	(0.140)	(0.184)	(0.163)	(0.132)	(0.127)	(0.174)
Year is 2012	0.00929	-0.176	-0.168	0.0949	-0.0266	-0.0318	-0.0462	-0.303***	-0.0454
	(0.532)	(0.395)	(0.118)	(0.202)	(0.226)	(0.177)	(0.159)	(0.0936)	(0.256)
Constant	-4.182***	-7.426***	-4.046***	-4.541***	-3.614***	-4.252***	-2.178***	-3.597***	-4.282***
	(0.563)	(0.312)	(0.124)	(0.129)	(0.175)	(0.144)	(0.0969)	(0.118)	(0.157)
Observations	942	942	942	942	942	942	942	942	942

Robust standard errors in parentheses. * p < 0.1, ** p < 0.05, *** p < 0.01

not, each dummy variable in the series should be interpreted compared to the one category left out. Candidates who are independent and not a member of the Republican or Democratic Parties are more likely to use inclusive words. Those vying for an open seat are more likely to use social and family words, inclusive words and use the word *we* than are challengers.

CONCLUSION

At this point, our evidence indicates that debate rhetoric may not be a function of word choice based on gender, at least when it comes to the words utilized by candidates during debates. The lack of difference between male- and female-candidate word choice is consistent with previous research on debates (Banwart & McKinney, 2005), but not on other communication styles such as tweets (Evans & Clark, 2015). However, previous work on word use indicates that women and men use language differently, particularly their use of inclusive and exclusive words, their use of words that demonstrated tentativeness versus certainty, and their use of the pronouns *I* and *we* (e.g., Newman et al., 2008). The literature demonstrated that women tended to be more tentative than men, use more pronouns, and used the word *we* more often than men did in natural language.

However, Figure 5.2 and Table 5.2 show these parts of language and also show that the women within these debates did not use these parts of language in the same manner that the previous literature would have predicted in comparison to men. The bivariate tests demonstrated that the female candidates actually used less-tentative word choice, were less inclusive, and used the word *we* less often than their male counterparts. All of these findings were also statistically significant. However, when subjected to an analysis with control variables, gender simply did not differentiate the candidates. Partisanship (or lack thereof) or whether the seat was open had more of an effect on word choice.

While finding almost no difference between male and female candidates is not what we expected, there is an explanation offered in the literature that makes sense of these findings. Because these female candidates are aware of gender norms and it has been demonstrated that traits that voters seek within political candidates tend to be more masculine, these female candidates are changing their language to present themselves to the debate audience in a more masculine manner than the natural language used by women (Jones, 2015). Indeed, this is an issue that merits more exploration as more women enter the political arena, especially as women vie for high executive offices such as the presidency. The C-SPAN Video Library provides scholars access to these debates. Certainly, this methodology does not limit scholars to that study; LIWC affords scholars the ability to analyze all levels of debates and a large number of them. Some of these differences may be more evident in offices that one may consider entry level (city council or school board). Large-scale text analysis cannot tell us whether a candidate's math adds up or not, but we argue it may provide leverage needed for analysis of language use and candidate popularity or success.

ACKNOWLEDGMENTS

The authors wish to thank the University of North Carolina's Charlotte Research Scholars program for the resources needed to complete this chapter. We also thank the C-SPAN Archives and Purdue University for the funds needed to present our research.

NOTES

1. Pearson and Dancey (2011) do not use the dictionaries created by Pennebaker and his colleagues (2007). Rather, they use the software for a word count of "women."

2. The 2007 version of the software (Pennebaker et al., 2007) is used to analyze all the text in the present research, as it was the most updated version when the project began.

3. For detailed information about reliability of the standard dictionary used in the software, see Pennebaker, Boyd, Jordan, & Blackburn (2015).

4. The authors state that the use of I is more likely from a depressed person and women are more likely to be depressed.

5. For this analysis, we use GLM regression with a logit link function to take into account the censored nature of the data (we also cluster on candidate: note our unit of analysis). The dependent variable is a proportion of the parts of the speeches that are each kind of word, so they vary from 0-1. However, we suspect that future iterations of this type of research will need to use a zero-inflated regression technique (not

zero-inflated negative binomial as one would for a count-dependent variable because of the heterogeneity in the number of words among speeches).

6. See "C-SPAN through the years . . ." (n.d.).

7. Note that CC transcripts are not available for all the debates. Where they were unavailable, we searched online for the transcripts. Thus, the use of the debates is not just driven by random sampling, but also by whether or not we could locate a transcript for the selected debate.

8. In other words, we have selected the debates using Kahn and Goldenberg's (1991) categorical groupings to obtain a relatively equal amount of all types of debates, i.e., male v. female, incumbent Republican v. Democrat challenger, etc.

9. Those transcripts from 2010 were particularly hard to come by; therefore the 2010 debates were simply used based on pure availability.

10. We coded Bernie Sanders as both independent and Democrat.

REFERENCES

Alexander, D., & Andersen, K. (1993). Gender as a factor in the attribution of leadership traits. *Political Research Quarterly*, *46*(3), 527–545.

Banwart, C. M., & McKinney, M. S. (2005). A gendered influence in campaign debates? Analysis of mixed-gender United States Senate and gubernatorial debates. *Communication Studies*, *56*(4), 353–373.

Benoit, William; Brazeal, L.M., Airne, D. (2007). A Functional Analysis of Televised US Senate and Gubernatorial Campaign Debates. *Argumentation & Advocacy*, *44*(2), 75-89.

Bystrom, D. G., Banwart, C. M., Kaid, L. L., & Robertson, T. A. (2004). *Gender and political candidate communication: Videostyle, webstyle, and newsstyle*. New York, NY: Routledge.

Center for American Women and Politics. (2016). Women in U.S. Congress 2015. Retrieved from www.cawp.rutgers.edu/women-us-congress-2015

C-SPAN through the years . . . . (n.d.). Retrieved from http://www.c-span.org/about/milestones/

Dolan, K. (2014). Gender stereotypes, candidate evaluations, and voting for women candidates: What really matters? *Political Research Quarterly*, *67*(1), 96–107.

Dolan, K., & Lynch, T. (2014). It takes a survey: Understanding gender stereotypes, abstract attitudes, and voting for women candidates. *American Politics Research*, *42*(4), 656–676.

Edelsky, C., & Adams, K. (1990). Creating inequality: Breaking the rules in debate. *Journal of Language and Social Psychology, 9*(3), 171–190.

Evans, H. K. & Hayes Clark, J. (2015). "You tweet like a girl!" How female candidates campaign on Twitter. *American Politics Research.* http://dx.doi.org/10.1177/1532673X15597747

Fulton, S. (2012). Running backwards and in high heels: The gendered quality gap and incumbent electoral success. *Political Research Quarterly, 65*(2), 303–314.

Jones, J. (2015). *"Talk like a man": The linguistic appeal of Hillary Rodham Clinton.* Paper prepared for presentation at the 2015 meeting of the Western Political Science Association. Retrieved from http://wpsa.research.pdx.edu/papers/docs /jjjones_HRC_talk_like_a_man_3_30_15.pdf

Kahn, K. F. & Goldenberg, E. N. (1991). Women candidates in the news: An examination of gender differences in US Senate campaign coverage. *Public Opinion Quarterly, 55*(2), 180–199.

Kropf, M. (2014). *The impact of ranked choice voting on election cooperation and civility: Measuring public sentiment through a content analysis of campaign-related communications.* Paper presented at Stanford University Workshop on Electoral System Reforms, March 14–15, 2014 (part of larger project; this part sole-authored). Retrieved from http://cddrl.fsi.stanford.edu/multimedia/electoral-system-reform-6. Also presented at the 2014 North Carolina Political Science Association Conference, Cary, NC, February 27, 2014.

McKinney, M., & Carlin, D. B. (2004). Political campaign debates. In L. L. Kaid (Ed.), *Handbook of political communication research* (pp. 203–234). Mahwah, NJ: Lawrence Erlbaum.

Newman, M. L., Groom, C. J., Handelman, L. D., & Pennebaker, J. W. (2008). Gender differences in language use: An analysis of 14,000 text samples. *Discourse Processes, 45*(3), 211–236.

Pearson, K., & Dancey, L. (2011). Elevating women's voices in Congress: Speech participation in the House of Representatives. *Political Research Quarterly, 64*(4), 910–923. http://dx.doi.org/10.1177/1065912910388190

Pennebaker, J. W., Boyd, R. L., Jordan, K., & Blackburn, K. (2015). *The development and psychometric properties of LIWC2015.* Austin: University of Texas. http://dx .doi.org/10.15781/T29G6Z. Retrieved from http://liwc.wpengine.com/wp-content /uploads/2015/11/LIWC2015_LanguageManual.pdf

Pennebaker, J. W., Chung, C. K., Ireland, M., Gonzales, A., & Booth, R. J. (2007). *The development and psychometric properties of LIWC2007.* Austin, TX: LIWC.net.

Pennebaker, J. W., Francis, M. E., & Booth, R. J. (2001). *Linguistic inquiry and word count: LIWC 2001.* Mahway, NJ: Lawrence Erlbaum.

Pennebaker, J. W., Mehl, M. R., & Niederhoffer, K. G. (2003). Psychological aspects of natural language use: Our words, our selves. *Annual Review of Psychology, 54,* 547–577.

Schwartz, H. A., Eichstaedt, J. C., Kern, M. L., Dziurzynski, L., Ramones, S. M., Agrawal, M., . . . Ungar, L. H. (2013). Personality, gender, and age in the language of social media: The open-vocabulary approach. *PLoS ONE, 8*(9), e73791. Retrieved from http://journals.plos.org/plosone/article?id=10.1371/journal.pone.0073791

Yu, B., Kaufmann, S., & Diermeier, D. (2008). Exploring the characteristics of opinion expressions for political opinion classification. *Proceedings of the 9th Annual International Digital Government Research Conference.* Retrieved from http://beiyu.syr.edu/DGO2008.pdf

CHAPTER 6

MICROANALYSIS OF THE EMOTIONAL APPROPRIATENESS OF FACIAL DISPLAYS DURING PRESIDENTIAL DEBATES: C-SPAN COVERAGE OF THE FIRST AND THIRD 2012 DEBATES

Patrick A. Stewart and Spencer C. Hall

"Debates," it has been aptly put, "are for losers," with the potential losses from mistakes greatly outweighing possible gains from candidate performance during general-election debates (Schrott & Lanoue, 2008). More precisely, by the time the presidential candidates from both political parties are ready to confront each other face-to-face in the days leading up to the general election, they have been thoroughly vetted by the media, public, and their respective political parties on their policy positions, political and social values, personality traits, and quirks. What remains for the voters, especially those who are undecided or wavering in their support, is a final verification of candidate authenticity. While presidential debates have been referred to as side-by-side press conferences (Lanoue & Schrott, 1991; Racine Group, 2002), they offer enough spontaneity and surprise to potentially alter electoral outcomes through inappropriate or unexpected behavior by the candidates. As a result, they are among the most-viewed political events, with the first 2012 presidential debate between Barack Obama and Mitt Romney drawing 67.2 million viewers, more than the Summer Olympics opening ceremony earlier that year.

Not doing your political homework can certainly lead to embarrassment and ultimately withdrawal from even the most well-planned and -funded of presidential campaigns. Texas Governor and presidential candidate Rick Perry learned this hard lesson during the 9 November 2011 primary debate when he promised to cut three federal agencies, but was only able to name two of his targets. His resultant "oops" moment diminished his credibility as a front-running candidate and was perceived as leading to his exiting from 2012 presidential Republican Party primary, as well as his early exit from the 2016 race. Even minor verbal gaffes can be amplified by the mass media in the postdebate spin (Norton & Goethals, 2004), as experienced by President Gerald Ford in his 1976 debate with Jimmy Carter when he stated that the Soviet Union did not dominate Eastern Europe (Brownell, 2014). While this assertion did not play an immediate role in how Ford's performance was evaluated, the postdebate media spin raised questions as to his leadership ability (Exline, 1985).

Despite the influence of misstatements such as these on electoral prospects, a major means by which candidates apparently lose their edge is through inappropriate behavior. While the focus of much debate research has been on the verbal, textual elements (e.g., Benoit & Harthcock, 1999; Racine Group, 2002), what may matter more is the nonverbal delivery and response by the participants. In other words, what a candidate says is important; how it is delivered and, in turn, reacted to is perhaps even more important. This is especially the case when norms and expectations are deviated from. Whether this is through general "impoliteness" (Dailey, Hinck, & Hinck, 2005) or through specifically identified nonverbal behavior (Gong & Bucy, 2015; Gong & Bucy, 2016; Seiter & Harry Weger, 2005; Seiter, Weger Jr, Jensen, & Kinzer, 2010), inappropriate behavior has had a substantial and negative effect upon a candidate's electoral chances (Schrott & Lanoue, 2008). In other words, while talk by the candidates may be seen as cheap, it is nonverbal behavior—especially that at odds with the verbal utterances—that more honestly signals the capability, intent, and reliability of the candidates (Mehu & Scherer, 2012).

The first televised presidential debate between John F. Kennedy and Richard M. Nixon in 1960 is the benchmark of how appearing like a leader, or not, can have a major influence on electoral success (Brownell, 2014; Bucy

& Ball, n.d.). Here Nixon's sickly and sweaty appearance led to him apparently being upstaged by the more youthful-looking and tanned Kennedy, leading viewers to the conclusion that the latter had won—even though listeners came to the opposite conclusion (Druckman, 2003). In other words, by violating the *emotional appropriateness heuristic* (Burgoon & Hale, 1988), Nixon in the crucial latter stages of the campaign likely raised questions in the minds of supporters and potential supporters as to his suitability for office. Although research has not developed clear causal linkages, inappropriate *display behavior* during debates has been implicated in precipitous drops in public opinion support for candidates such as Ronald Reagan, Michael Dukakis, George H. W. Bush, Al Gore, and George W. Bush (Schrott & Lanoue, 2008). More promising in the teasing out of the influence of inappropriate display behavior is the multimethod research by Gong and Bucy concerning Barack Obama's perceived weak debate performance against Mitt Romney (Gong & Bucy, 2015; 2016), which we cover and expand upon in this chapter.

This leads us to the question as to just what can be considered emotionally appropriate for a leader, or individuals aspiring to leadership positions. This chapter will explore emotional appropriateness, and conversely inappropriateness, by first discussing research by Erik Bucy and colleagues pertaining to both televised news stories and, more recently, presidential debates. From there, we consider connections between nonverbal signals and emotions in order to systematically approach display behavior. Here, we utilize the state of the art in emotion research, the Componential Processing Model (CPM) of emotion appraisal, to characterize facial displays as coded using the Facial Action Coding System (FACS) to take a closer look at the 2012 presidential debates between incumbent President Barack Obama and challenger Mitt Romney. In the first debate the former was thought to have performed poorly by behaving passively in a "lackluster performance" (MacAskill, 2012a), whereas in the third and final debate, Romney was judged the loser by virtue of his having "appeared unsure at times" (MacAskill, 2012b).

Using as a baseline those video clips Bucy and Gong have identified as examples of either appropriate or inappropriate candidate display behavior, through their analysis of focus groups, response dial testing, and eye-tracking methodologies, we consider discrete utterances from within the clips (Gong & Bucy, 2015; 2016). We coded video clips of the listening candidate's nonverbal behavior on a frame-by-frame basis using FACS, allowing us to more precisely identify the emotion(s) signaled by the listening candidates during their (in) appropriate displays. We next consider whether viewers accurately identify CPM-predicted emotions as displayed by the listening candidates as well as the influence of the opponent's verbal utterances on the viewers' evaluations. We do so by carrying out an experiment that randomly assigns participants to view the video clips in either an audiovisual or visual-only condition. It is here that we attempt to disentangle the nonverbal influence on emotion identification from the verbal information provided by discrete utterances. We conclude by discussing the implications our findings have for understanding just what is appropriate display behavior during presidential debates.

THE EMOTIONAL APPROPRIATENESS HEURISTIC

Extensive research by Bucy and colleagues considering the effect of presidential display behavior during television news stories found that there was an emotional appropriateness heuristic used by viewers (Bucy, 2003; Bucy & Newhagen, 1999; Bucy, 2000; Bucy & Bradley, 2004). Here, when display behavior by the president was considered appropriate in terms of both its valence and its intensity, viewers engaged in automatic and cognitively effortless processing of information. On the other hand, when this behavior did not match the news story, thus violating nonverbal expectancies, viewers engaged in higher levels of cognition to interpret and understand this behavior.

This leads to the question of what, exactly, determines appropriateness. Burgoon and Hale (1988) posit nonverbal expectancies based upon communicator characteristics, the context, and the relationship between the receiver and the communicator. In this case, violations lead to more cognitively involved processing as the "discrepancy between the emotional cues displayed and the assumed emotional experience associated with the event is taken as a possible indicator that the content of symbolic signals should not be trusted" (Mehu & Scherer, 2012, p.402).

In their application of this model to mass-media news coverage, Bucy and Newhagen (1999) suggest that appropriateness in televised news stories relies both upon conformity with social and cultural norms and with being meaningfully related to the message that preceded the display behavior. When considering news stories involving President Bill Clinton's leadership across a range of domestic and international news stories (Bucy & Newhagen, 1999), as well as President George W. Bush's response to the 11 September 2001 terrorist attacks (Bucy, 2003), participants expected and deemed low-intensity presidential reactions, in which strong emotions were either absent or subdued, as most appropriate. On the other hand, when President Clinton was shown experiencing high-intensity reactions displaying strong emotions such as anger or happiness, respondents used more cognitive capacity to consider this violation of nonverbal expectancies (Bucy & Newhagen, 1999), findings in turn supported by psychophysiological analyses (Bucy & Bradley, 2004). These results are presumably due to the preference for leaders to be in control of themselves when facing challenging circumstances.

However, it should be noted that these studies relied upon news stories that focused on anxiety-inducing events requiring leadership behavior that rallies support (Schubert, Stewart, & Curran, 2002). The behavior studied does not consider the activity of leaders and putative leaders in competitive contexts such as debates. We next turn to this special, albeit compellingly important, context.

EMOTIONAL APPROPRIATENESS DURING PRESIDENTIAL DEBATES

Since the 1960 debate between Richard Nixon and John F. Kennedy, televised coverage of presidential debates has played a powerful role in the perception and choice of America's preeminent leader. Presidential debates not only help citizens understand the domestic and foreign policy positions of the contenders, it allows for a side-by-side comparison of candidate performance. Perhaps more important, the candidates' verbal and nonverbal behavior provides viewers insights into candidate traits and potential performance (Patterson, Churchill, Burger, & Powell, 1992).

According to Gong and Bucy (2016, p. 4), during debates "the appropriateness of nonverbal expressions indexes the congruency between the candidate's nonverbal expressions and immediate rhetorical context, where situationally consistent responses are classified as appropriate and situationally inconsistent responses as inappropriate. In competitive settings, appropriate nonverbal behavior thus entails an assertive response to challenge or verbal attack." Again, context plays a major role in whether display behavior is appropriate or not; however, there is greater fluidity and different expectations during debates. For instance, angry display behavior is expected in response to attacks by the opponent or by the moderator. An example of what may be perceived as a violation of expected behavior occurred when Michael Dukakis did not respond with anger to moderator Bernard Shaw's opening question in the 1988 presidential debate with George H. W. Bush. When asked whether Dukakis would support the death penalty if his wife were raped, Dukakis dispassionately discussed his policy position instead of showing the expected anger. As a result, it was popularly perceived that Dukakis was lacking in the emotions necessary for leadership (Grabe & Bucy, 2009).

On the other hand, some display behavior may be considered inappropriate for a leader regardless of context. In this case, leaders are expected to not display fear or sadness except in exceptional cases. For example, participants in an experiment were shown video of President Bill Clinton during his grand jury testimony regarding his sexual relations with Monica Lewinsky, and attributed more power and status when he displayed anger than when he displayed sadness in his face and body language (Tiedens, 2001), suggesting sadness—a submissive emotion—is generally not expected from leaders.

Thus, a major factor in assessing a leader is evaluating the appropriateness of the leader's facial display behavior. Specifically, while candidates often rely upon prepared, vetted, and memorized scripts when answering questions and making statements during debates, when a candidate listens to a comment, question, or even an attack from either the moderator or the opponent, the unexpectedness of such utterances can reveal pertinent emotional and behavioral information through the candidate's nonverbal response (Bucy, 2000; Gong & Bucy, 2015; Lancaster, Vrij, Hope, & Waller, 2013). In turn, the nonverbal behavior displayed may be seen by the audience as either appropriate or inappropriate. However, this behavior might be so subtle and/ or fleeting as to not be cognitively attended to, or lead to emotional response that is more of a gut feeling. In this latter case, viewers might engage in non-heuristic, effortful information processing only after perceiving inappropriate display behavior. As a result, in the cases where subtle or fleeting micro-expressions occur, being able to code at the lowest level, the *molecular level*, is highly important, especially as research shows that leaders (Porter & ten Brinke, 2008; Stewart, Waller, & Schubert, 2009; ten Brinke & Adams, 2015) as well as criminals (Porter & ten Brinke, 2008) display through their facial displays their anxiety, sadness, even delight at duping someone. In other words, being able to identify the emotional state being signaled thus becomes the most important first step towards understanding the matching or violation of nonverbal expectancies.

CONNECTIONS BETWEEN EMOTIONS AND NONVERBAL CUES

Nonverbal behavior is inherently complex due to there being multiple redundant and unique signals communicating many different forms of information. Furthermore, the sender's intent is influenced by the context within which this information is sent. While strides have been made in recent years, much of the research concerning politicians over the past 30 years has relied on *molar* interpretations of behavior that rely upon more general gestalt definitions of emotional displays to understand support towards these representatives (Dumitrescu, Gidengil, & Stolle, 2015; Masters, Sullivan, Lanzetta, McHugo, & Englis, 1986; McHugo, Lanzetta, Sullivan, Masters, & Englis, 1985; Sullivan & Masters, 1988). With molar approaches, behavior is clustered into a limited number of discrete categories, albeit with the understanding that the stochastic nature of nonverbal interaction limits precision concerning the identification of emotions and behavioral intent that may be inferred (Salter, 2007).

Regardless of the advances made concerning how different nonverbal channels signal different forms of behavioral intent and emotions (App, McIntosh, Reed, & Hertenstein, 2011) and how it informs evaluation of politicians (Shah, Hanna, Bucy, Wells, & Quevedo, 2015), much work remains concerning the untangling of the multiple nonverbal components. Below we focus on what is typically in view during presidential debates—the face, head, and the upper torso—albeit with the understanding that this represents an incomplete picture of a complex system of communication. This is best considered through the theoretical lens of the CPM of emotion appraisal which has been developed to consider nonverbal cues ranging from facial displays, to vocalics, to body language, in order to understand how people interpret this behavior (Scherer, 2013; Scherer & Meuleman, 2013; Scherer, Schorr, & Johnstone, 2001).

THE COMPONENTIAL PROCESSING MODEL (CPM) OF EMOTION APPRAISAL

It has long been suggested that nonverbal behavior provides signals of emotional stress and behavioral intent more so than spoken words (Darwin, Ekman, & Prodger, 2002; Ekman, 2009; Ekman, Friesen, & Ancoli, 1980; Ekman & Friesen, 2003; Segerstråle & Molnár, 1997). While it is generally accepted that individuals can alter their nonverbal behavior by masking or minimizing displays, cognitive control over specific nonverbal behavior is limited (Mehu, Mortillaro, Bänziger, & Scherer, 2011). Specifically, due to there being multiple channels for nonverbal behavior to be communicated, along with a broad range of information being signaled, there is a high likelihood that even the most accomplished and careful politician will inadvertently signal information concerning the politician's own emotional state. Therefore, attempts to determine the emotional state, and concurrently the behavioral intent of individuals, should consider indicators from multiple channels. Furthermore, these indicators need to be reliable and valid by being easily observed and coded so they can be connected with behavioral intent.

To test whether emotions are perceived in the facial displays of presidential candidates during the presidential debates, we first characterize these displays by the listening candidate on a frame-by-frame basis using the FACS in conjunction with the CPM of emotion appraisal. The CPM provides an approach to understanding how emotions are encoded in nonverbal display behavior, and more important, allows for predictions as to what emotions will be perceived.

Emotions are notoriously difficult to define, although recent years have seen a convergence of research suggesting they are componential systems involving (1) situational appraisal; (2) action tendencies; (3) physiological reactions; (4) motor expressions; and (5) subjective feelings. Taken together as a summary of emotion concepts, especially in the latter case of subjective feelings, it can be posited that there are natural families of emotion, and within each of these families more finely grained constructs (Scherer & Grandjean, 2008). With the CPM, semantic representations of emotion (e.g., anger, fear, disgust, happiness) are seen as the result of seven sequential, albeit reciprocal and interactive (Scherer, Mortillaro, & Mehu, 2013), appraisal checks by individuals (consciously or unconsciously) in terms of: relevance regarding novelty (1) concerning the suddenness and (2) the familiarity and predictability of the stimuli, (3) intrinsic pleasantness, and goal/need relevance; the implications of the stimuli for the individual in terms of who the causal agent is, and what their motivations are in terms of an outcome's probability, as well as how (4) discrepant it is from expectations, and how (5) conducive and urgent the implications are; (6) the person's coping potential regarding their control, power, and adjustments required; and finally, (7) the normative significance of the event based upon the individual's internal and external standards (Mehu & Scherer, 2012; Mortillaro, Mehu, & Scherer, 2011; Scherer et al., 2013). On the basis of these appraisal checks, and resultant physiological changes that occur, their presence may in turn be signaled through facial display behavior that may in turn be coded using FACS.

In this study, we focus on those basic *folk* emotions that are most closely linked with political behavior. We draw from the work of the Dartmouth Group and their followers (Masters et al., 1986; Salter, 2007; Stewart, Salter, & Mehu, 2009; Sullivan & Masters, 1994; Sullivan & Masters, 1988), albeit with elaborations made possible by advances in human ethology through the CPM (Mehu & Scherer, 2012; Scherer et al., 2013; Scherer & Meuleman, 2013). Specifically, we consider the six emotion clusters connected with the political behaviors of dominance (anger and disgust), submission (fear and sadness), and affiliation (happiness and contentment), which are then presented as choices to participants when identifying the behavior of the candidates.

Taken together with the theoretical precision offered by the CPM, greater accuracy in the definition of emotion and the constructs associated with it can be carried out. Specifically, facial displays can now be defined more precisely than previously done by the Dartmouth Group and their adherents (Bucy & Newhagen, 1999; Salter, 2007; Stewart, 2012; Sullivan & Masters, 1988). This does not preclude other definitions or approaches to emotion, it just allows for a more finely honed appreciation for the preconscious and conscious appraisal of those nonverbal display elements that make up the basis for folk psychological understandings of definitions of emotion. Below we look at the potential indicators of these emotions and how they might influence perceptions.

Eyes and Eye Blinks

There is no doubt that the face and eyes are the focal points of human interaction (Darwin et al., 2002; Ekman & Friesen, 2003; Harrigan, Rosenthal, & Scherer, 2005; Kobayashi & Kohshima, 1997; Kobayashi & Kohshima, 2001;

Segerstråle & Molnár, 1997). Nonverbal displays associated with the eyes and eyebrows provide useful, noninvasive information concerning an individual's emotions, mood, and cognitive processing, mainly through eye blinks (Stern, Walrath, & Goldstein, 1984).

Televised presidential debates have long provided copious and salient research material concerning eye-blink rates, due to their importance for the democratic process. Frank's (1977) evaluation of the 1972 Democratic Party primary debate between George McGovern and Hubert Humphrey found that, of multiple verbal and nonverbal indicators considered, blink rates differentiated best between most and least stressful political issues addressed by the candidates. Likewise, Exline (1985) found differences in blink rates during President Gerald Ford's rebuttals of challenger Jimmy Carter's responses in comparison with the moderator's questions during the first 1976 Ford-Carter debate. More recently, analysis of the first 2004 debate between John Kerry and George W. Bush found both candidates had much higher blink rates than the norm (Stewart & Mosely, 2009), whereas Bucy and Ball's exploration of the classic 1960 Nixon-Kennedy debate found the former's eye-blink rate was substantially higher than JFK's (Bucy & Ball, n.d.). In all these studies, increased eye-blink rates were associated with speaking, and concomitantly with increased stress and anxiety. As a result, it is expected that higher eye-blink rates will be considered inappropriate display behavior due to association with enhanced anxiety and fear.

Facial Muscular Movements

While gains in understanding emotion have been made on a variety of fronts, arguably the most robust and interesting insights resulted from the use of the FACS. FACS comprises 46 movements in the face and additional movements involving the head, the eyes, and gross movement behaviors (Ekman & Friesen, 2003), and is a robust research tool. This is due to its comprehensive and finely honed measurement of muscular movements in the face (i.e., action units [AUs]) made possible by frame-by-frame analysis of video. FACS coding provides information not only about the presence of muscular movements, but also their strength and their onset and offset. In turn, FACS reveals the incredible complexity and fluidity of facial display behavior, even in brief video clips, and with it, changing emotional states that provide the basis for our predicting their presence by using the CPM.

Head Movements

Although head movements are coded as separate AUs using FACS, the head movements can best be defined as auxiliary to the muscular movements of the face by either enhancing or diminishing facial displays. However, social context must also be taken into account. Presidential debates in the United States provide such contextual fluidity, with different types of behavior appropriate at different times. For instance, Exline's (1985) study of the first Jimmy Carter–Gerald Ford 1976 presidential debate found that looking directly at the television audience and emphasizing statements through head movements increased perceived competence. This finding was elaborated on by Patterson and colleagues' analysis of the second 1984 debate between Ronald Reagan and Walter Mondale in which "Reagan's gaze changes and head movements seemed to punctuate and emphasize verbal comments. In contrast, Mondale stared straight ahead at the camera," which led study participants to rate Reagan more favorably and see him as more expressive and attractive (Patterson et al., 1992). On the other hand Gong and Bucy's (2016) analysis of the 2012 Romney-Obama debates, on which this current study is based, found Obama's looking down, presumably to study his notes, but also potentially to mask his facial display behavior, led to him being perceived as passive, disengaged, disinterested, dismissive, and disrespectful towards Romney. As a result, we expect that looking downward with the chin lowered may be considered a submissive and fearful gesture, whereas concomitantly staring with a raised chin may be perceived as threatening and angry behavior (Salter, 2007).

CONTENT-ANALYSIS OF C-SPAN VIDEO OF THE FIRST AND THIRD 2012 PRESIDENTIAL DEBATES

The study we cover in this chapter relies upon C-SPAN Video Library video for our evaluation of appropriate and inappropriate emotions. Specifically, we consider facial display behavior during the 2012 first and third presidential debates between Barack Obama and Mitt Romney, downloaded from the C-SPAN Video Library and edited using Adobe Premier Pro video software. The C-SPAN Video Library provides a voluminous and rich source of data that is incredibly easy to search and access if research questions are adequately delineated. While this research project addresses high-profile debates that may be expected to be easily accessible, previous research carried out by the first author using C-SPAN archival material (e.g., Stewart & Mosely, 2009) suggests that not only have C-SPAN production choices (particularly, the use of split-screen technology since the 2004 presidential debates) provided for greater transparency regarding candidates and their display behavior, the delivery of archival material has kept abreast of, if not surpassed, current trends. Specifically, whereas in the past DVDs were the main means of video delivery, online methods are currently in place with a range of video outputs available.

In this study, the extracted clips were previously identified as examples of appropriate and inappropriate nonverbal behavior (Gong & Bucy, 2015). Due to each of these clips taking from 1 to 2 minutes and involving substantial variation in display behavior, shorter clips were extracted based first upon their communicating a policy position or making an attack on the other candidate in an utterance comprising two-to-three sentences, and second upon containing identifiable and discrete facial display movements that may be effectively coded from onset to offset. The clips are analyzed first through frame-by-frame molecular-level content coding by a FACS-certified coder (the first author). This allows us to evaluate the influence of acclaims, defense, and attacks by the opposing candidate on the emotions displayed by the listening candidate. Specifically, for each candidate we consider one acclaim, in which the candidate discusses positive characteristics about themselves or their existing or future policy positions or goals, and either two or three attacks, in which they criticize their opponent's policy position or character, and two or three defenses by the candidate regarding their policies or personal characteristics (Benoit & Harthcock, 1999).

Behavioral Analysis

This section discusses the coding of the facial display behavior of the candidate listening and nonverbally responding to the opponent, using the FACS (Ekman & Friesen, 2003). Part of FACS coding involves eye blinks (AU 45); however, well before FACS coding, eye blinks were analyzed. Although studies have shown that baseline eye-blink rates during normal activities are relatively low (12–18 per minute) (Stern et al., 1984), highly stressful competitive activities such as political debates can be expected to elevate eye blinks substantially. Previous research concerning presidential debates suggests that the average ranges from a low of 28.5 eye blinks per minute for John F. Kennedy during his first 1960 debate, to a high of nearly one blink a second for his opponent in that debate, Richard Nixon (59.7) (Bucy & Ball, n.d.), a rate nearly matched by his eventual Vice President Gerald Ford (57.0) when he debated Jimmy Carter in 1976 (Exline, 1985). Despite these extremes, the average eye blinks per minute during the debates studied tends to be in the mid-40s, as evidenced for not only Carter (44.4), but also for George W. Bush (44.2) and John F. Kerry (45.7) in their first 2004 debate (Stewart & Mosely, 2009).

However, average eye-blink rate over an entire debate obscures such factors as whether the candidate is attacking or defending a position (Frank, 1977) as well as whether they are responding to the moderator, rebutting the opponent, or listening (Stewart & Mosely, 2009). In their analysis of the first 2004 debate, and taking advantage of the first use of split-screen camera shots by C-SPAN, Stewart and Mosely (2009) found that Kerry (31.8) and Bush (42.8) displayed greatly different eye-blink rates when listening, likely reflecting felt anxiety. Indeed, the complete split-screen coverage provided by C-SPAN allowed for identification of emotionally charged moments such as when Kerry hit peaks of 62.0 and 63.6 eye blinks per minute. For his part, George W. Bush had eye-blink rates of 67.7 and 84.0 and a peak average of 104.4 during his 2-minute closing statement. Due to our clips considering only brief utterances in a side-by-side camera context, the Bush-Kerry debate study provides a useful comparison for interpreting emotional state.

In addition to the eye blinks, the facial and head movements considered by FACS provide information concerning the presence, strength, and timing of AUs in the face. We characterized this information in terms of emotional and behavioral intent that was communicated using the CPM (Scherer et al., 2013; Scherer & Ellgring, 2007). Tables 6.1 and 6.2 list the CPM-predicted emotions felt and communicated by the candidates through their facial displays in response to the utterances of the opponent. The tables also provide information concerning the nature and content of the utterances the listening candidate was responding to. We briefly summarize our findings below and in Tables 6.1 and 6.2 (interested readers should contact the first author for the methods appendix).

Table 6.1 Obama's Componential Processing Model (CPM) predicted emotional response to Romney utterances. CPM predictions premised upon FACS coded facial displays and eye blink rate with strong predictions in **bold**.

Video Clip (Time)	CPM-FACS Predicted Emotions	CANDIDATE (Type of Utterance): Text
Obama – Clip 1 (17.23)	**Angry** Happy	ROMNEY (defense): I said that we would provide guarantees, and—and that was what was able to allow these companies to go through bankruptcy, to come out of bankruptcy. Under no circumstances would I do anything other than to help this industry get on its feet. And the idea that has been suggested that I would liquidate the industry, of course not. Of course not.
Obama – Clip 2 (12.03)	**Happy** Fearful Sad	ROMNEY (defense): But I'm not going to reduce the share of taxes paid by high-income people. High-income people are doing just fine in this economy. They'll do fine whether you're president or I am. The people who are having the hard time right now are middle-income Americans.
Obama – Clip 3 (17.11)	**Angry** **Disgusted** Happy	ROMNEY (attack): But not due to his policies. In spite of his policies. Mr. President, all of the increase in natural gas and oil has happened on private land, not on government land. On government land, your administration has cut the number of permits and licenses in half.
Obama – Clip 4 (10.27)	**Angry** Fearful	ROMNEY (defense): . . . look, I'm not looking to cut massive taxes and to reduce the—the revenues going to the government. My—my number-one principal is, there will be no tax cut that adds to the deficit.
Obama – Clip 5 (12.18)	**Angry**	ROMNEY (attack): But don't forget, you put $90 billion, like 50 years' worth of breaks, into—into solar and wind, to Solyndra and Fisker and Tesla and Ener1.
Obama – Clip 6 (14.23)	**Angry** Fearful	ROMNEY (acclaim): We don't want another Iraq, we don't want another Afghanistan. That's not the right course for us. The right course for us is to make sure that we go after the—the people who are leaders of these various anti-American groups and these—these jihadists, but also help the Muslim world.

Table 6.2 Mitt Romney listening to Barack Obama utterances. CPM predictions premised upon FACS coded facial displays and eye blink rate with strong predictions in **bold**.

Video Clip (Time)	CPM-FACS Predicted Emotions	CANDIDATE (Type of Utterance): Text
Romney–Clip 1 (9.01)	Happy	OBAMA (defense): Social Security is structurally sound. It's going to have to be tweaked the way it was by Ronald Reagan and Speaker—Democratic Speaker Tip O'Neill. But it is—the basic structure is sound.
Romney–Clip 2 (16.24)	Happy Angry Fearful	OBAMA (acclaim): My grandmother died three days before I was elected president. And she was fiercely independent. She worked her way up, only had a high school education, started as a secretary, ended up being the vice president of a local bank. And she ended up living alone by choice.
Romney–Clip 3 (12.07)	**Disgusted**	OBAMA (defense): Because if it's just us that are imposing sanctions—we've had sanctions in place a long time. It's because we got everybody to agree that Iran is seeing so much pressure.
Romney–Clip 4 (8.21)	**Happy** Contented	OBAMA (attack): Well, first of all, I think Governor Romney's going to have a busy first day, because he's also going to repeal Obamacare, which will not be very popular among Democrats as you're sitting down with them.
Romney–Clip 5 (14.22)	**Angry** **Disgusted**	OBAMA (attack): Unfortunately, Governor Romney's plan doesn't do it. We've got to do it in a responsible way by cutting out spending we don't need, but also asking the wealthiest to pay a little bit more. That way we can invest in the research and technology that's always kept us at the cutting edge.
Romney–Clip 6 (15.05)	**Angry** Happy	OBAMA (attack): Does anybody out there think that the big problem we had is that there was too much oversight and regulation of Wall Street? Because if you do, then Governor Romney is your candidate.

Barack Obama's Nonverbal Response

All utterances by Mitt Romney, which Barack Obama listened and nonverbally responded to, addressed policy. Specifically, with the acclaims, attacks, and defenses by Romney, whether financial or, in just one case, foreign policy, we see no personal attacks or critiques of the opposition party. However, we do see a high level of variation in how Obama responded nonverbally to these utterances.

With the great majority of the video clips, Obama signaled mixed emotions. Specifically, in Clips 1–3 he displayed posed smiles involving the lip-corner pull-up and at an angle of the *zygomaticus major* muscle (AU 12) that may be associated with masking his felt emotions. However, it should be noted that the unilateral smile, combined with the tightening of the lip corners (AU 14) in Clip 3, is associated with contempt (Stewart, Bucy, & Mehu, 2015). This lip-corner tightener is likewise seen in Clips 4–6, where it can be viewed as most strongly connected with anger—especially in Clip 5 where it is paired with his lips being tightened (AU 23). However, it should be noted that Obama's looking downward likely led to the misperceptions of his emotional state, as noted by Gong and Bucy (2015, 2016), especially in Clips 3–5 where his face was averted downward for more than half of the clip (see Figure 6.1).

Mitt Romney's Nonverbal Response

The utterances that were nonverbally responded to by Mitt Romney, whether appropriately or inappropriately, nearly mirrors those utterances by Obama. Here Obama makes three attacks, two defenses, and one acclaim. However, while all six of Romney's utterances were focused on policy, two of the six Obama utterances had a personal component.

The first considered the effect of Social Security on his grandmother's independence, while the second considered the effect of Romney's proposed repeal of Obamacare on his opponent's ability to negotiate with congressional Democrats. In both of these clips, Romney's facial display behavior is quite subtle, with smiles that pulled his lip corners up and slightly at an angle, yet not affecting his eyes. On the other hand, his posed smile in Clip 4 suggests he is at the very least pleased with Obama's suggesting that Romney would be president, although not to the extent of an enjoyment or amusement smile

Figure 6.1   2Obama_2:09-2:27 (Romney attack): "But not due to his policies. (*Obama AU R12 & 14*) In spite of his policies. Mr. President, all of the increase in natural gas and oil has happened on private land, not on government land. On government land, your administration has cut the number of permits and licenses in half."

(which would be seen with the muscles around the eyes—the *orbicularis oculi*—contracting). In Clips 3 and 5, his thrusting his tongue out likely indicates his rejection of Obama's assertions and felt disgust (see Figure 6.2). Finally, Romney's moderately pushing his lower lip up (AU 17) may be seen as indicating anger in both Clips 5 and 6.

Experimental Analysis

Although it is not possible to know what a politician is thinking and feeling during presidential debates, behavioral microanalysis can provide insights into their thoughts and emotions. As we have seen, by analyzing a candidate's nonverbal responses to the opposition's utterances through such techniques as the FACS, we can detect subtle nonverbal signals. While it may be argued that presidential candidates are heavily coached, highly scripted, and well-practiced performers who have proven their aptitude through their ascent to the top of their respective political parties, and as such have a high degree of control over their verbal and nonverbal performance, even subtle indicators of emotion can "leak." This is especially the case when the opponent engages in unpredicted attacks or makes unanticipated statements.

Figure 6.2 8Romney_1:29-1:44 (Obama attack): "Unfortunately, Governor Romney's plan doesn't do it. We've got to do it in a responsible way (*Romney AU 17, 19, 25 & 26*) by cutting out spending we don't need, but also asking the wealthiest to pay a little bit more. That way we can invest in the research and technology that's always kept us at the cutting edge."

Vigilant observers may see such signals as slight facial muscular movements, increased eye-blink rates, or head movements in response to unexpected acclaims, attacks, and defenses by the opposition or moderators. Ultimately it is the viewing audience that is most important for understanding and interpreting candidate response, whether accurate (as predicted by CPM application of FACS coding) or not. As a result, the next section first considers how accurately the CPM predicts viewer identification of emotions when applied through our FACS coding of the listening candidates' facial display behavior. It next considers what influence the opposition candidate's verbal utterances have on the accuracy of viewer interpretation of the listening candidate's felt emotions.

This study was carried out on an iPad by showing staff members at the University of Arkansas, Fayetteville, 12 video clips that alternated between showing Mitt Romney and Barack Obama debate each other. The use of a tablet computer to carry out the experiment not only reproduced the second-screen experience of many Americans, it also served to standardize the delivery of the audiovisual stimuli while at the same time respecting workplace dynamics of this more externally valid sample. Half of the participants were randomly assigned to view these clips with sound, and the other half without; all were asked to identify the emotion felt by the listening candidate after each clip was finished. We analyzed the data using the chi-square statistic to assess the probability of emotion identification being random and the likelihood ratio statistic to compare the visual-only and audiovisual clips.

Discussion

As can be expected from nonverbal display behavior that is complex, subtle, and often influenced by a multitude of external factors, the findings here are not necessarily straightforward. They do, however, provide insight into the processing of facial signals of emotions that may be considered appropriate or inappropriate for presidential candidates during their debates. Perhaps more important, it suggests future research directions when considering what exactly is inappropriate display behavior, especially as the CPM predicted the plurality of emotions identified by participants in 5 of 12 video clips shown.

A major finding from our study is that attempts by a candidate listening to acclaims, attacks, or defenses to minimize viewer perceptions of their nonverbal behavior by averting gaze might backfire. Specifically, while looking down is a good way to mask facial display behavior such as elevated eye-blink rates (Stewart & Mosely, 2009), as well as potentially inappropriate smiles (Keltner, 1995), this behavior might also be interpreted as submissive behavior. Namely, in both anxiety and sadness there is a lowering of the chin and directing of gaze downward (Salter, 2007, pp. 146–147).

A second major finding is that looking downward likely affects the interpretation of facial movements. Here, Obama's looking downward in Clip 4 (Table 6.1 & Figure 6.1) led to a majority of participants perceiving him as feeling happiness despite there not being muscle movements associated with happiness (Stewart, Bucy, & Mehu, 2015; Stewart & Ford Dowe, 2013). Instead, the angle of the face downward likely led to the lip-corner tightening (AU 14), which is associated with negative emotions such as anger and contempt, being seen as a smile, even a smirk.

Furthermore, there appears to be a bias towards identifying the behavior of Barack Obama, and to a lesser extent Mitt Romney, as indicating some form of positive emotion such as happiness or contentment. Specifically, even when not predicted for by the CPM, one-quarter to one-half of participant deviations to select either of these two emotion clusters occurred with both candidates. This high level of deviation may be due to two factors. First, there is a bias towards identifying the affiliation clusters of happiness and contentment. This is likely due to the accurate selection of prototypical expressions of the emotion of happiness, often over 90% (Ekman & Friesen, 2003; Scherer & Grandjean, 2008; Stewart, Méhu, & Salter, 2015). Additionally, there might be a propositivity bias with errors tending towards seeing happiness, even when it does not occur, especially with political leaders in more egalitarian systems like the United States (Masters & Sullivan, 1989; Warnecke, Masters, & Kempter, 1992).

A second factor influencing the interpretation of emotions might reflect the facial characteristics of the candidates themselves (Trichas & Schyns, 2012). Specifically, Barack Obama has more of a *neotonous* face, with baby-faced features such as larger eyes and ears—especially when compared with Mitt Romney's more masculine face. This in turn might lead to systematic errors in the interpretation of emotion as recent research suggests that facial characteristics such as strong cheekbones and brows bias individuals towards perceiving dominant emotions such as anger and/or disgust (Gill, Garrod, Jack, & Schyns, 2014).

The treatment randomly assigning participants to receive the verbal utterance in addition to the nonverbal display behavior (the audiovisual condition) or solely receive the nonverbal channel of communication (the visual-only condition) appeared to have a minimal impact upon the identification of emotion felt by the listening candidate. In Barack Obama's case, participants were significantly affected in their identification efforts in only one video clip. Although Mitt Romney's displays were likewise not systematically and significantly affected, with only one equation showing highly significant differences between participants in the two conditions, three other clips approached significant differences. In these cases, the added channel of verbal and audio information led to a pattern of slightly greater accuracy in the identification of CPM-predicted emotions. The relatively low power of this study with its small number of participants limits our conclusions. This, combined with the Gong and Bucy (2015, 2016) finding that participants engaged in variable scanning of both candidates, suggests that multiple components in the interaction between candidates likely plays an important role in the processing of information.

Likewise, although it does not appear that the type of utterance, whether an acclaim, attack, or defense, played a role in the interpretation of the emotional response of the listening candidate, our set of video clips was limited. Specifically, verbal utterances might have a different effect on viewers depending on whether they were policy focused—as was the case with most of the video clips in our study—or focused on the character of the candidate and those the candidate represents. Furthermore, how the utterance is delivered, whether politely or impolitely (Dailey et al., 2005), and/or with or without humor (Stewart, 2012), influences not just the perception of the speaker, but also the listener.

CONCLUSION

The study carried out here advanced the literature by more directly testing whether the perceived display behavior by the listening candidate, whether Barack Obama or Mitt Romney, reflected the emotional intent as predicted by the CPM, and whether interpretation of the emotions signaled through a facial display is affected by verbal information. It also provided further insight into the nature of inappropriate displays by party nominees during presidential debates, as well as likely other political events, by more proximately and precisely exploring the role of nonverbal display behavior. More specifically, by using the work of Gong and Bucy (2015, 2016) as a starting point, we are able to "drill down" to discrete moments in the first and third 2012 presidential debates that were identified as having either Obama or Romney engaging in behavior inappropriate for a leader. By focusing on the display behavior of the candidate listening to utterances by the opposition party's representative, we are able to identify moments that are likely unanticipated, leading to natural, unrehearsed, and revealing responses.

Although the CPM of emotion appraisal may not be considered as effective as initially posited, in light of its relative difficulty in predicting participant choice of emotion clusters, it should be noted that subtle and quick facial displays are often interpreted by different individuals in various ways, especially if they might be considered inappropriate. As stated by Mehu and Scherer, "A discrepancy between the emotional cues displayed and the assumed emotional experience associated with the event is taken as a possible indicator that the content of symbolic signals should not be trusted"

(2012, p. 11). Specifically, the Brunswikian lens model for the study of emotion communication, upon which the CPM builds, suggests multiple social and perceptual factors influence the interpretation of emotion, and concomitantly, behavioral intent.

Studies considering the influence of nonverbal signals will likely increase in importance as our media environment continues its trend of being increasingly dominated by visuals and images that are often fleeting and taken out of context. This media environment in turn can be expected to influence how citizens perceive and interact with their government, especially as research suggests many individuals are more visually than verbally oriented, especially as concerns their search for and recall of political information (Grabe & Bucy, 2009; Prior, 2014). As noted by Brownell (2014), scholars wishing to understand connections between U.S. citizens and their government should use minimally mediated video content such as that provided by the C-SPAN Video Library to "go beyond the red/blue electoral divide and examine the more complicated and nuanced political reality on the ground" (p. 53).

Just as the introduction of split-screen debate coverage of the 2004 debates between George W. Bush and John Kerry likely affected the perceptions of both candidates (Cho, Shah, Nah, & Brossard, 2009; Scheufele, Kim, & Brossard, 2007; Stewart & Mosely, 2009), due to the ability to monitor the listening candidate, new technologies are changing how presidential debates are watched and evaluated. Currently debate watching is often accompanied by second-screen real-time response by viewers who use their smartphones and tablet computers to comment via Twitter, Facebook, and other social media sites (Shah et al., 2015). Further, in an increasingly Internet-connected world, memes and tweets drawing upon such moments where candidates act seemingly inappropriately have the potential to reach and influence a large audience. While these moments, whether considered appropriate or not, may be subtle, in the aggregate they potentially may have substantial effects on the perceptions of candidates, and as a result, the electoral process.

REFERENCES

App, B., McIntosh, D. N., Reed, C. L., & Hertenstein, M. J. (2011). Nonverbal channel use in communication of emotion: How may depend on why. *Emotion, 11*(3), 603.

Benoit, W. L., & Harthcock, A. (1999). Functions of the great debates: Acclaims, attacks, and defenses in the 1960 presidential debates. *Communication Monographs, 65*, 341–357.

Brownell, K. C. (2014). Going beyond the headlines: The C-SPAN archives, grassroots '84, and new directions in American political history. In R. X. Browning (Ed.), *The C-SPAN Archives: An interdisciplinary resource for discovery, learning, and engagement* (pp. 45–58). West Lafayette, IN: Purdue University Press.

Bucy, E. P. (2000). Emotional and evaluative consequences of inappropriate leader displays. *Communication Research, 27*(2), 194–226.

Bucy, E. P. (2003). Emotion, presidential communication, and traumatic news. *International Journal of Press/Politics, 8*(4), 76–96.

Bucy, E. P., & Ball, J. (n.d.). Quantifying the claim that Nixon looked bad: A visual analysis of the Kennedy-Nixon debates [Typescript].

Bucy, E. P., & Bradley, S. D. (2004). Presidential expressions and viewer emotion: Counterempathic responses to televised leader displays. *Social Science Information, 43*(1), 59–94.

Bucy, E. P., & Newhagen, J. E. (1999). The emotional appropriateness heuristic: Processing televised presidential reactions to the news. *Journal of Communication, 49*(4), 59–79.

Burgoon, J. K., & Hale, J. L. (1988). Nonverbal expectancy violations: Model elaboration and application to immediacy behaviors. *Communications Monographs, 55*(1), 58–79.

Cho, J., Shah, D. V., Nah, S., & Brossard, D. (2009). "Split screens" and "spin rooms": Debate modality, post-debate coverage, and the new videomalaise. *Journal of Broadcasting & Electronic Media, 53*(2), 242–261.

Dailey, W. O., Hinck, E. A., & Hinck, S. S. (2005). Audience perceptions of politeness and advocacy skills in the 2000 and 2004 presidential debates. *Argumentation and Advocacy, 41*(4), 196–210.

Darwin, C., Ekman, P., & Prodger, P. (2002). *The expression of the emotions in man and animals.* New York, NY: Oxford University Press.

Druckman, J. N. (2003). The power of television images: The first Kennedy-Nixon debate revisited. *Journal of Politics, 65*(2), 559–571.

Dumitrescu, D., Gidengil, E., & Stolle, D. (2015). Candidate confidence and electoral appeal: An experimental study of the effect of nonverbal confidence on voter evaluations. *Political Science Research and Methods, 3*(01), 43–52.

Ekman, P. (2009). *Telling lies: Clues to deceit in the marketplace, politics, and marriage.* New York, NY: W. W. Norton.

Ekman, P., & Friesen, W. V. (2003). *Unmasking the face*. Cambridge, MA: Malor Books.

Ekman, P., Friesen, W. V., & Ancoli, S. (1980). Facial signs of emotional experience. *Journal of Personality and Social Psychology, 39*(6), 1125–1134.

Exline, R. V. (1985). Multichannel transmission of nonverbal behavior and the perception of powerful men: The presidential debates of 1976. In S. L. Ellyson & J. F. Dovidio (Eds.), *Power, dominance, and nonverbal behavior* (pp. 183–206). New York, NY: Springer.

Frank, R. S. (1977). Nonverbal and paralinguistic analysis of political behavior: The first McGovern-Humphrey California primary debate. In M. G. Hermann & T. W. Milburn (Eds.), *A psychological examination of political leaders* (pp. 62–79). New York, NY: Wiley.

Gill, D., Garrod, O. G., Jack, R. E., & Schyns, P. G. (2014). Facial movements strategically camouflage involuntary social signals of face morphology. *Psychological Science, 25*(5), 1079–1086.

Gong, Z. H., & Bucy, E. P. (2015). Image bite analysis of presidential debates. In R.X. Browning (Ed.), *Exploring the C-SPAN Archives: Advancing the research agenda* (pp. 45–75). West Lafayette, IN: Purdue University Press.

Gong, Z. H., & Bucy, E. P. (2016). When style obscures substance: Visual attention to display appropriateness in the 2012 presidential debates. *Communication Monographs*, (online) 1–24.

Grabe, M. E., & Bucy, E. P. (2009). *Image bite politics: News and the visual framing of elections*. Oxford, England: Oxford University Press.

Harrigan, J. A., Rosenthal, R. E., & Scherer, K. R. (Eds.). (2005).*The new handbook of methods in nonverbal behavior research*. New York, NY: Oxford University Press.

Keltner, D. (1995). Signs of appeasement: Evidence for the distinct displays of embarrassment, amusement, and shame. *Journal of Personality and Social Psychology, 68*(3), 441–454.

Kobayashi, H., & Kohshima, S. (1997). Unique morphology of the human eye. *Nature, 387*(6635), 767–768.

Kobayashi, H., & Kohshima, S. (2001). Unique morphology of the human eye and its adaptive meaning: Comparative studies on external morphology of the primate eye. *Journal of Human Evolution, 40*(5), 419–435.

Lancaster, G. L., Vrij, A., Hope, L., & Waller, B. (2013). Sorting the liars from the truth tellers: The benefits of asking unanticipated questions on lie detection. *Applied Cognitive Psychology, 27*(1), 107–114.

Lanoue, D. J., & Schrott, P. R. (1991). *The joint press conference: The history, impact, and prospects of American presidential debates*. Westport, CT: Greenwood Press.

MacAskill, E. (2012a, 4 October). Mitt Romney comes out on top as Obama stumbles in first debate. *Guardian*. Retrieved from https://www.theguardian.com /world/2012/oct/04/romney-obama-first-presidential-debate

MacAskill, E. (2012b, 23 October). Obama and Romney clash over foreign policy in final presidential debate. *Guardian*. Retrieved from https://www.theguardian .com/world/2012/oct/23/third-presidential-debate-obama-wins

Masters, R. D., & Sullivan, D. G. (1989). Nonverbal displays and political leadership in France and the United States. *Political Behavior, 11*(2), 123–156.

Masters, R. D., Sullivan, D. G., Lanzetta, J. T., McHugo, G. J., & Englis, B. G. (1986). The facial displays of leaders: Toward an ethology of human politics. *Journal of Social and Biological Structures, 9*, 319–343.

McHugo, G. J., Lanzetta, J. T., Sullivan, D. G., Masters, R. D., & Englis, B. G. (1985). Emotional reactions to a political leader's expressive displays. *Journal of Personality and Social Psychology, 49*(6), 1513–1529.

Mehu, M., Mortillaro, M., Bänziger, T., & Scherer, K. R. (2011). Reliable facial muscle activation enhances recognizability and credibility of emotional expression. *Social Psychological and Personality Science, 2*(3), 262–271.

Mehu, M., & Scherer, K. R. (2012). A psycho-ethological approach to social signal processing. *Cognitive Processing, 13*(2), 397–414.

Mortillaro, M., Mehu, M., & Scherer, K. R. (2011). Subtly different positive emotions can be distinguished by their facial expressions. *Social Psychological and Personality Science, 2*(3), 262–271.

Norton, M. I., & Goethals, G. R. (2004). Spin (and pitch) doctors: Campaign strategies in televised political debates. *Political Behavior, 26*(3), 227–248.

Patterson, M. L., Churchill, M. E., Burger, G. K., & Powell, J. L. (1992). Verbal and nonverbal modality effects on impressions of political candidates: Analysis from the 1984 presidential debates. *Communication Monographs, 59*(3), 231–242.

Porter, S., & ten Brinke, L. (2008). Reading between the lies. *Psychological Science, 19*(5), 508–514.

Prior, M. (2014). Visual political knowledge: A different road to competence? *Journal of Politics, 76*(01), 41–57.

Racine Group. (2002). White paper on televised political campaign debates. *Argumentation and Advocacy, 38*, 199–218.

Salter, F. K. (2007). *Emotions in command: Biology, bureaucracy, and cultural evolution*. New Brunswick, NJ: Transaction.

Scherer, K. R. (2013). The evolutionary origin of multimodal synchronization in emotional expression. *Journal of Anthropological Sciences*, *91*, 1–16.

Scherer, K. R., & Ellgring, H. (2007). Are facial expressions of emotion produced by categorical affect programs or dynamically driven by appraisal. *Emotion*, *7*(1), 113–130.

Scherer, K. R., & Grandjean, D. (2008). Facial expressions allow inference of both emotions and their components. *Cognition and Emotion*, *22*(5), 789–801.

Scherer, K. R., & Meuleman, B. (2013). Human emotion experiences can be predicted on theoretical grounds: Evidence from verbal labeling. *PloS One*, *8*(3), e58166.

Scherer, K. R., Mortillaro, M., & Mehu, M. (2013). Understanding the mechanisms underlying the production of facial expression of emotion: A componential perspective. *Emotion Review*, *5*(1), 47–53.

Scherer, K. R., Schorr, A., & Johnstone, T. (Eds.). (2001). *Appraisal processes in emotion: Theory, methods, research*. New York, NY: Oxford University Press.

Scheufele, D. A., Kim, E., & Brossard, D. (2007). My friend's enemy: How split-screen debate coverage influences evaluation of presidential debates. *Communication Research*, *34*(1), 3–24.

Schrott, P. R., & Lanoue, D. J. (2008). Debates are for losers. *PS: Political Science and Politics*, *41*(03), 513–518.

Schubert, J. N., Stewart, P. A., & Curran, M. A. (2002). A defining presidential moment: 9/11 and the rally effect. *Political Psychology*, *23*(3), 559–583.

Segerstråle, U. C. O., & Molnár, P. (1997). *Nonverbal communication: Where nature meets culture*. Mahwah, N.J: Lawrence Erlbaum Associates.

Seiter, J. S., & Weger, H., Jr. (2005). Audience perceptions of candidates' appropriateness as a function of nonverbal behaviors displayed during televised political debates. *Journal of Social Psychology*, *145*(2), 225–236.

Seiter, J. S., Weger, H., Jr., Jensen, A., & Kinzer, H. J. (2010). The role of background behavior in televised debates: Does displaying nonverbal agreement and/or disagreement benefit either debater? *Journal of Social Psychology*, *150*(3), 278–300.

Shah, D. V., Hanna, A., Bucy, E. P., Wells, C., & Quevedo, V. (2015). Examining social media influence: The power of television images in a social media age: Linking biobehavioral and computational approaches via the second screen. *ANNALS of the American Academy of Political and Social Science*, *659*, 225–307.

Stern, J. A., Walrath, L. C., & Goldstein, R. (1984). The endogenous eyeblink. *Psychophysiology*, *21*(1), 22–33.

Stewart, P. A. (2012). *Debatable humor: Laughing matters on the 2008 presidential primary campaign*. Lanham, MD: Lexington Books.

Stewart, P. A., Bucy, E. P., & Mehu, M. (2015). Politician smiles: A biobehavioral assessment of attempts to connect with followers by 2012 Republican party presidential candidates. *Politics & the Life Sciences, 34*(1), 73–92.

Stewart, P. A., & Ford Dowe, P. K. (2013). Interpreting President Barack Obama's facial displays of emotion: Revisiting the Dartmouth Group. *Political Psychology, 34*(3), 369–385.

Stewart, P. A., Méhu, M., & Salter, F. K. (2015). Sex and leadership: Interpreting competitive and affiliative facial displays based on workplace status. *International Public Management Journal, 18*(2), 190–208.

Stewart, P. A., & Mosely, J. (2009). Politicians under the microscope: Eye blink rates during the first Bush-Kerry debate. *White House Studies, 9*(4), 373–388.

Stewart, P. A., Salter, F. K., & Mehu, M. (2009). Taking leaders at face value: Ethology and the analysis of televised leader displays. *Politics and the Life Sciences, 28*(1), 48–74.

Stewart, P. A., Waller, B. M., & Schubert, J. N. (2009). Presidential speechmaking style: Emotional response to micro-expressions of facial affect. *Motivation and Emotion, 33*(2), 125–135.

Sullivan, D. G., & Masters, R. D. (1988). 'Happy warriors': Leaders' facial displays, viewers' emotions, and political support. *American Journal of Political Science, 32*(2), 345–368.

Sullivan, D. G., & Masters, R. D. (1994). Biopolitics, the media, and leadership: Nonverbal cues, emotions, and trait attributions in the evaluation of leaders. In A. Somit & S. A. Peterson (Eds.), *Research in biopolitics: Biopolitics in the mainstream* (2nd ed., pp. 237–273). Somerville, MA: Emerald Group.

Ten Brinke, L., & Adams, G. S. (2015). Saving face? When emotion displays during public apologies mitigate damage to organizational performance. *Organizational Behavior and Human Decision Processes, 130*, 1–12.

Tiedens, L. Z. (2001). Anger and advancement versus sadness and subjugation: The effect of negative emotion expressions on social status conferral. *Journal of Personality and Social Psychology, 80*(1), 86–94.

Trichas, S., & Schyns, B. (2012). The face of leadership: Perceiving leaders from facial expression. *Leadership Quarterly, 23*(3), 545–566.

Warnecke, A. M., Masters, R. D., & Kempter, G. (1992). The roots of nationalism: Nonverbal behavior and xenophobia. *Ethology and Sociobiology, 13*(4), 267–282.

CHAPTER 7

PRESIDENT WILLIAM J. CLINTON AS A PRACTICAL ETHNOMETHODOLOGIST: A SINGLE-CASE ANALYSIS OF SUCCESSFUL QUESTION-ANSWERING TECHNIQUES IN THE 1998 GRAND JURY TESTIMONY

Angela Cora Garcia

Previous conversation analytic research has addressed how the organization of interaction in talk in institutional settings differs from ordinary conversation (e.g., Antaki, 2011; Boden & Zimmerman, 1991; Clayman & Heritage, 2002; Drew & Heritage, 1992; Garcia, 2013; Heritage & Clayman, 2010; Heritage & Maynard, 2006; Sacks, 1992; Sacks, Schegloff, & Jefferson, 1974). While the speech exchange system of ordinary conversation provides for maximum flexibility in such things as the organization of turns at talk, types of turns produced by participants, and topics of talk, talk in workplace settings is often more highly structured or constrained on these types of dimensions (e.g., see Clayman & Heritage, 2002; Heritage, 1985). For example, talk in airplane cockpits (Nevile, 2004), medical settings (Heritage & Maynard, 2006), television news interviews (Clayman

& Heritage, 2002; Heritage, 2002), and mediation hearings (Garcia, 1991; Greatbatch & Dingwall, 1997) differs from talk in ordinary conversational settings in a variety of ways.

The term *talk in institutional settings* is commonly used in conversation analytic research not to claim that talk in workplace interactions is always different from that in everyday life, in fact ordinary conversation takes up a good part of the workday of many people. In addition, the work-specific talk that does occur in institutional settings is typically based on many of the same procedures and techniques that are used in everyday contexts. However, the organization of interaction differs in systematic ways in institutional settings because that is how the work of that setting is done and institutional roles are accomplished. Heritage and Clayman (2010) focus on how questions and answers are organized as they explain what they mean by "talking institutions into being" (p. 32):

> We do not mean by this to suggest that every time persons talk they invent institutions from scratch. Far from it: the institutions of education, news, courts, and medicine plainly antedate the lives and actions of the persons who participate in them. But these institutions do draw life from, and are reproduced in, those actions. The word we have used for this in this chapter is "instantiate." By this we mean that the sequences of talk we have examined are aligned with, and embody, some of the basic imperatives of the institutions within which they are found. Talking in these ways is, in part, how these institutions are realized: that is, are rendered observable and consequential in everyday life as the real entities that persons take them to be. Talking in these ways is part of being a teacher or a student, an interviewer, a lawyer or a doctor. These roles are enacted by talking in these ways. Failing to talk in these ways, by contrast, can lead to difficulties in realizing, or being recognized in, these institutional roles and activities. Speakers in these institutions are accountable for bringing off their question-answer sequences in these ways, and institutions are accountably reproduced in these sequences. (p. 32)

Talk in institutional settings is designed by participants to accomplish the goals of that particular institutional context. In the case of talk in legal settings, this often involves not just the elicitation of information through questions and answers but also a contest between opposing sides in a dispute or legal case. The holders of different institutional roles therefore may be in an oppositional relationship (as in a prosecuting attorney interviewing a defense witness). How each participant constructs an action will take account of the role the participant is playing in the interaction.

Previous conversation analytic research has revealed a variety of techniques that can be used to evade answering questions. In televised news interviews, Clayman (2001) found that interviewees used a range of techniques to avoid answering questions, such as first answering the question, but then elaborating the answer in a way that redirects the interaction; reformulating a more favorable version of the question before answering it; or providing incomplete or hypercomplete responses (Clayman, 2001). Lynch and Bogen (1996) analyzed the Iran-Contra hearings, and found that Col. Oliver North used several of these techniques to avoid direct answers to questions in order to deflect blameworthy implications. Another technique that can be used is to first answer a question and then take advantage of having the floor to switch the agenda and attack the questioner. This strategy was used by then-Vice President George H. W. Bush in a televised news interview with news anchor Mr. Dan Rather (Clayman & Whalen, 1988/89).

President Clinton's 1998 grand jury testimony was subpoenaed as part of the Paula Jones case in which she accused President Clinton of sexual harassment. The questions asked by the attorneys during this testimony revolved around the nature of his relationship with former White House intern Monica Lewinsky and whether he had perjured himself in previous statements in a deposition in the Paula Jones case. President Clinton's grand jury testimony in the Paula Jones case is important historically because it was part of the charges involved in his presidential impeachment trial (Starr, 1998). In terms of reactions from Congress, the press, and the public at the time, it seemed to be a Watergate moment for the Clinton presidency with at least the potential to bring his presidency down by either impeachment or resignation (Baker, 2000; Posner, 2000; Wilson, 2015). It also arguably crystalized a trend that had been occurring in recent American history towards increasingly less division between the public and private spheres of the lives of Presidents (see, e.g., Perloff, 1999). Some also argued that it contributed to the trend of diminishing news-media control over access to information (e.g., Williams & Carpini, 2004).

Research on President Clinton's 1998 grand jury testimony has been conducted from a variety of analytical perspectives including sociolinguistic, pragmatic, and conversation analytic approaches, each of which focuses on different aspects of the testimony. In addition, there is research on the effectiveness of the speech President Clinton gave after the testimony (e.g., Kramer & Olson, 2002; Simons, 2000; Wilson, 2015), as well as media framing of the coverage of the scandal (e.g., Larson & Wagner-Pacifici, 2001; Yioutas & Segvic, 2003). Wilson (2015) analyzed the pragmatics of President Clinton's grand jury testimony. Some studies are concerned with whether the President was telling the truth during his testimony (e.g., Hirsch & Wolf, 2001; Upchurch & O'Connell, 2000). These studies examined a range of verbal and nonverbal behaviors including pauses, hesitation markers, qualifiers, expanded contractions, speech errors, and body language and gestures. However, these behaviors are studied independently of the immediate sequential context they occur within (Sacks, 1992). Jaworski and Galasinski (2002) analyze media reporting of President Clinton's nonverbal behaviors during his grand jury testimony, and conclude that there was little agreement in terms of what mood or emotion his nonverbal behavior signified to the media. They found that the British press media's portrayal of President Clinton's emotions and honesty in the pictures, captions, and text of news articles differed with type of publication.

However, in spite of the embarrassing details of President Clinton's relationship with Ms. Lewinsky, which were revealed during the testimony, and the potentially injurious accusations of perjury, President Clinton's popularity during this crisis did not take the plunge that many predicted it might (Larson & Wagner-Pacifici, 2001; Simons, 2000; Yioutas & Segvic, 2003). Some previous studies have addressed this public response in terms of the motivations of particular subgroups. For example, Danielson (2013) argued that African Americans typically continued to support President Clinton because of his previous actions and their strong belief in the sincerity of his advocacy of their concerns. In general, the public, while extremely interested in the grand jury testimony and the subsequent impeachment trial, did not seem to share the same concern with the issues that Congress and others in government and in the media did.

In this chapter I will consider how President Clinton's construction of his grand jury testimony may have contributed to the relative loyalty of the public during this crisis. In particular, I will utilize Locke and Edward's (2003) conversation analytic study of the techniques President Clinton used to successfully avoid implications of blame and how he used framing devices to manage the impressions given by his answers to the attorneys' questions. Locke and Edwards' study of the grand jury testimony focused on how references to emotions and psychological states were used to construct favorable accounts. For example, they show how President Clinton distances himself from Ms. Lewinsky by attributing emotions to her rather than to himself.

Locke and Edwards (2003) also investigated how President Clinton works to recast potentially damaging facts into ordinary, routine actions. They showed how President Clinton reformulated aspects of the attorneys' questions to remove the implications of blame or guilt by presenting the events or situations as normal or routine, at least in the context of the role of president in the White House. For example, they describe how President Clinton invokes the routine process of exchanging Christmas gifts to provide a rationale for one of his meetings with Ms. Lewinsky. This provides an alternative to the implication of the attorney's question, which raised the possibility that the purpose of the meeting was to interfere with her testimony in response to the subpoena she had received. President Clinton also uses the routine expectation that a "going away" gift is a suitable rationale for the large number of gifts he gave her. He argues that they were not just Christmas gifts, but also "going away" gifts. Finally, President Clinton uses commonsense assumptions about the membership categories *man* and *woman* to explain that people in those categories can give each other gifts without a romantic relationship being implied (Locke & Edwards, 2003).

In sum, Locke and Edwards (2003) identified a range of ways that President Clinton answered questions while avoiding some of the negative and potentially damaging implications of them. In this chapter I will extend their analysis of his testimony to include a range of ways in which President Clinton uses a *practical ethnomethodological* approach pedagogically—instead of simply answering the question, he explains how his answers are consistent with routine, ordinary procedures and techniques that people typically use. This explanation instructs the recipient (the questioning attorney and the grand jury itself) in how to understand and interpret his answers. Following Garfinkel's (1967) work on the commonsense background assumptions and everyday procedures used to accomplish social organization, and Sacks' (1984b) work on how people "do being ordinary" in everyday interactions, I will show how

President Clinton used everyday commonsense reasoning to provide alternative interpretations of his actions. This work as a practical ethnomethodologist enabled him to deflect negative interpretations of his actions and substitute ordinary, everyday, and innocent interpretations of, and explanations for, his actions in specific contexts. I will also draw on conversation analytic research on evasive answering in legal and other institutional contexts (e.g., Clayman, 1993; 2001; Clayman & Heritage, 2002) and apply it to understanding President Clinton's testimony.

The chapter begins with a description of the methods and data used. I will then analyze President Clinton's use of evasive answering techniques and his pedagogical use of commonsense knowledge and understandings of how things are routinely done to show how he effectively defended himself against attorneys' accusatory questions.

DATA AND METHODS

The theoretical and analytical perspective used in this project is conversation analysis, a qualitative method of analyzing talk in interaction that grew out of the ethnomethodological perspective developed by Harold Garfinkel (1967). Conversation analysts study talk in its sequential context in order to discover the commonsense understandings and procedures people use to shape their conduct in particular interactional settings (Heritage, 1984; Sacks, 1984a; Schegloff, 2007). Members' shared interactional competencies not only enable them to produce their own actions but also to interpret the actions of others. Roles do not just affect behavior by providing a set of rights, obligations, and expectations; people instantiate their roles by their actions (Halkowski, 1990).

In this chapter I use a single-case analysis approach. The purpose of a single-case analysis is not to create new findings but to use findings from previous conversation analytic research to understand a particular event, in order to gain insights and understandings of that event (e.g., Osvaldsson, Persson-Thunqvist, & Cromdal, 2012; Schegloff, 1987; Whalen, Zimmerman, & Whalen, 1988). By means of this single-case analysis, I will show how President Clinton successfully used a wide range of evasive answering techniques and other defensive moves to avoid and counter blame-implicatory moves on the part of the interrogating attorneys.

I analyzed the 4 hours of video of grand jury testimony by President Clinton in the *Jones v. Clinton* case regarding allegations of sexual harassment by Ms. Paula Jones. This testimony was given on August 17, 1998. The video of this testimony is available online in the C-SPAN Video Library. Selected excerpts from this video have been transcribed using a simplified version of conversation analytic conventions (Jefferson, 1984, 1985, 2004). While the official transcripts produced by the Office of the Independent Counsel (published online by JURIST, 1998) are of high quality, there are several ways in which they are not adequate for conducting an analysis of the interaction that occurred during the testimony. In order to facilitate the analysis, additional details have been added, including timing of pauses (estimated), indications of stress or emphasis or noticeable changes in volume, repetitions and errors in speech, and where relevant, indications of nonverbal behavior such as facial expressions, gestures, or body movements. The transcribing conventions used are in the Appendix to this chapter. Some of the more common symbols and transcribing conventions used in this chapter include the use of punctuation to indicate intonation rather than grammatical structure, the timing of pauses, the use of underlining to indicate a word was stressed, and capitalization to indicate loud speech. Simultaneous talk is marked by brackets showing where the simultaneity began and ended.

The benefits of using the C-SPAN Video Library as the source for this data are several. First, the entire 4 hours of testimony are available in an easy-to-access format that anyone can use. This makes the data available to anyone who wants to check the transcription of the excerpts quoted in the chapter, or who wants to listen to more of the hearing than can be excerpted in a short book chapter, in order to gain more understanding of the interaction as a whole. The public availability of the data is especially important to conversation analysts. From the perspective of conversation analysis, the data (at least in detailed transcript form) should be available to the readers so that they can understand the analysis and check the data themselves to see if the analysis is sound (Psathas, 1995). Readers can easily listen to the original data to verify or challenge the interpretations presented in the research. Second, the video is set up on the C-SPAN website such that it is easy to play, start, stop, and rewind, and to make clips of specific parts of the testimony for use in conference presentations. For those studying the communication style and practices of public figures, whether presidential or otherwise, the C-SPAN Video Library is an excellent source of public-domain examples of their speeches, testimony, and other public appearances.

In the analysis that follows I will extend two previous lines of conversation analytic investigation in talk in legal settings in general and the presidential grand jury testimony in particular. First, I will extend and apply the analysis of how witnesses can evade answering or construct answers to avoid damaging implications of questions. Second, I will extend the consideration of the techniques used to present actions or interpretations as normal or routine by investigating President Clinton's pedagogical use of commonsense understandings and assumptions in his testimony. I will show that he uses it to instruct the questioner and the overhearing grand jury in commonsense background assumptions for his actions that enable him to sidestep blame-implicative aspects of the attorney's questions. In the concluding section of this chapter I summarize the results of the analysis and discuss its implications for understanding question-answering techniques and President Clinton's successful performance of them.

EVASIVE ANSWERING: MANAGING THE IMPLICATIONS OF ANSWERS

In this section of the analysis I apply findings from previous conversation analytic studies of talk in legal and other institutional contexts to show how President Clinton is able to successfully to resist the implication of blame in attorneys' questions and transform any negative implications of his answers to their questions to more favorable formulations. Here I build on Atkinson and Drew's (1979) analysis of the *prospective management* of accusations in trials and tribunals, and Clayman's (1993; 2001) analysis of the techniques interviewees use to avoid answering challenging questions in television news interviews. I will analyze the construction of questions and answers in the grand jury investigation and explore how accusation-implicative questions and morally accountable evasive answers are constructed. The problem for the witness is how to avoid answering potentially damaging questions while appearing to answer the question.

One way witnesses can resist potentially damaging implications of an attorney's question (or what Atkinson and Drew [1979] call the prospective management of accusations) is to resist the answer categories the question provides. For example, in Excerpt 1 the first two questions the interrogator asks (in lines 1–2 and lines 5–6) are yes/no questions. Both questions are designed with a preference for a yes answer (Pomerantz, 1984; Sacks, 1987). They are both answered quickly by President Clinton in lines 3 and 8, respectively.

Excerpt 1: Presidential Grand Jury Testimony 1998 (45:26)

1	Q:	have you reviewed thuh <u>rec</u>ords for december twenty eighth,
2		nineteen ninety seven, mister president?
3	A:	<u>yes</u> sir, I have.
4		(0.2)
5	Q:	do you be<u>lieve</u> that miss lewinsky was at thuh white house, (0.2)
6		and saw <u>you</u> on December twenty eighty, nineteen ninety seven?
7		(0.2)
8	A:	yes, sir, i do.
9		(1.5)
10	Q:	and (0.2) do you remember talking with miss lewinsky (0.2) about
11		her subpoena that she had received for thuh paula jones case on
12		that day.
13		(1.4)
14	A:	<u>I</u> remember talking with miss lewinsky about her <u>tes</u>timony, (0.4)
15		u:h or about thuh <u>pros</u>pect that she <u>might</u> have to give testimony.
16		(0.8) A:nd=u:h (0.3) she uh (1.7) she talked to me about that. °I
17		remember that.°

The third question, however (lines 10–12) is answered only after a delay (note the 1.4-second pause in line 13). When President Clinton answers the question in lines 14–17, his answer avoids the categories projected by the question (yes or no). Instead President Clinton describes what he remembered but avoids answering the main point of the question which was to establish the day on which it happened. He avoids mentioning the subpoena, and avoids stating whether he discussed the subpoena with Ms. Lewinsky. He instead reports that he remembers talking about her testimony (lines 14–15). He then repairs this utterance (Jefferson, 1974; Schegloff, Jefferson, & Sacks, 1977), and replaces it with a statement about "thuh <u>pros</u>pect that she <u>might</u> have to give testimony." Note that this is not the same thing as talking about the testimony itself. Note also that President Clinton does not admit to remembering talking about the subpoena or the Paula Jones case in particular.

Locke and Edwards (2003) describe how President Clinton uses claims to remember or not remember specific facts as a strategic move. President Clinton uses explicit statements about what he can and cannot remember, to avoid appearing to evade answering specific questions:

> The everyday categories 'remember', 'recall', 'forget', and so on, are not merely references to inner, psychological processes, but coins of verbal exchange that have a public, discursive use in managing accountability (Coulter, 1990; Lynch & Bogen, 1996). Clearly we are not looking simply at recall on Clinton's part, in the sense of pure memory at work, but at testimony produced under cross-examination—at memory as a participant's discourse category, as a social psychological phenomenon (Middleton & Edwards, 1990). Potentially threatening implications are worked up by Q and handled, re-worked, or warded off in Clinton's responses. This echoes findings from a variety of close studies of courtroom dialogue, including Bogen and Lynch (1996), and also Drew's (1990, 1992; cf. Atkinson & Drew, 1979) demonstration of how questions and responses in court re-work descriptive content and implications for culpability. (Locke & Edwards, 2003, p. 244)

Drew (1992) notes that witnesses can use "I don't remember" as a strategy to avoid having to confirm information in an interrogating attorney's question:

> As a sequential object *I don't remember* not only avoids confirming what is proposed in the question, but also avoids disconfirming it: that is, the witness thereby avoids directly challenging or disputing a version proposed by the attorney, but nevertheless neutralizes that version, at least for the present. (p. 483)

Drew also notes that by stating "I don't remember," the witness is claiming that it is not something that one would typically notice, for example, due to its unimportance or insignificance.

In sum, the third question in Excerpt 1 is answered quite differently from the first two questions because it is a different type of question. Atkinson and Drew (1979) would describe it as a question that foreshadows a prospective accusation. It may be leading up to an implication that President Clinton coached Ms. Lewinsky on her testimony or intervened in some way with her testimony. Mr. Clinton's answer as constructed preemptively avoids any such implications that might ensue.

In Excerpt 2, the questioner next shifts the topic to the Christmas gifts that President Clinton had given Ms. Lewinsky:

Excerpt 2: Presidential Grand Jury Testimony (45:04)

19	Q:	and, you also gave her uh- <u>chris</u>tmas! gifts, is that not correct,
20		mister president?
21		(0.3)
22	A:	th- That <u>is</u> correct. They were christmas gifts and they were going
23		a<u>way</u> gifts. she was moving to new york (0.5) to, aye uh taking
24		aye new job, starting uh new life. and uh i gave her: some gifts.

Mr. Bittman's question in lines 19 and 20 is also formulated as a yes or no question. President Clinton begins with a brief hesitation (line 21), then says "th- That <u>is</u> correct," thus answering the question with something approximating the type of answer requested. However, instead of stopping and waiting for the next question, as would be typical for a witness in a legal proceeding, the President continues speaking and elaborates his response (lines 22–24). This elaboration is a repair of the original question: the gifts were not just Christmas gifts, they were also "going away gifts." No doubt anticipating the questioner's subsequent questions about the large number of gifts he had given Ms. Lewinsky, President Clinton preemptively challenges their categorization as Christmas gifts by reframing them as also going away gifts. This additional reason for the gifts provides a preemptive defense for the large number of gifts he had given, thus taking some of the steam out of the interrogator's line of questioning. This elaboration could be seen to be prospectively responsive to the questioning trajectory that Mr. Bittman is establishing here. The interrogator's questions implied a prospective accusation (Atkinson & Drew, 1979) that the gifts were evidence of a romantic relationship. President Clinton's responses, here and elsewhere in the testimony, work to convey a more mundane interpretation of his actions. Locke and Edwards (2003) describe this strategy of supplanting a problematic explanation for his actions with an ordinary explanation:

This is a robust rhetorical pattern, where the notion that one is specially accountable for an action or situation, such that a motive or
account is required, is resisted by defining that action as commonplace, normal, or 'scripted' (Edwards, 1994, 1995, 1997; cf. Sacks,
1992). (Locke & Edwards, 2003, p. 245)

This strategy is consistent with the concept from the communications
literature of *framing* (e.g., Fairhurst, 2011a; Yioutas & Segvic, 2003). For example, Fairhurst (2011b, p. 43) describes this skill: "Framing involves the
ability to shape the meaning of a subject—typically the situation here and
now—to judge its character and significance through the meanings chosen."

Another line of questions about the gifts appears in Excerpt 3:

Excerpt 3: Presidential Grand Jury Testimony (45:20)

40	Q:	you were alone with her on december twenty eighty, nineteen
41		ninety se[ven,]
42	A:	[yes,] sir i was.
43	Q:	the gifts that you gave her (0.2) was aye (0.2) were aye CANvas
44		bag from thuh blackdog restaurant at martha's vineyard, is that
45		right?
46		(0.3)
47	A:	well, that was just, that was just something I had in thuh place to-
48		(0.3) to contain thuh gifts.= but (0.2) I believe that thuh gifts I gave
49		her were- I put 'em in that bag. that's what I had there, and I <u>knew</u>
50		she- liked things from thuh black dog.=so, I gave her- (0.2) i pu- i
51		<u>think</u> that's what I put thuh presents in. i remember what thuh
52		presents were, .h i don't remember what thuh bag was i gave them
53		in.
54		(0.2)
55	Q:	Did you also give her aye marble bear bear's head carving from
56		vancouver, canada?
57	A:	i <u>did</u> do that. i remember that.
58	Q:	and you also gave her a rockettes blanket? that has thuh famous
59		rockettes from new=york?
60		(0.1)
61	A:	tch i <u>did</u> do that. i had that, i had had that in my possession for a

62		couple of years but had never used it, and she was <u>go</u>ing to- new
63		york. so, I thought it would be uh nice thing to give=ʼer.
64		(0.1)
65	Q:	you gave her aye box of cherry chocolates, is that right?
66		(2.8)
67	A:	i don't remember that, sir. i mean, it th- there could have been. i-
68		(0.6) i- i just don't remember. i remember giving thuh BEAR,
69		(0.4) and thee (.) throw.

As Locke and Edwards (2003) note, at times President Clinton conveys that he does not always recall events referred to in the attorneys' questions. While Drew (1992) notes the strategic uses of "I don't remember" in hostile questioning environments, overuse of this technique can also be problematic for a witness. Note that President Clinton is very careful to balance these "I don't remember" answers with some very quick responses to questions (e.g., line 42 overlaps the prior question). In addition there are times when he specifically states his ability to remember. In line 57 President Clinton answers a yes/no question with "i <u>did</u> do that. i remember that." This lengthy way of saying "yes," plus the addition of "i remember that" may serve to display that he does not always fail to remember. There were times he didn't remember, and said so, but when he does remember, instead of just saying so, he flags it as something he remembered by stating that explicitly.

In his response to the question about the Rockettes blanket Mr. Bittman asks about in lines 58–59 President Clinton displays his ability to remember by detailing unsolicited information about why he gave her the blanket. Note that in lines 68–69 President Clinton reformulates "blanket" to "throw"—a blanket being something you might put on a bed, while a throw could be draped over an arm chair. Because Ms. Lewinsky was moving to New York, something from New York was relevant. These are ways of displaying that he's not always saying he can't remember, sometimes he does remember. Also, this information serves to normalize the gifts by displaying reasons for them that are not romantic reasons (cf. Locke & Edwards, 2003). When he is next asked a question, about the "box of cherry chocolates" (line 65), there is a 2.8-second pause and he then replies, "i don't remember <u>that</u>, sir" (line 67). Again, the "I don't remember" answers look less like he's trying to hide something when they are balanced by other answers in which he clearly does remember.

However, note also that the box of cherry chocolates is a gift that could be construed as a romantic gift, and this is the one he's not remembering.

President Clinton also uses elaborations of his answers to questions as a form of resistance to the questioner's implications. In Excerpt 4 below President Clinton takes advantage of having the floor to answer the question to do much more than take the floor. He uses his turn to accuse the opposing side in the lawsuit of various things, including illegally leaking information about the case to the press. Baker (2000) argues that Clinton prepared several such minispeeches prior to the testimony, with the intention of inserting them in relevant places to strengthen his position.

Transcript Excerpt 4: Presidential Grand Jury Testimony (52.25)

7	Q:	do you agree that she was up<u>set</u> about being
8		subpoenaed?
9		(0.5)
10	A:	tch oh, yes, <u>sir</u>, she was upset. she- well- she- (0.4) we she didn't
11		<u>we</u> didn't (0.2) <u>talk</u> about uh subpoena.=but she was <u>upset</u>.=she
12		said, <u>I</u> don't want to testify. (0.2) I know <u>nothing</u> about this. (0.2) I
13		<u>certainly</u> know nothing about sexual harassment. (0.4) <u>why</u> do
14		they want me (0.2) to testify. (1.5) and uh (1.5) I ex<u>plained</u> to
15		her?, (0.2) why they were (0.2) <u>doing</u> this, and why all these
16		women were on these lists, and (0.2) people that they knew good
17		and well had nothing to do with any sexual harassment. (0.4) I
18		ex<u>plained</u> to her that it was uh po<u>litical</u> lawsuit. (0.2) they wanted
19		to get <u>what</u>ever they could under oath that was damaging to me,
20		and then they wanted to leak it in violation of thuh judge's orders,
21		.hh and turn up their nose and say, well, you can't <u>prove</u> we did it.
22		(0.5) now, that was their strategy. and that- (0.2) they were <u>very</u>
23		<u>fru</u>strated because everything they'd leaked so far was old news.
24		so, they <u>desperately</u> were trying to validate this <u>ma:</u>ssive amount of
25		money they'd spent (0.9) uhm by finding some (0.3) <u>new</u> news.
26		and-
27		(0.4)
28	Q:	(you [were familiar)]
29	A:	[and she] didn't want to be caught up in that, and <u>I</u>
30		didn't blame her.

President Clinton's elaboration of his answer to the question fills similar purposes, as does Vice President George H. W. Bush's initial answer in the controversial interview he did with Mr. Dan Rather in the 1980s. Clayman and Whalen (1988/89) noted that in the first question/answer sequence of that interview, Vice President Bush first briefly answered the question he was asked by Mr. Rather and then continued to speak at length. In the extension and elaboration of his response, he departed from answering the question and made several topic shifts, which included complaints and accusations directed at Mr. Rather.

Similarly, in Excerpt 4, above, President Clinton uses his answer slot to produce more than an answer. His elaboration and extension of his answer is an attempt to reframe, not only this line of questioning, but the whole hearing and the legal case in general. In line 10 President Clinton first provides a yes answer, which is the preferred response to Mr. Bittman's question from lines 7–8. He then repairs his response, to clarify that she (Ms. Lewinsky) was upset. He also reiterates his earlier point that they did not "<u>talk</u> about uh subpoena" (lines 10–11). Note the latches (equal signs) in the transcript in line 11. These symbols indicate that there was no pause at all between those words. President Clinton ran them together so that these possibly complete *turn constructional units* (Sacks et al., 1974) would not be treated as *transition relevance places* (would not signal to the questioner that he was done with his turn). What he continues with is an elaboration of his answer, which is not just a topic shift but a shift in utterance type— instead of responding to Mr. Bittman's question, he is now introducing a complaint about the whole case.

Excerpt 5 below illustrates several avoidance strategies. First of all, notice that President Clinton does not answer the question Mr. Bittman has asked in lines 17–18 and 21.

Excerpt 5: Presidential Grand Jury Testimony (105:40)

17	Q:	she professed her love to you in these cards after thee end of thuh
18		relationship, didn't she?
19		(3.0)
20	A:	well,-=

21   Q: =she said she loved you?

22   (6.0) ((President Clinton puts his hand up in a "stopping"
gesture—palm raised toward the questioner—nonverbal request for the questioner
to wait until he produces his response))

23   A: sir, (5.0) thuh <u>truth</u> is (0.8) that most of thuh ti:me, (0.4) even when

24   she was: expressing her (0.2) feelings for me in affectionate terms,

25   (0.5) <u>I</u> believe that she had accepted, understood (3.0) <u>my:</u> decision

26   (0.5) to stop this inappropriate contact. (0.5) she knew from thuh

27   very be<u>gi</u>nning of our relationship that I was apprehensive about it.

28   (0.5) and I think that (4.0) in uh way she felt uh little freer to be

29   affectionate, (0.3) tch because she knew that nothing else was

30   going to happen. I can't explain en<u>tire</u>ly what was in her mind.

31   (0.7) but <u>most</u> of these messages (0.4) were not what you would

32   call over thuh top. they weren't things that, (0.4) if you read them,

33   you would say, oh, my goodness, these people are having some

34   sort of sexual affair.

35   (0.4)

36   Q: mister president, thuh question=

37   A: =but some of them were quite

38   affectionate.

Notice the long silence in line 22 prior to President Clinton's answer to the question "=she said she loved you?" This question, on the face of it, is straightforward, asking for a simple yes or no answer. But clearly, in the context of the hearing the answer is very sensitive. The lengthy 6-second pause could have negative implications for President Clinton. However, the video and transcript show that President Clinton "puts his hand up in a 'stopping' gesture" during this pause. He raised his palm toward the questioner in a gesture that conveyed a nonverbal request for the questioner to wait until he produced his response. This request transforms the meaning of the silence from simply not answering the question to asking for more time to produce his answer. By means of this gesture President Clinton makes the 6-second pause accountable. In addition, through this gesture he transforms any negative implications of his delay in responding into a visual demonstration of the questioner's interruption of him (Mr. Bittman's line 21 interrupted President Clinton's line 20 where he had already started to answer the question).

Once President Clinton produces his answer (lines 23–34), it must be apparent to the questioning attorney (and probably the overhearing audience as well) that Mr. Clinton has not answered the question that was asked. He used the technique of producing an elaborated answer that transforms the question (Clayman, 2001).

In sum, President Clinton used a wide range of techniques for evading answering or avoiding the damaging implications of answers as he responded to the attorneys' questions during the grand jury testimony. In the next section I show how President Clinton used commonsense understanding of everyday terms, contexts, and situations in order to challenge the construction or implications of attorneys' questions.

THE PEDAGOGICAL USE OF COMMONSENSE KNOWLEDGE

In the 4 hours of grand jury testimony I have identified at least 20 instances in which President Clinton uses his practical knowledge of everyday procedures (Garfinkel, 1967; Sacks, 1984b, 1992) as a resource when constructing his response to questions. By this I mean that he uses this everyday knowledge about how things ordinarily work to instruct the questioning attorneys and the overhearing grand jury in alternative or blameless interpretations of his actions. These instances fell within five broad categories of commonsense knowledge and assumptions. First, there is the contrasting of the legalistic meaning of a term (e.g., *sex*, *oral sex*, or *alone*) with a commonsense meaning of that term. Second, there is the provision of an alternative (typical, ordinary) interpretation/explanation of actions that supplants the blame-implicative interpretation of the question. For example, President Clinton used several explanations for the gifts he gave Ms. Lewinsky; these explanations worked to challenge the assumption that the gifts implied a romantic relationship. He proposed that gift-giving is an ordinary thing at Christmas time or as a going away gift. He also argued that gift-giving between men and women did not necessarily imply a romantic relationship. In addition, when challenged as to Ms. Lewinsky's use of the word *love* in her letters to him, he argued that the use of this word was an ordinary occurrence between male and female friends and did not necessarily imply a romantic relationship. Third, President Clinton challenged implications of questions by providing explicit instruction in how interaction works. For example, he explained how people typically answered questions in order to show how the attorney's interpretation of his responses was inaccurate. He explained how questions are routinely interpreted in context—in terms of the flow of questions that occurs. He also explained that an answer to a question may span more than one exchange of turns at talk. Thus what the attorney was treating as his answer to a question was actually an incomplete or partial answer rather than a falsehood. Fourth, the President instructs hearers as to the ordinariness of being vague and the nonordinariness of remembering every single detail (see Sacks, 1984b). Fifth, the President calls upon the audience's commonsense understanding of how the job of president is different from that of an ordinary citizen, and how the work of the White House legitimately involves construction of a public face in order to justify and explain actions taken. While the scope of this chapter does not allow examination of all of the examples of these categories of actions that occurred in the 4 hours of testimony, I will analyze some selected excerpts here to illustrate how President Clinton worked to recast the implications of his actions and his testimony through his pedagogical use of commonsense knowledge of how things are typically done.

Defining Terms: Challenging Commonsense Understandings of Terms

Perhaps the most famous instance of a challenge of the commonsense definition of a term in the grand jury testimony is President Clinton's definitions of sex and sexual relationships (cf. Wilson, 2015). In response to an attorney's question about his relationship with Ms. Lewinsky and her prior affidavit in which she had denied a sexual relationship with President Clinton, President Clinton challenges the attorney's taken-for-granted understanding of the term *sexual relationship* and instead instructs him on the ordinary way of defining it. On page 52 of the JURIST (1998) transcript of the grand jury testimony, President Clinton says about the term *sexual relationship*, "I was using those terms in the normal way people use them. You'll have to ask them what they thought I was saying." This use of commonsense knowledge echoes Harvey Sacks' (1984b) construction on how people do "being ordinary" in everyday life.

Excerpt 6 shows President Clinton explaining why Ms. Lewinsky was able to truthfully deny having a sexual relationship with him. He invokes the perspective of people having ordinary conversation, including the grand jurors themselves, and argues that they would assume that the term *sexual relationship* implies intercourse.

Excerpt 6: (JURIST [1998] Transcript, p. 11-12; C-SPAN Video 3:13:50)

1	A:	I believe at the time that (0.8) <u>she::</u> filled out this affidavit, (0.4) if
2		<u>she</u> believed that- thuh definition of sexual relationship was two
3		people having intercourse?, (0.2) then this is accurate. (0.2) And I
4		believe <u>that</u> is thuh definition that <u>most</u> (0.2) ordinary Americans
5		would give it. If you said s- (0.2) Jane and Harry have uh sexual
6		relationship, (0.5) and you're <u>not</u> talking about people being drawn
7		into uh lawsuit and being given definitions, and then uh great effort
8		to <u>trick</u> them in some way, but you're just talking about people in
9		ordinary conversation, (0.2) I'll bet thuh grand jurors, if they were
10		talking about two people they know, and said <u>they</u> have uh sexual
11		relationship, (0.2) they meant they were <u>sleeping</u> together, they
12		meant they were having <u>in</u>tercourse together. (0.2) so, I'm not at
13		all sure that this affidavit is not true!, (0.3) and was not true in Ms.
14		Lewinsky's mind at thuh time she swore it out.

President Clinton uses a similar tactic in his response to a question about whether he was ever alone in the White House with Ms. Lewinsky. He argues that being alone does not just mean being out of eyesight, it means the lack of aural access as well as the absence of open or unlocked doors through which others have permission to enter. By this understanding of the term *alone*, President Clinton argues that he was not alone with Ms. Lewinsky:

Excerpt 7: Definition of "alone" (JURIST [1998] Transcript, pp. 65–66; C-SPAN Video 3:13:50)

1	Q:	Do you <u>agree</u> with me that thuh statement, "I was never a<u>lone</u> with
2		her", (0.8) is incorrect? (0.2) You <u>were</u> alone with Monica
3		Lewinsky, weren't you?
4		(3.0)

5	A:	Well, again, it depends on how you define alone. yes, we were
6		alo:ne (0.5) from time to time, even during 1997, even when there
7		were absolutely no improper contact occurring. Yes, there- that is
8		accurate. u::h (0.5) bu:t there were also uh lot of times when, uh
9		even though no one could- <u>see</u> us, thuh doors were open to thuh
10		ha:lls, on both ends of the hall, people could hear. uh thuh Navy
11		stewards could come in and out at will, (0.2) if <u>they</u> were around.
12		<u>o</u>ther things could be happening. so- there were uh lot of times
13		when we were alone, but I never really <u>thought</u> we were. (0.3) and
14		sometimes when we, when- (0.2) but, as far as I know, what <u>I</u> was
15		trying to determine, if I might, is that Betty was always <u>aro:und</u>,
16		and I believe she <u>was</u> always <u>aro:und</u>. (0.2) where I could
17		((coughs)) basically call her or get her if I needed her.

In sum, President Clinton uses a technique of challenging the questioner's use of a term, and explaining how an alternative commonsense understanding of the term could replace it.

Precision, Vagueness, and Memory

President Clinton uses commonsense knowledge about how things work to justify his frequent failure to remember things he was asked about by the attorneys. He argues that things that look important in retrospect are not necessarily seen as important while they are occurring, therefore memories may be vague and imprecise. When an attorney asked about a previous problematic answer President Clinton had given to a question about when Ms. Lewinsky got her subpoena, the President first admitted that that answer was "sort of a jumbled answer" (JURIST [1998] transcript, p. 36), and then went on to offer this explanation for the lack of precision of his memory:

Excerpt 8: (JURIST [1998] Transcript, pp. 36–37; C-SPAN Video 1:49:06; Mr. Wisenberg)

1	A:	<u>Again</u>, I say, sir, (3.0) just from thuh tone of your voice, and thuh
2		way you are asking questions here, (0.2) it's obvious that- (0.8)

3		this is thuh most important thing in thuh wo:rld, uh (0.5) and that
4		<u>e</u>verybody was focused on all thuh details at the ti:me. (0.8) u::h
5		(0.5) but that's not thuh way it worked. I was, I was doing my best
6		to remember.

A few minutes later he makes a similar argument in his attempt to explain why an "I don't know" answer was not perjurious. He provides a commonsense explanation of why his memory is not as detailed as the attorney would like it to be, and explains how actions that in retrospect may seem important did not necessarily seem important at the time they occurred. Excerpt 9 shows part of President Clinton's answer to a question as to whether he thought it was okay to say "I don't know" when he really did know the answer to a question (JURIST [1998] transcript, p. 39). In his response he uses a commonsense understanding of how memory works and when details are memorable or not in order to justify his "I don't know" responses:

Excerpt 9: (JURIST [1998] Transcript pp. 39–40; C-SPAN Video 1:57:16; Mr. Wisenberg)

1	A:	<u>All</u> of you are intelligent people. you've worked <u>hard</u> on this.
2		you've worked for a long ti:me. (0.5) you've gotten all thuh facts.
3		you've seen uh lot of evidence that <u>I</u> haven't seen. (3.0) and it's,
4		it's an em<u>bar</u>rassing and personally painful thing, (0.5) thuh <u>truth</u>!,
5		about my relationship with Miss Lewinsky. (0.2) so, thuh natural
6		assumption, is (0.5) that while all this was going on, I must have
7		been focused on <u>no</u>thing but this; therefore, I must remember
8		<u>e</u>verything about it (0.2) .h in thuh sequence and form in which it
9		occurred. All I can tell you is, I was con<u>cerned</u> about it. I was
10		glad she saw a lawyer. I was glad she was doing an affidavit. But
11		there were a <u>lot</u> of other things going on, and I <u>don't</u> necessarily
12		remember it all. And I don't know if I can convince you of that!
13		(0.5) but I tried to be honest with you about my mindset, about this
14		deposition. (0.3) and I'm just trying to explain that I- I <u>don't</u> have
15		thuh memory that you assume that I should about some of these
16		things.

In sum, by pointing out commonsense understandings about how interaction typically works, he is both defending himself against the specific charge in the attorney's question, and also displaying that, by contrast, the attorney's failure to understand these aspects of interaction may indicate either imprecision or disingenuousness on the attorney's part.

Explaining How Interaction Works

On several occasions President Clinton uses an explanation of how interaction works in order to explain or justify his response to a question. For example, in Excerpt 10 he challenges an attorney's critique of one of his responses. The attorney had represented his previous testimony as contradicting his later representations about when he knew that Ms. Lewinsky had been subpoenaed. President Clinton explains that answers to questions have to be understood in the context in which they occur. In the context of legal testimony, this means a series of questions and answers. President Clinton refers to this as the "<u>con</u>text of thuh flow of questions" (line 2). He goes on to explain that his answer was not complete in one turn at talk, and was actually continued and finished in the next turn.

Excerpt 10: (JURIST [1998] Transcript p. 33; C-SPAN Video 1:34:50; Mr. Wisenberg)

1	A:	well, mister Wisenberg, I think you have to- (0.5) <u>again</u> you have
2		to- (0.8) put this in thuh <u>con</u>text of thuh flow of questions, (0.4)
3		and I've already testified to this <u>once</u> today. I will testify to it (0.2)
4		again. (3.0) u::h (5.0) my answer to thuh <u>next</u> question, I think, is
5		uh way of (0.2) finishing my answer to thuh question and the
6		answer you've said here. I was trying to remember (0.2) who thuh
7		first person, other than mister- mister Bennett- I don't think Mr.
8		Bennett- who the first person told me that, who told me Paula
9		Jones had, I mean, excuse me, Monica Lewinsky had uh subpoena.
10		and I <u>thought</u> that Bruce Lindsey was thuh first person. And <u>that's</u>
11		<u>how</u> I was trying to remember that.

At another point in the grand jury testimony (Excerpt 11, lines 11–13), President Clinton argues that inconsistent answers are not necessarily a sign of something wrong with his testimony, because "people don't always hear thuh same questions in thuh same way. they don't always answer them in thuh same way." He then provides an account for the discrepancy between his answers in which he presents himself as working hard to make his answer as "honest" as possible, thus justifying the differences.

Excerpt 11: (JURIST [1998] Transcript p. 35, C-SPAN Video 1:41:19; Mr. Wisenberg)

1	Q:	Do you understand that if you answered, "I don't <u>think</u> so", to thuh
2		question, has anyone <u>o</u>ther than your attorneys (0.5) uh (0.2) told
3		you that Monica Lewinsky has been served with uh subpoena in
4		this case, that if you answered, "I don't think so", but you really
5		<u>kne:w</u> Vernon Jordan had been (0.2) telling you all about it, you
6		understand that that would be aye (0.2) false statement,
7		presumably perjurious?
8		(3.0)
9	A:	Mister Wisenberg, (1.5) I have testified about this three times.
10		now, I will do it thuh fourth time. (0.2) I am not going to answer
11		your trick questions. (2.0) I:: (0.2) people don't always hear thuh
12		same questions in thuh same way. they don't always <u>a</u>nswer them
13		in thuh same way. (1.5) <u>I</u> was so con<u>cerned</u> about thuh question
14		they asked me (1.0) that thuh next question I was asked, (6.0) I
15		went back to the previous question, trying (0.5) to gi:ve (0.5) an
16		honest answer (0.5) about thuh <u>first</u> time I heard (0.2) about thuh-
17		Lewinsky subpoena.

President Clinton instructs the questioner ("Mister Wisenberg") in the commonsense knowledge that "people don't always hear thuh same questions in thuh same way. they don't always <u>a</u>nswer them in thuh same way." He thereby makes it look like the attorney's assumptions about his answers were unfairly legalistic rather than based in commonsense knowledge of how people interact.

On "Doing Being Ordinary" in the White House

For some of his responses to questions, President Clinton invoked the ways in which the role of president differs from the role of an ordinary citizen, or how the White House as a political entity routinely conducts business. First, he describes how the demanding nature of the role of president challenges his memory, and makes it harder for him to remember things than it ordinarily would be. In Excerpt 12 he argues that his bad memory results from the "crowded" life of a president. In addition, he notes that the events being asked about were not important at the time they occurred; it is only in retrospect that the need for a detailed memory of these events has arisen (Excerpt 12 lines 17–19, see also Excerpt 8 and Excerpt 9 lines 5–12). In response to a question about his meetings with Vernon Jordan, President Clinton explains his failure to remember details in terms of the pressures of life as president:

Excerpt 12: (JURIST [1998] Transcript p. 35; C-SPAN Video 1:42:55; Mr. Wisenberg)

1	A:	It's <u>a</u>lso- if I could say one thing about my memory. I have been
2		blessed and advantaged in my life with uh good memory. (2.0)
3		now, I have been shocked, and so have members of my family and
4		friends of mine, (3.0) at how (0.5) <u>many</u> things that I have
5		forgotten (0.2) in thuh last six years, I think because of thuh
6		pressure and thuh pace and thuh volume of events in uh president's
7		life, (0.2) compounded by thuh pressure of your four year (0.2)
8		inquiry, (2.0) tch and all thee other things that have happened, I'm
9		amazed there are lots of times when I literally can't remember last
10		week. if you ask me, did you talk to Vernon- when was the last
11		time you talked to Vernon Jordan?, what time of day was it, when
12		did you see him, what did you say?, (0.2) my answer was thuh last
13		you know, if you answered me, when was thuh last time you saw
14		u::h (1.0) friend of yours in California, if you asked me uh lot of
15		questions like that?, my <u>mem</u>ory is not what it was when I came
16		here, because my <u>life</u> is so crowded. (0.5) and <u>now</u> that- as I said,
17		<u>you</u> have made this thuh most important issue in America!, (2.0)
18		eh (0.5) I mean, <u>you</u> have made it thuh most important issue in

19	America!, from <u>your</u> point of view. At the time this was occurring,
20	even though I was con<u>cerned</u> about it, and I <u>hoped</u> she didn't have
21	to testify, and I <u>hoped</u> this wouldn't come out, (0.5) I felt I will say
22	again, that she could honestly <u>fill</u> out an affidavit that, under
23	reasonable circumstances, would relieve her of thuh burden of
24	testifying.

In Excerpt 13 below, President Clinton provides a routine, everyday (in the life of the White House) explanation for why he spoke to Ms. Currie about his meetings with Ms. Lewinsky. As a "political organization" (i.e., the White House), "when you are subject to a barrage of press questions of any kind, (1.0) you always try to make thuh best case you <u>can</u> consistent with thuh facts; that is, while being truthful." (lines 12–15).

Excerpt 13: (JURIST [1998] Transcript p. 70, C-SPAN Video 3:26:54; Mr. Bennett)

1	Q:	If I understand uh your current line of testimony, (0.5) you are
2		saying that your <u>only</u> interest in (0.5) speaking with (0.5) uh (0.5)
3		Ms. Currie in thee uh days after your deposition was to refresh
4		your own recollection?
5		(1.0)
6	A:	tch yes.
7	Q:	It was not to impart instru:ctions on how she was to recall things in
8		thuh future?
9		(2.0)
10	A:	tch no, and certainly not under oath. that- (0.5) every day, sir-
11		mister Bennett, (3.0) uh (2.0) in thuh White House, and in every
12		other political organization when you are subject to a barrage of
13		press questions of any kind, (1.0) you always try to make thuh best
14		case you <u>can</u> consistent with thuh facts; that is, while being
15		truthful. uh but- so, I was concerned for uh day or two there, about
16		this as a <u>press</u> story only. I had no idea you were involved in it for
17		a couple of days. (0.5) I think Betty Currie's testimony will be that
18		I gave her expli:cit instructions (0.5) or encouragement to just go
19		in thuh grand jury and <u>tell</u> thuh <u>truth</u>. That's what I told her to do
20		and I thought she would.

In short, in the workplace that is the White House, specific types of actions must be performed on a regular basis (e.g., managing the public face of the White House to the media). In addition, the social role of president entails demands that ordinary people typically do not work under. In his ad hoc analysis of talk at work in this institutional setting, President Clinton constructs an argument for why coordinating his response with Ms. Currie (the White House secretary) was a normal, typical thing to do, rather than indicating some nefarious intent. In addition, his failure to remember is not a result of his pretending not to remember, but simply the result of the demands of the job of president.

DISCUSSION AND CONCLUSION

This chapter has built on previous sociological research on the interactional organization of question/answer sequences in a range of institutional settings by applying it to the study of the 1998 presidential grand jury testimony. It has also extended prior research showing how President Clinton used common-sense knowledge and understanding to instruct the questioning attorneys and the overhearing audience (in particular the grand jury) on how to understand and interpret his actions and his previous testimony.

In terms of the techniques used to answer questions with accusatory implications, this analysis focused on how answers to attorneys' questions were designed to avoid damaging implications and present a positive face to the questioner, the grand jury, and the listening audience. In sum, this analysis has shown how President Clinton used several interactional techniques to avoid problematic implications of questions and/or to avoid answering them. These include evasive answering, reframing, reformulating, and extending or deviating from the answering role. For example, the analysis showed how President Clinton used techniques for resisting answer categories (such as yes/no or correct/incorrect), managing the moral accountability of silence (e.g., through gestures or facial expressions used to account for delays in responding), highlighting aggressive interrogation techniques (e.g., by flagging interruptions), and using "I remember" and "I don't remember" *turn prefaces* strategically. President Clinton volunteered the "I remember" frame to display cooperation and manage the interpretation of his subsequent "I don't remember" responses. He also provides information or details not asked for by the questioner to display his ability to remember and to prospectively manage accusations. President Clinton also took advantage of having the floor to produce an answer to elaborate, shift the topic, and/or make accusations. These actions enabled him to take control of the agenda and the framing of the line of questions from the questioning attorney. President Clinton also often reformulated the question, and reframed or reformulated facts, person references, or events to change their meaning or implications. For example, President Clinton reformulated "gifts" to "Christmas gifts," and then reformulated "Christmas gifts" to "both Christmas and going away gifts"; he also reformulated "blanket" to "throw." Finally, he used nonverbal behaviors (e.g., wagging a finger, shaking his head) to challenge the questioner's assumptions and to flag an interruption.

In terms of his pedagogical use of commonsense knowledge and background assumptions about how interaction works and how things are done in the White House or when one is president, President Clinton used a range of approaches. This analysis showed President Clinton's pedagogical use of commonsense assumptions and background knowledge (e.g., Garfinkel, 1967; Sacks, 1984b) about how things work or how people ordinarily behave. He persuasively used commonsense understandings of what is ordinarily done and how ordinary people do things, either in an everyday context or in the specific context of the ordinary life of a president within the White House. Through these arguments he was able to explain his answers to problematic questions and to provide alternative contexts to interpret them, which contrasted with the legalistic context provided by attorneys' questions. President Clinton's success in defending himself against the blame-implicative questions of the attorneys in the grand jury testimony, and in maintaining relatively high public approval in spite of the potentially damaging information revealed, may be due in part to his use of these techniques rather than just to external political actions by others and media representations of the case at the time. The institutional role of president of the United States undoubtedly contributed to President Clinton's ability to make these arguments and rebuttals in the way that he did. More-ordinary witnesses in legal proceedings would most likely have been instructed to follow the requested answer format and avoid providing answers that deviated from what was asked (Atkinson & Drew, 1979).

What does it mean to be a "great communicator"? One answer to that question is that President Clinton's pedagogical use of commonsense understandings and shared background knowledge enabled him to successfully reach his public through this testimony. These techniques provide an everyday, understandable explanation for his actions that may have resonated better with the general public than the intrusive, legalistic, and often embarrassing questions asked by the attorneys during the testimony.

In sum, President Clinton's grand jury testimony was important historically because it was a defining moment of his presidency, as Watergate was for President Nixon. In addition, it may well become relevant for the 2016 presidential campaign if former First Lady Hilary Clinton is tied to President Clinton's history. Finally, the goal of conversation analysis is to discover how work is done in a variety of different interactional contexts, both informal and institutional. President Clinton's use of a wide range of techniques to avoid answering or to manage the implications of answering hostile questions in a legal setting provides an exemplar of how things are done in this type of talk in institutional settings. Further research should examine what it means to be a "great communicator" by comparing different approaches to evading questions in adversarial settings such as the grand jury testimony. For example, while both Presidents Reagan and Clinton are among those presidents commonly viewed as good communicators, do they use the same techniques or strategies to explain their positions and make connections with the public?

REFERENCES

Antaki, C. (Ed.). (2011). *Applied conversation analysis: Intervention and change in institutional talk*. Basingstoke, England: Palgrave-MacMillan.

Atkinson, J. M., & Drew, P. (1979). *Order in court: The organization of verbal interaction in judicial settings*. London, England: MacMillan Press.

Baker, P. (2000). *The breach: Inside the impeachment and trial of William Jefferson Clinton*. New York, NY: Scribner.

Boden, D., & Zimmerman, D. H. (1991). *Talk and social structure: Studies in ethnomethodology and conversation analysis*. Berkeley: University of California Press.

Clayman, S. E. (1993). Reformulating the question: A device for answering/not answering questions in news interviews and press conferences. *Text, 13*(2), 159–188.

Clayman, S. E. (2001). Answers and evasions. *Language in Society, 30,* 403–422.

Clayman, S. E., & Heritage, J. (2002). *The news interview: Journalists and public figures on the air.* Cambridge, England: Cambridge University Press.

Clayman, S. E., & Whalen, J. (1988/89). When the medium becomes the message: The case of the Rather-Bush encounter. *Research on Language and Social Interaction, 22,* 241–272.

Coulter, J. (1990). *Mind in action.* Oxford, England: Polity Press.

Danielson, C. (2013). *The color of politics: Racism in the American political arena to-day.* Santa Barbara, CA: Praeger.

Drew, P. (1990). Strategies in the context between lawyers and witnesses. In J. N. Levi & A. G. Walker (Eds.), *Language in the judicial process* (pp. 39–64). New York, NY: Plenum Press.

Drew, P. (1992). Contested evidence in courtroom cross-examination: The case of a trial for rape. In P. Drew & J. Heritage (Eds.), *Talk at work: Interaction in institutional settings* (pp. 470–520). Cambridge, England: Cambridge University Press.

Drew, P., & Heritage, J. (Eds.). (1992). *Talk at work: Interaction in institutional settings.* Cambridge, England: Cambridge University Press.

Edwards, D. (1994). Script formulations: A study of event descriptions in conversation. *Journal of Language and Social Psychology, 13*(3), 211–247.

Edwards, D. (1995). Two to tango: Script formulations, dispositions, and rhetorical symmetry in relationship troubles talk. *Research on Language and Social Interaction, 28*(4), 319–350.

Edwards, D. (1997). *Discourse and cognition.* London, England: Sage.

Fairhurst, G. T. (2011a). *The power of framing: Creating the language of leadership.* San Francisco, CA: Jossey-Bass.

Fairhurst, G. T. (2011b, Summer). Leadership and the power of framing. *Executive Forum, 2011*(61), 43–47.

Garcia, A. C. (1991). Dispute resolution without disputing: How the interactional organization of mediation hearings minimizes argument. *American Sociological Review, 56,* 818–835.

Garcia, A. C. (2013). *An introduction to interaction: Understanding talk in formal and informal settings.* London, England: Bloomsbury Academic Press.

Garfinkel, H. (1967). *Studies in ethnomethodology*. Cambridge, United Kingdom: Polity Press.

Greatbatch, D., & Dingwall, R. (1997). Argumentative talk in divorce mediation sessions. *American Sociological Review, 62,* 151–170.

Halkowski, T. (1990). Role as an interactional device. *Social Problems, 37,* 564–577.

Heritage, J. (1984). *Garfinkel and ethnomethodology*. Cambridge, England: Cambridge University Press.

Heritage, J. (1985). Analysing news interviews: Aspects of the production of talk for an overhearing audience. In T. A. van Dijk (Ed.), *Handbook of discourse analysis, Vol. 3. Discourse and dialogue* (pp. 95–119). London, England: Academic Press.

Heritage, J. (2002). The limits of questioning: Negative interrogatives and hostile question content. *Journal of Pragmatics, 34,* 1427–1446.

Heritage, J., & Clayman, S. E. (2010). *Talk in action: Interactions, identities, and institutions*. Boston, MA: Wiley Blackwell.

Heritage, J., & Maynard, D. W. (Eds.). (2006). *Communication in medical care: Interaction between primary care physicians and patients*. Cambridge, United Kingdom: Cambridge University Press.

Hirsch, A. R., & Wolf, C. J. (2001). Practical methods for detecting mendacity: A case study. *The Journal of the American Academy of Psychiatry and Law, 29*(4), 438–444.

Jaworski, A., & Galasinski, D. (2002). The verbal construction of non-verbal behaviour: British press reports of President Clinton's grand jury testimony video. *Discourse & Society, 13*(5), 629–649.

Jefferson, G. (1974). Error correction as an interactional resource. *Language in Society, 13*(2), 181–199.

Jefferson, G. (1984). Transcription notation. In J. M. Atkinson & J. Heritage (Eds.), *Structures of social action: Studies in conversation analysis* (pp. ix–xvi). Cambridge, United Kingdom: Cambridge University Press.

Jefferson, G. (1985). An exercise in the transcription and analysis of laughter. In T. A. Van Dijk (Ed.), *Handbook of discourse analysis, Vol. 3. Discourse and dialogue* (pp. 25–34). London, England: Academic Press.

Jefferson, G. (2004). Glossary of transcript symbols with an introduction. In G. H. Lerner (Ed.), *Conversation analysis: Studies from the first generation* (pp. 43–59). Amsterdam, Netherlands: John Benjamins.

JURIST. (1998). Official transcript of the Office of the Independent Counsel. Presidential grand jury testimony. Available at https://www.gpo.gov/fdsys /pkg/GPO-CDOC-105hdoc311/pdf/GPO-CDOC-105hdoc311-3.pdf

Kramer, M. R., & Olson, K. M. (2002). The strategic potential of sequencing apologia stases: President Clinton's self-defense in the Monica Lewinsky scandal. *Western Journal of Communication, 66*(3), 347–368.

Larson, M. S., & Wagner-Pacifici, R. (2001). The dubious place of virtue: Reflections on the impeachment of William Jefferson Clinton and the death of the political event in America. *Theory and Society, 30,* 735–774.

Locke, A., & Edwards, D. (2003). Bill and Monica: Memory, emotion and normativity in Clinton's grand jury testimony. *British Journal of Social Psychology, 42,* 239–256.

Lynch, M., & Bogen, D. (1996). *The spectacle of history: Speech, text, and memory at the Iran-Contra hearings.* Durham, NC: Duke University Press.

Middleton, D., & Edwards, D. (1990). Conversational remembering: A social psychological approach. In D. Middleton & D. Edwards (Eds.), *Collective remembering* (pp. 23–45). London, England: Sage.

Nevile, M. (2004). *Beyond the black box: Talk-in-interaction in the airline cockpit.* Aldershot, England: Ashgate.

Osvaldsson, K., Persson-Thunqvist, D., & Cromdal, J. (2012). Comprehension checks, clarifications, and corrections in an emergency call with a nonnative speaker of Swedish. *International Journal of Bilingualism, 17*(2), 205–220.

Perloff, M. (1999). Sex, lies, and First Ladies: A modest (Wittgensteinian) proposal. *Southwest Review, 84*(1), 31–42.

Pomerantz, A. (1984). Agreeing and disagreeing with assessments: Some features of preferred/dispreferred turn shapes. In J. M. Atkinson & J. Heritage, *Structures of social action: Studies in conversation analysis* (pp. 57–101). Cambridge, England: Cambridge University Press.

Posner, R. A. (2000). *An affair of state: The investigation, impeachment, and trial of President Clinton.* Cambridge, MA: Harvard University Press.

Psathas, G. (1995). *Conversation analysis: The study of talk-in-interaction.* Thousand Oaks, CA: Sage.

Sacks, H. (1984a). Notes on methodology. In J. M. Atkinson & J. Heritage (Eds.), *Structures of social action: Studies in conversation analysis* (pp. 21–27). Cambridge, England: Cambridge University Press.

Sacks, H. (1984b). On doing "being ordinary." In J. M. Atkinson & J. Heritage (Eds.), *Structures of social action: Studies in conversation analysis* (pp. 413–429). Cambridge, England: Cambridge University Press.

Sacks, H. (1987). On the preferences for agreement and contiguity in sequences in conversation. In G. Button & J. R. E. Lee (Eds.), *Talk and social organisation* (pp. 54–69). Clevedon, England: Multilingual Matters.

Sacks, H. (1992). *Lectures on conversation* (Vol. 1). G. Jefferson (Ed.). Oxford, UK: Blackwell.

Sacks, H., Schegloff, E. A., & Jefferson, G. (1974). A simplest systematics for the organization of turn-taking for conversation. *Language, 50*(4), 696–735.

Schegloff, E. A. (1987). Analyzing single episodes of interaction: An exercise in conversation analysis. *Social Psychology Quarterly, 50*(2), 101–114.

Schegloff, E. A. (2007). *Sequence organization in interaction: A primer in conversation analysis* (Vol. 1). Cambridge, England: Cambridge University Press.

Schegloff, E. A., Jefferson, G., & Sacks, H. (1977). The preference for self-correction in the organization of repair in conversation. *Language, 53*, 361–382.

Simons, H. W. (2000). A dilemma-centered analysis of Clinton's August 17th apologia: Implications for rhetorical theory and method. *Quarterly Journal of Speech, 86*(4), 438–453.

Starr, K. (1998). *The Starr Report: The Independent Counsel's complete report to Congress on the investigation of President Clinton*. New York, NY: Pocket Books.

Upchurch, C. M., & O'Connell, D. C. (2000). "Typical Clinton: Brazen it out." *Journal of Psycholinguistic Research, 29*(4), 423–431.

Whalen, J., Zimmerman, D. H., & Whalen, M. (1988). When words fail: A single case analysis. *Social Problems, 35*(4), 335–362.

Williams, B. A., & Carpini, M. X. D. (2004). Monica and Bill all the time and everywhere: The collapse of gatekeeping and agenda setting in the new media environment. *American Behaviorial Scientist, 47*(9), 1208–1230.

Wilson, J. (2015). *Talking with the president: The pragmatics of presidential language*. Oxford, England: Oxford University Press.

Yioutas, J., & Segvic, I. (2003). Revisiting the Clinton/Lewinsky scandal: The convergence of agenda setting and framing. *Journalism & Mass Communication Quarterly, 80*(3), 567–582.

APPENDIX: TRANSCRIBING CONVENTIONS

Symbol	Definition
.h	Inhalations and exhalations, respectively
ta::lk	A syllable is drawn out
that-	Word cut off abruptly
lot	Stress or emphasis
YOU	Increased volume
°cost°	Decreased volume
(1.4)	Length of pauses (in seconds)
(talk)	Tentative transcriptions
.,?!	Punctuation indicates intonation, not grammatical structure
A: [a copy of it] B: [I have]	Brackets indicate simultaneous speech
A: yeah= B: =in order	Equal signs indicate one utterance or word is attached to another
A: are yuh gonna?	Words spelled as pronounced

CHAPTER **8**

C-SPAN UNSCRIPTED: THE ARCHIVES AS REPOSITORY FOR UNCERTAINTY IN POLITICAL LIFE

Joshua M. Scacco

M ost political communications that individuals encounter on a regular basis could be easily classified as neat, orderly, planned, sterile, or sanitized. Presidents speak from manuscripts electrified by teleprompter. Members of Congress post press releases documenting their activities. Journalists prepare questions to interview political officials. In one extreme example of planned politics, 2012 Republican presidential candidate Mitt Romney's tweets had to be approved by 22 staffers before being posted online (Kreiss, 2014). Few political surprises abound amid an endless stream of talking points.

What then are scholars to do if they want to study the "natural" parts of American politics? The first step is finding the proper setting or context where political officials, journalists, citizens, or other political actors are forced from manuscripts and talking points. These settings arguably would create greater uncertainty for political and citizen actors, meaning that the audio, verbal, nonverbal, and visual material may capture this uncertainty as well. The C-SPAN Video Library is an appropriate place to begin this search. Because of the unedited way C-SPAN covers public affairs content, the material captured in some contexts represents those unscripted, natural moments in United States politics.

The previous three chapters focus on two unscripted venues captured in the C-SPAN political debates and investigations. In each of the chapters, the authors document the convergence of planned politics and uncertainty. These chapters offer insights on what these unscripted moments tell us about expectations for candidate behavior, gender norms, and institutional power.

POLITICAL DEBATES

Political debates are critical moments in the course of election campaigns in the United States. For prospective voters, the format allows for learning and direct comparisons (Benoit & Hansen, 2004; Pfau, 2002), as well as the opportunity to correct misperceptions (Popkin, 1994) and rally around the "home team" candidate (Scheufele, Kim, & Brossard, 2007). For candidates, political debates are risky affairs where scripted talking points meet the uncertainty of press questions and oppositional attacks. The previous chapters by Patrick Stewart and Spencer Hall as well as Martha Kropf and Emily Grassett provide a window into one of the most unscripted moments in campaign communication.

The chapter by Martha Kropf and Emily Grassett unpacks the language patterns of male and female candidates in debates for seats in the United States Senate. Statements heard one at a time may reveal little in terms of patterns. In their computerized textual analysis of 942 candidate statements in 16 debates, Kropf and Grassett observe few differences in the communication styles of Senate candidates based on gender. Indeed, the analysis illustrates how debate communication style may contradict past research finding gendered differences in speaking styles. The authors creatively posit that female candidates for the U.S. Senate may change "their language to present themselves to the debate audience in a more masculine manner than the natural language used by women." Even in a relatively uncertain environment, the authors claim that women candidates engage in a high level of language monitoring. Kropf and Grassett's work should encourage scholars to delve into the repository of debate material in the Archives to extend their work.

Patrick Stewart and Spencer Hall focus on another potentially natural part of political debates—candidate facial displays. In their microanalysis of candidate nonverbal communication in presidential debates, the authors illustrate how the small facial expressions of individuals reveal particular emotional responses. These responses, in turn, are judged by individuals to be either appropriate or not (Bucy & Newhagen, 1999). Their work is a nice illustration of how the visual material in the Archives can be used to assess emotional, physiological, and potentially psychological components of American politics. Stewart and Hall write, "In an increasingly Internet-connected world, memes and tweets drawing upon such moments where candidates act seemingly inappropriately have the potential to reach and influence a large audience." Indeed, scholars who research in this area have a wealth of material to explore in the C-SPAN Archives.

POLITICAL INVESTIGATIONS

The third chapter addresses a similarly unscripted format in one area where law and politics collide: political investigations. Seared in the political consciousness are moments where wrongdoings were brought into sunlight—the abuse of power with Watergate or the personal exploits of the Monica Lewinsky affair. It is the latter which continues to occupy the attention of scholars of the contemporary presidency. Research has focused on media coverage of the Lewinsky scandal that engulfed Bill Clinton's presidency (Williams & Delli Carpini, 2000), the communicative responses President Clinton gave as a result (Kramer & Olson, 2002), and the progression and influence of public opinion (Lawrence & Bennett, 2001).

Angela Garcia's chapter enriches these perspectives by examining the detailed question-answering and evasion strategies in Clinton's 1998 grand jury testimony. Using conversation analysis, she extends prior research looking at question/answer strategies in interviews to a heated legal investigation of the president. Despite the uncertainty created by interrogatory questioning,

President Clinton controlled the agenda at key moments during his testimony, employing a practical ethnomethodology, "he persuasively used common-sense understandings of what is ordinarily done and how ordinary people do things," Garcia writes. The chapter presents an interesting portrait of how the small linguistic ways in which the president answered questions protected and insulated the institutional presidency.

RESEARCH PATHS FORWARD

The previous three chapters illustrate that the material in the C-SPAN Archives serves as a rich communicative collection of unscripted moments. These unscripted moments can tell researchers quite a bit about the health of democratic institutions as gauged by both political elites and citizens. I wish to touch on two additional communicative venues included in the Archives that both illustrate unscripted political moments and offer insights on the pulse of democratic governance: press conferences and call-in programming. These venues offer clear paths forward for continued archival research that seeks relatively unscripted political material.

Press Conferences

The C-SPAN Archives are an important repository for moments where press officials attempt to question and probe political elites on matters of import. A search of the C-SPAN Archives for "news conference" or "news briefing" contains approximately 18,000 videos, a wealth of material for scholars to assess unscripted moments where political officials meet the press. These texts include remarks by the president, secretary of state, the White House press secretary, and congressional leaders, among many other political actors.

Why should scholars consider press conferences as a site for analysis? First, the actors that participate in press conferences strongly dislike them (see Hart & Scacco, 2014). Press conferences combine both antiseptic transactions (which the press dislikes) with the inherent uncertainty embedded in the format (which political officials dislike). This recipe makes press conferences radioactive for journalists and political elites, but promising for researchers. The opportunity to assess the planned language of opening statements and press questions against the unscripted nature of responses and follow-up questions in one venue is replicated in few other political communication formats. Second, the press conference often represents a public clash of institutions, between the press (Cook, 2006) and another political actor. This venue can provide keen insights on how news norms and practices are publicly performed and have evolved over time, how political actors negotiate uncertain circumstances, and how two or more disparate institutions comingle.

Although scholars have assessed a number of facets of press conferences, there is still much to investigate. For instance, researchers have assessed the type and tone of questions posed by journalists at press conferences (Clayman, 2004; Clayman, Elliot, Heritage, & McDonald, 2006). This trajectory of research could be extended with the Archives by pairing the type and tone of questions with the visual responses of political officials. In this manner, scholars can assess not only unscripted verbal responses, but also nonverbal responses as well. The chapter by Patrick Stewart and Spencer Hall in this volume on microanalysis of debates could be instructive in this manner. Other research has looked at other aspects of the dialogic dance between political and press officials. Recent work that Roderick P. Hart and I (2014) completed on rhetorical negotiations in the presidential press conference assesses the language patterns of presidents and journalists across 12 presidencies. Using DICTION, a computer-assisted textual analysis program, we document how presidents have increasingly gotten the better of the press over 6 decades. Yet, the Archives present the opportunity to compare the language of presidents and their corresponding press secretaries, as well as other cabinet members. These comparisons could shed light on how organizational pressures within the executive branch lead to similar and different rhetorical patterns when managing press relationships.

Call-In Programming

The C-SPAN Archives also are home to a repository of call-in programming from the *Washington Journal.* Over the course of three and a half decades, C-SPAN has featured relatively unscripted calls from individuals who wish to comment on contemporary topics. The incorporation of call-in programming on C-SPAN in 1980 presaged other participatory mass-media developments that would occur in the late 1980s and 1990s, including talk-radio formats in shows like those of Rush Limbaugh and Larry King (Davis & Owen, 1998; Owen, 2013). The archived material would allow researchers the ability to track citizens' sentiment, as represented by their communication, over an extended period of time.

Citizen communications can reflect deep-seated concerns, as well as hopes and opportunities, within the body politic. Although call-in programming does not constitute a representative sample of public concerns, the material in the Archives can allow for comparisons over time and the estimation of rough trajectories. Similar approaches have been applied to other news media venues, including letters to the editor. In his research examining letters, Roderick Hart (2000) observes that a picture of the citizenry can be constructed in a number of manners, including with public opinion polling or letters to the editor. Hart's research uncovers that citizen communication in letters to the editor operates as a tonal intermediary between journalists and politicians. Indeed, his work points to the importance of considering citizen sentiment outside public polling formats. In an age with numerous newer media venues, I add call-in programming to this list of promising venues to gauge citizen sentiment.

Scholarship in the area of citizen talk could benefit from a careful examination of the call-in programming in the C-SPAN Archives. Because of the often-provocative nature of the programming, talk radio formats have received quite a bit of scholarly attention (for reviews, see Barker, 2002; Jamieson & Cappella, 2008). Richard Davis and Diana Owen (1998) were among the first scholars to tout C-SPAN's call-in programming as part of a new generation of media formats designed to engage individuals. Public affairs–focused formats, like *Washington Journal*, encourage callers to mention pertinent political information that may not be on the show's or the public's policy agenda, as found in a content analysis conducted by David Kurpius and Andrew Mendelson (2002). Although citizen call-ins create uncertainty for the hosts (a possibility that also could warrant research attention), the unscripted nature of caller responses could shed light on the emotional and information richness inherent in citizen political communications.

The C-SPAN Archives represent a wealth of public affairs material for scholars to explore the more unplanned moments in American politics. The previous three chapters offer a clear starting point for understanding the often unscripted nature of political debates and investigations. Although we acknowledge how so much of our politics is neatly planned, these chapters illustrate that there is still much to know where planned politics meet uncertain contexts.

REFERENCES

Barker, D. C. (2002). *Rushed to judgment: Talk radio, persuasion, and American political behavior*. New York, NY: Columbia University Press.

Benoit, W. L, & Hansen, G. J. (2004). Presidential debate watching, issue knowledge, character evaluation, and vote choice. *Human Communication Research, 30*(1), 121–144. http://dx.doi.org/10.1111/j.1468-2958.2004.tb00727.x

Bucy, E. P., & Newhagen, J. E. (1999). The emotional appropriateness heuristic: Processing televised presidential reactions to the news. *Journal of Communication, 49*(4), 59–79. http://dx.doi.org/10.1111/j.1460-2466.1999.tb02817.x

Clayman, S. E. (2004). Arenas of interaction in the mediated public sphere. *Poetics, 32*(1), 29–49. http://dx.doi.org/10.1016/j.poetic.2003.12.003

Clayman, S. E., Elliot, M. N., Heritage, J., & McDonald, L. L. (2006). Historical trends in questioning presidents, 1953-2000. *Presidential Studies Quarterly, 36*(4), 561–583. http://dx.doi.org/10.1111/j.1741-5705.2006.02568.x

Cook, T. E. (2006). The news media as a political institution: Looking backward and looking forward. *Political Communication, 23*, 159–171. http://dx.doi.org/10.1080/10584600600629711

Davis, R., & Owen, D. (1998). *New media and American politics*. New York, NY: Oxford University Press.

Hart, R. P. (2000). *Campaign talk: Why elections are good for us*. Princeton, NJ: Princeton University Press.

Hart, R. P., & Scacco, J. M. (2014). Rhetorical negotiation and the presidential press conference. In R. P. Hart (Ed.), *Communication and language analysis in the public sphere* (pp. 59–80). Hershey, PA: IGI Global.

Jamieson, K. H., & Cappella, J. N. (2008). *Echo chamber: Rush Limbaugh and the conservative media establishment*. New York, NY: Oxford University Press.

Kramer, M. R., & Olson, K. M. (2002). The strategic potential of sequencing apologia stases: President Clinton's self-defense in the Monica Lewinsky scandal. *Western Journal of Communication, 66*(3), 347–368. http://dx.doi.org/10.1080/10570310209374741

Kreiss, D. (2014). Seizing the moment: The presidential campaigns' use of Twitter during the 2012 electoral cycle. *New Media & Society*. Advance online publication. http://dx.doi.org/10.1177/1461444814562445

Kurpius, D. D., & Mendelson, A. (2002). A case study of deliberative democracy on television: Civic dialogue on C-SPAN call-in shows. *Journalism & Mass Communication Quarterly*, *79*(3), 587–601. http://dx.doi.org/10.1177/107769900207900304

Lawrence, R. G., & Bennett, W. L. (2001). Rethinking media politics and public opinion: Reactions to the Clinton-Lewinsky scandal. *Political Science Quarterly*, *116*(3), 425–446. http://dx.doi.org/10.2307/798024

Owen, D. (2013). "New media" and contemporary interpretations of freedom of the press. In T. E. Cook & R. G. Lawrence (Eds.), *Freeing the presses: The First Amendment in action* (Revised ed., pp. 141–160). Baton Rouge: Louisiana State University Press.

Pfau, M. (2002). The subtle nature of presidential debate influence. *Argumentation and Advocacy*, *38*, 251–261.

Popkin, S. L. (1994). *The reasoning voter: Communication and persuasion in presidential campaigns* (2nd ed.). Chicago, IL: University of Chicago Press.

Scheufele, D. A., Kim, E., & Brossard, D. (2007). My friend's enemy: How split-screen debate coverage influences evaluation of presidential debates. *Communication Research*, *34*(1), 3–24. http://dx.doi.org/10.1177/0093650206296079

Williams, B. A., & Delli Carpini, M. X. (2000). Unchained reaction: The collapse of media gatekeeping and the Clinton–Lewinsky scandal. *Journalism*, *1*(1), 61–85. http://dx.doi.org/10.1177/146488490000100113

CHAPTER **9**

PROTECTING (WHICH?) WOMEN: A CONTENT ANALYSIS OF THE HOUSE FLOOR DEBATE ON THE 2012 REAUTHORIZATION OF THE VIOLENCE AGAINST WOMEN ACT

Nadia E. Brown[1] and Sarah Allen Gershon

The most dangerous time for a woman is when she is trying to escape her perpetrator, when she is trying to do something about it, when she is trying to turn her life around, hers and her children's.

—Rep. Gwen Moore (D-WI)

In my years of service in law enforcement, not once did a domestic assault or rape victim question where the help was coming from or which political party or organizations endorsed the law that made that funding possible.

—Rep. Sandy Adams (R-FL)

Domestic violence, also known as domestic abuse, spousal abuse, or intimate partner violence (IPV), is broadly defined as a pattern of abusive behaviors by one or both partners in an intimate relationship such as marriage, dating, family, friends, or cohabitation. One in four women in the United States will experience domestic violence at some point in her life. In an effort to ameliorate the effects and consequences of domestic violence, Congress enacted the Violence Against Women Act (VAWA) in 1994 under the leadership of then-Senator Joe Biden (D-DE). Signed by President Bill Clinton, this law orchestrated a national strategy to end domestic violence and sexual assault in the United States. Not only did the act strengthen laws and penalties for perpetrators of domestic and sexual violence, it also provided funding for services to help victims of violence, in the form of crisis centers and hotlines (Laney, 2010). This bill improved services for victims; revised how the criminal justice system responds to domestic violence and sex crimes; and as a way to change the attitudes of Americans around intimate partner violence, shone a national spotlight on domestic violence.

Since its passage in 1994, this bill has been reauthorized three times through bipartisan support. Both Democrats and Republicans lauded VAWA as a useful measure to curb dating violence, sexual assault, domestic violence, and stalking, through the use of grant programs to state, tribal, and local governments. Indeed, both parties cited the weak response by police and prosecutors and numerous blind spots in existing law as the primary reasons why VAWA was necessary. However, unlike the previous reauthorizations, the Violence Against Women Act proposed in 2012 saw intense partisan politics that exposed major differences in which types of women the lawmakers deemed as legitimate victims worthy of legal protections and governmental funds. Democrats accused Republicans of waging a war on women. Republicans charged Democrats with using identity-based politics to create special categories for certain groups of people and with not seeking to protect all women. These intense debates were captured by C-SPAN in the May 16, 2012, congressional session in which House members hotly debated the bill, proposed amendments, and sought to reconcile the Republican-initiated bill to the Senate version that previously passed. Legislators on both side of the aisle spoke passionately about this act, drawing on personal stories, petitions from various organizations, and previous experiences with the law.

In contrast to many partisan exchanges in the House, congresswomen dominated this debate, comprising over 79% of all Republican speakers, and 60% of all Democratic speakers. Thus, the debate on H.R. 4970 offers a unique chance to examine how partisan and gender identity shape debate over women's issues. While the literature in gender politics indicates that female representatives in particular should consistently act on behalf of women when confronted with so-called women's issues (such as domestic violence), these debates reveal the uniquely quantitative and qualitative differences that this representation takes when congresswomen differ in their partisan, racial, and ethnic identity.

The differences in how Republicans and Democrats frame women's issues are a telling indicator of the party's policy priorities. Women (as well as Latinos, Blacks, and other people of color) are the face of America's new electorate. Political parties must court these new voters in order to win elected office. For example, President Obama was reelected due in part to winning 56% of women's votes compared to Mitt Romney's 44% (Jones, 2012). To be sure, women have often voted differently than men, and that has led scholars to explore the gender gap in presidential elections (Freeman, 1999). Women have also outvoted their male counterparts in every presidential election since 1964 (CAWP, 2015). The gender gap in women's political participation demonstrates that parties must seriously address issues of concern to women and have party platforms that embrace women's policy interests. Since the 2012 election, conservatives and GOP leadership have been rolling out specific strategies to help their party and political ideology connect with women—particularly, young and unmarried women. Republicans have been trying to counter their party's negative image among women. As such, debates like those surrounding the Reauthorization of the Violence Against Women Act are opportunities for the political parties and members of Congress to signal to women voters that they care about women's issues and are able to protect victims of domestic violence, who are popularly framed as women.

An intersectional analysis of both the policy itself and legislators' political discussion on the bill reveals the complexity of how multiple identities are often ignored in the examination of legislative decision making. First, H.R. 4970 centered on specific challenges that specific demographic groups face when trying to access services for victims of domestic violence. Next, the personal background, partisanship, and constituency wishes of lawmakers themselves offer a unique examination of how the multiplicative and interlocking identities and wishes of members of Congress underscore their positions on this legislation. Lastly, the discussion of the Reauthorization of the Violence Against Women Act forcefully illustrates the multifaceted political understanding of women's issues and women's representation. The use of VAWA as a case study reveals the continued importance of intersectionality research in political science. Our use of mixed methods provides scholars with a nuanced articulation of identity politics—both in the policy formation and the legislative behavior of members of Congress—to uncover rich differences in political calculations between Democrats and Republicans, men and women lawmakers, as well as White and ethnic/racial minority legislators.

In this chapter, we explore the differences in how members of the 112th Congress advocate for victims of domestic violence through their support or opposition to H.R. 4970. Relying on a content analysis of floor speeches, we examine House member's speeches on this highly partisan and contentious bill. The contemporary issue of domestic violence is complex, spanning immigrant, tribal, and sexual identity. How will women representatives—traditionally known for bipartisan support on bills concerning women's issues—discuss and debate this unusually partisan issue? The results of this research reveal the intersecting impact partisanship, gender, and racial/ethnic identity play in shaping representational behavior concerning domestic violence. Before turning to the analysis, we explore existing theories regarding descriptive and symbolic representation of women's issues.

IDENTITY, REPRESENTATION, AND COMMUNICATION: PREVIOUS LITERATURE

Communication from elected officials is a critical component of symbolic representation. Through messages to constituents, representatives may clarify their issue positions, claim credit for their actions, and enhance electoral support (Fenno, 1978; Maltzman & Sigelman, 1996; Mayhew, 1974; Rocca, 2007). Floor speeches broadcast on C-SPAN allow elected officials to explain their beliefs and behaviors to constituents in the same way they do through other communicative mediums such as websites, press releases, and newsletters. Thus, floor debates, like those concerning H.R. 4970, offer an important measure of representational style.

Previous research highlights the importance of both identity—partisan, gender, racial/ethnic identities—and representational style in shaping the ways in which elected officials explain their beliefs and behaviors. Scholars often suggest that descriptive representation for women, racial, and ethnic minorities may have some tangible benefits, most notably that these elected officials will emphasize the needs of their descriptive constituencies, increasing government responsiveness towards these groups (Canon, 1999; Darcy, Welch, & Clark, 1987; Mansbridge, 1996, 1999; Thomas, 1994; Zilber & Niven, 2000a).

Research in the fields of gender, racial, and ethnic studies does support expectations of substantively different messaging among men and women, Whites, and minority elected officials. For instance, female candidates and elected officials more frequently discuss issues associated with women as well as their gender identities (Bystrom, Banwart, Kaid, & Robertson, 2004; Fox, 1997; Gershon, 2008; Herrnson, Lay, & Stokes, 2003; Kahn, 1996; Niven & Zilber, 2001). Considerably less has been written on race and ethnicity and representational style, even less on the intersection of race, ethnicity, and gender in this area. However, existing research indicates that racial and ethnic minorities (including women) are more likely to emphasize issues related to race in their messages, as well as highlight their own gender, racial, and ethnic identities, as well as those of their constituents (Brown & Gershon, 2016; Canon, 1999; Zilber & Niven, 2000a, 2000b.)

Partisanship may also interact with gender in shaping communication style. Research often suggests there are widely held beliefs regarding the issue expertise of Democrats and Republicans (Petrocik, 1996), with "women's issues" consistently being associated with Democrats. Party attachment has been found to significantly influence representatives' messages generally (e.g., Sulkin, Moriarty, & Hefner, 2007), and in gender studies (e.g., Fox, 1997; Fridkin & Woodall, 2005), scholars typically find that Democrats more frequently mention issues related to gender in their communications. Research has further found partisan differences in the messages women candidates and elected officials communicate. For example, in her content analysis of congressional campaign websites, Schneider (2014) found that compared with male candidates, female candidates more often emphasized issues congruent with their gender (e.g., abortion, general women's issues, health care), and that these congruent messages were most pronounced among Democratic women.

While this analysis is exploratory, previous research does give us some preliminary expectations. Partisanship should exert a significant influence over a representative's speech. Unlike other venues for communication (e.g., district speeches, websites, press releases), these speeches are being made in the context of a very partisan debate over a divisive bill. Thus, representatives should be expected to tow the party line in support or opposition to H.R. 4970. We further expect that Democrats, the party historically associated with women's issues, will highlight the needs of women more prominently in their speeches. Within partisan identities, we expect representatives' remarks to be shaped by their gender, racial, and ethnic identities. For example, previous research indicates that White women, minority women, and minority men should discuss their descriptive constituencies at a higher rate than their White male peers, and should do so in qualitatively different ways. Thus, we expect that women legislators will more frequently highlight the concerns of women in their speeches and that minority representatives will pay particular attention to minorities in their floor debates. To explore differences in discussion of H.R. 4970, we rely on a content analysis.

METHODS AND DATA

To examine debate on the 2012 reauthorization of VAWA, we relied on C-SPAN Video Library from May 16, 2012 (C-SPAN, 2012). These videos provide a unique measure of representational style and priorities. The hearings, debates on the House floor, and written remarks all provide firsthand accounts of what the legislators said, and allows for study of their body language and interactions with colleagues. This is the only place where scholars can obtain such nuanced and complete depictions of lawmakers' policy priorities. In contrast to roll call votes, webpages, constituent communication, or media interviews, C-SPAN Video Library recording of the debates captures the stylized real-time discussion and votes on particular legislation. The bulk of research concerning representatives' symbolic representation through controlled communication utilize data drawn from speeches, press releases, newsletters, and (more recently) websites (e.g., Brown & Gershon, 2016; Bystrom, Robertson, Banwart, & Kaid, 2005; Canon, 1999; Dolan & Kropf, 2004; Dolan, 2005; Gershon, 2008; Grimmer, 2013; Gulati, 2004). Floor debate is substantively different than these mediums in a number of ways. First, the communication is likely more partisan, given the purpose and environment that it takes place in. Second, unlike press releases and websites, which offer almost limitless forums to discuss whatever topics the representative prioritizes, House members debating bills on the floor are constrained in the subject they will discuss and the time/space they have to discuss it in. Yet, variation in the ways they explain their beliefs and behaviors remain. In the debate analyzed for this chapter, representatives voiced their position on the reauthorization of VAWA using personal stories and statistics, some highlighting the experiences of different marginalized groups, others giving only general remarks. This variation tells us something about representational style, shaped by representatives' own identities, as well as that of their constituencies. Given the constraints on debate time, representatives must select only the most important messages to emphasize in their discussion. As such these floor debates provide a clear measure of the different ways representatives view the issue of domestic violence and the groups most impacted by it.

The Case

The political context during which this debate took place is a critical part of understanding the debate. The 112th Congress included a new class of Republican freshmen, many of whom were elected because of their association with the Tea Party movement. The Republican-dominated House introduced a number of bills restricting funding for programs widely associated with women, in particular women belonging to historically marginalized groups. Examples of these bills include H.R. 4970, but also legislation like H.R. 5855, which restricted access to abortion care for women being detained by Immigration and Customs Enforcement (ICE) (Camastra, 2012); H.R. 536 limiting abortion coverage of Native American women; H.R. 3541 criminalizing abortions based on fetus sex or race; and H.R. 3803, which banned late-term abortions in Washington, D.C. (Center for Reproductive Rights, 2013). While many of these bills died in committee, they, along with proposed legislation limiting contraceptive coverage rights under the Affordable Care Act (ACA), led to a the widespread discussion of the war on women (Torregrosa, 2012), a term attributed to the Republican effort. The 2012 debate on the reauthorization of VAWA reflects this political climate, with both Republicans and Democrats bringing up the war on women—in particular women belonging to marginalized groups—in their remarks. Thus, the debate offers a unique look at the differences in how Republicans and Democrats, especially female Republicans and Democrats, tie identity to the issue of domestic violence.

The Sample

The C-SPAN Video Library includes all speeches related to the reauthorization of VAWA on May 16, 2012, in the House of Representatives. This includes comments made during special-order speeches, during the consideration of the special rule for debate on VAWA, and during debate on the act itself (which included 1 hour of debate per party). Sixty-nine House members took part in this debate, including 25 Republicans and 44 Democrats (see Appendix A to this chapter for a list of representatives). Several of these representatives spoke more than once, resulting in 98 different segments being coded for this analysis. Both the Democrat and Republican speakers included disproportionate numbers of congresswomen. Women, 9% of all Republicans and 26% of all Democrats in the 112th House of Representatives, comprised 70% of the Republican and 60% of the Democratic speakers during this debate. Furthermore, women of color were overrepresented on the Democratic side, with over 80% of all Democratic women of color in the House speaking against the bill. In contrast, the two Republican women of color in the House, Representatives Ros-Lehtinen and Butler, did not speak in support of H.R. 4970. As these numbers indicate, partisan differences in the speakers are also representative of other differences, most notably, racial and ethnic differences. Of the Republican speakers, Rep. Tom Cole is Native American and the only racial or ethnic minority to offer remarks on the bill for his party. All other non-White representatives who spoke were Democrats. Thus, the correlation between partisanship and ethnoracial identity among the representatives who took the floor during this debate is sizable.

One final difference is the amount of time each member spoke. The frequency and content of representative's speeches varied widely. For example, while the average time spent speaking was 1.85 minutes, some representatives rose for just a few seconds to express opposition or support for the bill, and others spoke in depth on the bill for up to 7 minutes. Republicans averaged 2.07 minutes each time they rose to speak, compared with 1.73 minutes among Democrats. This difference is likely due to the fact that more Democrats spoke and both parties were restricted to a single hour of debate. and is further exaggerated by the fact that many Democrats used the 1-minute special-order speeches at the start of the day to address H.R. 4970. Furthermore, many more Democrats sought to speak in the time equally allotted.

Content Analysis

Relying on both quantitative and qualitative content analysis, we examined the content of representatives' debate on the reauthorization of the VAWA. The quantitative analysis includes manifest codes for the frequency and content of representatives' praises and critiques of the bill as well as their mentions of specific groups and identities (see Appendix B to this chapter for the code sheet)[2]. To conduct the qualitative analysis, several themes and reoccurring patterns were identified in the language that legislators used during the debate of the bill. We first loosely transcribed the video and then obtained the official transcript from www.congress.gov. The official transcript contained written remarks submitted by members of Congress who did not provide oral remarks. We organized the legislators' words thematically by context and legislator identity, once we discerned distinct patterns. In particular, our coding and analysis focuses on the representatives' discussion of whether or not the bill covers all women or merely some women as well as their discussion of particular groups. During the debate on this bill, much of the debate regarding this bill revolved around protections for Native American women on reservations, protections for members of the LGBTQ community, and protections for immigrant women.

We begin our discussion of the data by utilizing the quantitative content analysis data to show a broad picture of the content of the debate. We then use data from the qualitative analysis to flesh out the numbers presented, clearly articulating the differences in the debate presented. Utilizing this mixed approach, we are able to identify the systematic variation in representatives' statements, and explain the nuanced differences underlying this variance.

RESULTS

As outlined earlier, one of the primary differences in the content of debate across parties concerns whether or not H.R. 4970 was complete in its coverage (in particular, whether it covers all women, regardless of immigration status, sexual orientation, or ethnicity). To identity these differences in speech, we coded for the number of times the bill was praised for being complete or covering all women, as well as the number of times it was criticized for failing to cover some women. Table 9.1 shows the descriptive differences in this type of speech by party and gender.[3]

As the data in Table 9.1 reveal, there are statistically significant differences in the number of times House members praised and criticized the bill for the extent of its coverage. Specifically, Republicans praise the bill's coverage at a significantly higher rate, while Democrats criticized the limitations of this bill significantly more frequently. As the data in the table further indicate, these statistically significant differences remain when we break out only the female speakers, with congresswomen largely mirroring the partisan differences seen in the general sample.

Finally, Table 9.1 explores the impact of race, ethnicity, and gender on bill discussion. No minority women Republicans spoke on this bill, and only one minority male, Republican Tom Cole (OK), engaged in the debate on this bill, limiting our ability to examine the interaction between party and race. The data do indicate that Whites praised the bill significantly more often than non-White representatives. Breaking the groups down by race and gender, the data show that White men offered significantly more praise for the bill than any other group. White and minority men offered criticism at roughly the same rate for the lack of coverage of the bill, while White women criticized it the least[4].

To further explore the content of the praise and criticism leveled at the bill, we examine the groups mentioned in these representatives' discussion of the bill (results reported in Table 9.2). Those who criticized H.R. 4970 for failing to cover all women mentioned Native Americans, the LGBTQ community, and immigrants at a significantly higher rate than those who did not criticize the bill. In contrast, those who praised the bill did not differ significantly from other representatives in their mention of the LGBTQ or immigrant communities. These representatives did mention the bill's protections associated with age (in particular

Table 9.1 Discussion of VAWA by Representative Party Attachment, Gender, and Race

	All Republicans	All Democrats
Praise**	.64	.10
Criticism**	.05	1.04
N	34	64

	Republican Women	Democratic Women
Praise**	.629	.026
Criticism**	.037	.736
N	27	38

	White Representatives	Minority Representatives
Praise*	.400	.090
Criticism	.585	.939
N	65	33

	White Men	White Women	Minority Men	Minority Women
Praise†	.44	.383	.200	0
Criticism**	1.22	.340	1.20	.722
N	18	47	15	18

Note: †p < .10, *p < .05, **p < .01. Praise refers to the number of times VAWA is praised for being complete or for covering all women. Criticism refers to the number of times VAWA is criticized for being incomplete or for failing to cover all women.

for college-age women) at a significantly higher rate than their peers. Finally, due in large part to the speeches made by Tom Cole, speakers praising H.R. 4970 did mention Native Americans at a significantly higher rate than others.

Table 9.2 Groups Mentioned in Criticism and Praise for H.R. 4970

	Praise for H.R. 4970			Criticism of H.R. 4970	
	Praise	No Praise		Criticism	No Criticism
Gender/Women	1.95	1.55	Gender/Women	1.57	1.68
Race/Ethnicity	.181	.065	Race/Ethnicity	.1167	.052
Native Americans†	1.09	.565	Native Americans*	1.02	.466
LGBTQ Community	.636	.592	LGBTQ Community**	1.18	.233
Immigrants	.545	.828	Immigrants**	1.36	.383
Age-Related Groups†	.181	.052	Age-Related Groups	.052	.100
Children	.136	.157	Children	.078	.200
Disabled Americans	.045	.013	Disabled Americans	.000	.033
N	22	76	N	38	60

Note: †p < .10, *p < .05, **p < .01. Figures reflect the average number of mentions of each group per speech segment. Coding included other groups: Latinos, African Americans, Asian Americans, and the poor. None of these groups were mentioned during the course of the debate on the bill.

Taken together, these data indicate that at an aggregate level, many of the differences in the content of the language are partisan rather than gendered. However, given the sizable number of women speaking on both sides of the aisle, a more nuanced analysis is required to understand the ways in which women of different party, racial, and ethnic identities explain their support or opposition to this bill. Our qualitative content analysis reveals that there is substantive variance in how these representatives highlight the importance of symbolically representing specific demographic groups. There were other differences in how lawmakers framed the prevalence of domestic violence. These dissimilarities will now be explored in detail.

Representing All Women

The Republican-sponsored bill was touted as protecting all women rather than carving out special protections for specific groups. Indeed, Republican lawmakers claimed that because this bill was designed to protect all women there was not a specific need to address issues faced by certain demographic groups of women. For instance, Rep. Kristi Lynn Noem (R-SD) praised H.R. 4970 as a "piece of legislation which provides services to all victims without discrimination [and] has always enjoyed broad bipartisan support." Rep. Noem's comment is in direct response to Democrats' insistence that the 2012 Violence Against Women Act did not protect Native American women, immigrant women, and members of the LGBTQ community.

> Unfortunately, because some in Congress saw an opportunity to use abuse victims as a prop in a political game, today we're having a different discussion, and I feel it's shameful. House Republicans are not going to allow the Violence Against Women Act to get sidelined because of politics. It's simply too important. (Rep. Noem)

Republican rhetoric about protecting all women showcased the party's view that identity-based measures were an unnecessary and disruptive form of Washington-politics. The lead sponsor of the bill, Sandy Adams (R-FL), echoed Rep. Noem's sentiments by positing that the bill sought to protect all victims rather than play the so-called "oppression Olympics" (Martinez, 1993), where specific demographic groups of domestic violence victims compete to be the most oppressed to gain political attention and support of the dominant groups, saying, "I agree that all victims need to be covered, and that is what this piece of legislation does. We do not segment out. We do not pit victim against victim. It is all victims." Republicans viewed Democrats' resistance to this legislation as partisan politics, so much so that Rep. Sandy Adams frequently yielded small amounts of time to herself to refute several Democrats' claims that this bill failed to protect specific groups of victims. In response to challenges from her Democratic colleagues, Rep. Adams persistently refrained, "I will remind my colleagues on the other side that this bill and the current law protects all victims."

Likewise, Republicans Ann Marie Buerkle (R-NY) and Richard Nugent (R-FL) defended H.R. 4970 as being all-inclusive. Rep. Buerkle particularly found the Democrats' charge that Republicans are antiwomen distasteful, stating:

Madam Speaker, I just become so distressed when I hear the allegations that there is a war on women. When we sat down and we began discussing VAWA, we sat down with the understanding that Americans deserve equal protection under the law. We are not going to single out. We are not going to distinguish one victim from another. Any person who is a victim of domestic violence is a victim of domestic violence. Beyond that, it should be of no concern.

As indicated by Rep. Buerkle's remarks, many Republicans in the 112th Congress did not believe that there should be specific funding to target distinct groups of domestic violence victims. Republicans touted their bill for being gender neutral in that it protects all victims. Take Rep. Richard Nugent's assertion, for example:

The Violence Against Women Act protects and prevents all types of intimate partner crime regardless of the gender of either the criminal or the victim. This legislation funds the programs that not only help men and women who have been hurt, but it also helps law enforcement prevent these crimes from ever happening. I have heard a number of my colleagues talk about what isn't in the bill. They say, for example, it doesn't include "sexual orientation" as one of the protected classes. The Violence Against Women Act is and always has been gender-neutral. That's the beauty of this piece of legislation. It's gender-neutral.

While the legislation itself uses the gender-neutral words of *victim* and *abuser*, the law does not provide special funding for programs that target men as victims of domestic violence. House Democrats debating the bill wanted to include gender identity and sexual orientation in the legislation as a special category in order to change the cultural stereotype that men are the abusers and often women are the victims. Indeed, the name of the law itself—the Violence Against Women Act—assumes that victims of intimate partner violence are women. Rep. Nugent's statement reflects this belief, as it fails to address the pitfalls of using gender-neutral language.

Perhaps the most pointed rebuttal to Republicans claims was delivered by Rep. Betty McCollum (D-MN), in a statement in which she underscored the importance of VAWA as seeking to protect all women and the shortcomings of this particular piece of legislation:

All women who experience violence have the right to be protected. They need to know that their attackers will be tried in a court of law. And the purpose of VAWA has always been to ensure that all victims of violence are protected and that all their basic human rights are upheld no matter what one's sexual orientation, ethnicity, or legal status in this country is. This country failed to protect all women, and that's why this legislation failed to get the support from the advocates and from women all across this country.

Rep. McCollum is referring to the over 300 diverse organizations that opposed H.R. 4970. Democrats frequently reminded Republicans that the leading domestic violence prevention agencies and women's organizations publically denounced the legislation. Furthermore, John Conyers (D-MI), ranking member of the Judiciary Committee, informed Republicans in over half of his testimony that victim advocates vehemently disagreed with the GOP approach to combatting domestic violence. Many of the organizations that communicated their disapproval of the bill were traditional Republican allies such as conservative religious groups.

In response to Democrats, Rep. Lamar Smith (R-TX) provided the Republican rationale for not including specific provisions for marginalized demographic groups:

H.R. 4970 doesn't include language to provide special protected status to certain categories of people because they are already covered under VAWA. H.R. 4970 doesn't include language to allow Indian tribes to prosecute non-Indians because that is unconstitutional. H.R. 4970 does include provisions that prevent fraud and abuse in the immigration process.

However, Rep. Smith did not provide exact details about how this legislation covered Native American and immigrant women in his subsequent remarks. The insight we gain from his comments about VAWA being unable to protect Native American women from non-Indian abusers is the only mention of unconstitutionality in the transcript. Indeed, only the federal government has oversight within Indian country, whereas state and local laws and jurisdictions are unable to intervene in tribal courts (Miller, 2014). Rep. Smith's statement reiterates the Republican rhetoric that this bill protects all women rather than singling out certain groups of women that are already protected in this legislation, and that those groups are not specially protected because it is not within the legal scope of Congress to do so.

The clearest example of the partisan differences in how each party viewed the VAWA reauthorization is captured in the exchange between Reps. Virginia Foxx and Maxine Waters presented below:

> Mr. Speaker, it really pains me to see my colleagues across the aisle make the kind of accusations that they make about Republicans being unconcerned about the issue of violence against women. How could they possibly accuse us of not being concerned about that issue? All Republicans are concerned about violence against anyone. Violence, we are very concerned about that. I personally won't even watch any kind of movie that has any kind of violence in it because I can't stand to see violence perpetrated on another human being. So Republican men and women both abhor violence against women.
>
> —Rep. Virginia Foxx (R-NC)

> While my Republican colleagues may think many of these discarded provisions are unnecessary, there is ample proof that they are sadly mistaken. Just last year, cases of LGBT domestic violence had increased by 38 percent. Of those who sought help, 44 percent of LGBT victims were turned away from traditional shelters. As for Tribal victims, Native American women face the highest rate of domestic violence in the U.S.—three and a half times higher than the national average. Proposed changes to current VAWA protections for immigrant survivors create an even larger obstacle for immigrant victims seeking to report crimes and increase the danger to immigrant victims by eliminating important confidentiality protections. These changes threaten to undermine current anti-fraud protections in place while rolling back decades of Congress's progress and commitments towards the protection of vulnerable immigrant victims.
>
> —Rep. Maxine Waters (D-CA)

Both congresswomen note that their parties are concerned with violence and helping victims. In this case, descriptive representation does not fully tell the story of women's role in debating the reauthorization of the Violence Against Women Act. The comments of Representatives Foxx and Waters demonstrate key differences in how Democrats and Republicans communicate their support or opposition to this bill, and more generally, how they may represent women's issues. Rep. Virginia Foxx's quote is immaterial to changing the lived realities of domestic violence victims. She does not discuss the specifics of the bill, its intended results, nor the rationale for supporting this legislation. Compared to Representative Waters's quote, Rep. Foxx's inability to watch violent movies as an indicator for why Republicans are not waging a war on women skirts the contemporary debate over domestic violence. While Democrats largely debated the need for coverage of marginalized groups like Native American women and immigrants, the Republican comments on this bill focused on a general abhorrence of violence towards all women, largely ignoring the specific needs of vulnerable populations. The differences illustrated by these two women are indicative of the nature of the debate regarding the bill's protections for women from tribal, immigrant, and the LGBTQ communities.

Advocating for Immigrant Women

Democrats chided Republicans for failing to provide adequate support and federal funding for programs to protect immigrant women who are victims of domestic violence. For example, former rape counselor Rep. Judy Chu (D-CA) stated, "Let me be clear. This bill still rolls back existing law. For instance, with this bill, there is new, expedited deportation for any abused immigrant woman coming forth who has had even the slightest errors in her report." Similarly, Rep. Zoe Lofgren (D-CA) directly cites language in the bill during her testimony, and finds that "this bill changes the law that exists today and reduces protection for immigrant women in key ways." Rep. Lofgren points to changes in provisions for immigrant women needing to obtain a U visa prior to applying for a permanent visa. (A U visa is a nonimmigrant visa reserved for victims of crimes who have been physically or mentally abused. U visa holders agree to assist law enforcement and other government officials in the investigation of criminal activity (www.uscis.gov). The current law mandates that victims can only apply for residence if the abuser had been deported.) "So a U visa is for 4 years. If your abuser is serving a 5 year sentence, you have to be deported, and they—your abuser—will come after you the next year." In the spirit of collegiality Rep. Lofgren notes that this Republican-sponsored bill does not purposely seek to provide significant barriers to immigrant victims from obtaining protection from abusers. Instead, she notes that the bill sponsor is misguided in her efforts with this legislation. "I know Mrs. Adams is sincere, but that's what is in the bill. And that's why people object to the bill—that, among many other provisions that will endanger women and take us back to where we were."

In rebuttal, Republicans maintain that this bill is superior to the previous reauthorization of 2005. Bill sponsor Rep. Sandy Adams (R-FL) specified, "Let me first clarify. The bill requires that U visa holders actually assist law enforcement. Current law does not." Likewise, Rep. Sue Myrick (D-NC) affirmed Rep. Adams' articulation that the GOP's bill helps all women, particularly immigrant women. "We've streamlined and updated the immigrant provisions in the bill to address considerable fraud while still offering protections under the Violence Against Women Act, the statutes that are there to protect immigrant women." Representatives Adams and Myrick are among the very few Republican lawmakers that specifically addressed immigrant women in their remarks. The majority of statements made regarding immigrant victims came from Democrats like Rep. Rick Larsen (D-WA), who noted that the current bill "does not go far enough to strengthen those same protections that we established" in previous legislation.

Connecting her personal identity to her understanding of whom the bill fails to protect, Rep. Nydia Velasquez (D-NY) cited a "study from New York City [that] found that 51 percent of domestic violence homicide victims were foreign-born. Other research has suggested that, among undocumented Latina women, the rate of battering is as high as 34 percent." Congresswoman Velasquez noted that immigrant victims face specific barriers to seeking protection from their abusers, such as language barriers and the fear of deportation. Furthermore, "duplicate interviews with DHS would make it harder for those who are abused to secure assistance through the immigration system." In her revised remarks, Rep. Velasquez alleged that the Republican-sponsored bill will not reduce immigration fraud as the bill sponsors would have hoped. Instead, "there is not one shred of evidence suggesting female immigrants are misusing the Violence Against Women Act." As a Latina congresswoman, Rep. Velasquez was the only lawmaker to refute Republican claims by including specific statistics on the victims who share her ethnic and gender identity.

Safeguarding Native American Women

Perhaps the mostly hotly contested aspect of the Violence Against Women Reauthorization Act was the discussion of provisions to protect Native American women. As previously noted, Native women are victims of domestic violence at disproportionate and alarming rates. Democratic lawmakers focused on the abuse suffered by this specific population. For example, Rep. Hank Johnson (D-GA) provided statistics on this group to illustrate why it was so important for Democrats to protect Native victims, "Three out of five are victims of domestic and sexual violence are Native women. They are murdered at the rate of 10 times the national average, but yet H.R. 4970 denies protections to help those women." Similarly, Rep. Lucille Roybal-Allard (D-CA) stated that "Native women suffer domestic violence at epidemic proportions . . . and H.R. 4970 omits [the] provision . . . that ensures equal treatment and access to services."

Some Republican lawmakers rebuked their Democratic counterparts for calling for legislation to protect Native victims that they deemed unconstitutional. Rep. Jim Sensenbrenner (R-WI) accused Democrats of trying to "expand the scope of the law in a very controversial manner and by making an issue of whether a non-Indian can be prosecuted in a tribal court, which brings up huge constitutional issues because the Bill of Rights does not apply to tribal courts." Instead, Republican lawmakers such as Rep. Kristi Lynn Noem (R-SD) proposed, "Native women [should] petition individually the Federal courts or through their tribal courts for a Federal restraining order."

Yet, perhaps the most telling opposition to the bill's treatment of Native victims comes from Rep. Tom Cole (R-OK), who is Native American himself. For instance, Rep. Cole noted his belief that giving tribal courts the ability to prosecute non-Indians is constitutional. He noted that the bill sponsors met with him to "ensure that protections for tribal women were added and included in this bill." However, "these provisions aren't perfect, but they improve the current law considerably." Although his party's leadership included him in the development of the bill, as a Native American who represents a district with large numbers of American Indians, Rep. Cole respectfully disagreed with his party on this legislation.

Rep. Norm Dicks (D-WA), who represents a district with a sizable number of Native American constituents, disagreed with the Republican-led initiatives to protect Native victims in this bill. Rep. Dicks declared that the current bill did not go far enough in strengthening the authority of tribal courts to prosecute abusers, "Instead, tribal residents in my district would be forced to rely on Federal courts, located several hours away in Tacoma and Seattle, for help and protection. This puts a terrible and potentially dangerous burden on Indian victims in need of a protection order, many of whom do not have the means to travel this distance." Perhaps Rep. Cole's sentiments are similar to Rep. Dick's. As legislators who represent large numbers of Native Americans, these lawmakers are particularly aware of the needs of Native victims and the shortcomings of federal law to protect this population.

Protecting LGBTQ Victims

Unlike the bipartisan Senate bill, the proposed Reauthorization of Violence Against Women Act did not include gender-neutral language and specific provisions for queer victims. Republican sponsors of this legislation, again, noted the inclusivity of their bill as protecting all victims. Rep. Mike Quigley (D-IL) declared that including gender-neutral language in the legislation is not enough: "Gay men are not turned away from shelters because they are men; they're turned away because of discrimination based on their sexual orientation." As an active member in the Congressional LGBT Equality Caucus, Rep. Quigley has a long track record of advocating for the rights of queer Americans. He was inducted into the Chicago Gay and Lesbian Hall of Fame in 2009 for extending benefits to employees in his position as Cook County Commissioner, and has been a strong supporter of marriage equality (http://quigley.house.gov). Rep. Quigley views the Republican lack of support for LGBTQ issues as "folks who don't want to, in any way, have a pro-gay vote on it. But this is protecting human beings. It's the right thing to do."

Rep. Jerrold Nadler (D-NY) is also a member of the Congressional LGBT Equality Caucus who called for the House to include amendments in the Reauthorization of Violence Against Women Act that would protect queer

Americans. As a tireless supporter of equality for LGBTQ citizens, Rep. Nadler has championed legislation that will end discrimination based on sexual orientation and gender identity. He called for the House to adopt measures provided in the Senate bill that would protect gays and lesbians, "The bipartisan Senate bill would add sexual orientation and gender identity to the eligibility for grant programs under VAWA so that groups could focus on victims among this underserved population. The Senate bill would also include sexual orientation and gender identity as classes in the new VAWA antidiscrimination language." Rep. Nadler noted that the VAWA reauthorization did not protect all victims and that Republican majority sought to mislead the American public in who this bill actually protected, through the rhetorical use of the phrase "protect all women." This language failed to include men and trans women victims of domestic violence.

While both Representatives Quigley and Nadler are heterosexual, they are dedicated to procuring equal rights for queer Americans. In deciding to join the Congressional LGBT Equality Caucus, and subsequent vice-chairs of the caucus, these legislators indicate that sharing a similar sexual orientation or gender identity is not necessary for advocating for this marginalized population. Instead, these congressmen have chosen to represent a specific demographic group and affiliate with an identity-based caucus. Their remarks in opposition to the Reauthorization of the Violence Against Women Act showcases a deep commitment to issues that impact queer Americans.

CONCLUSION

The bipartisan support of the Reauthorization of the Violence Against Women Act seen in the 112th Congress indicates that both Republicans and Democrats are united in their efforts to create legislation to protect victims of domestic violence. However, the 2013 reauthorization signaled a substantive diversion in the lawmakers' abilities to uniformly agree on how to best assist victims. On the surface both parties, as well as men and women legislators, seek to strengthen federal law against batterers and abusers of women (and LGBTQ individuals). Yet we find that there are key differences in how the legislators are addressing domestic violence. Perhaps these differences are best seen in the consideration of H.R. 4970.

The articulation of substantive policy solutions to aiding victims of domestic violence is complicated by time and partisan constraints. What we have observed may be dictated by committee membership, time allotted for speech, and party-line directives. However, our findings are still instructive for viewing how legislators decide to use their time during debates. They may choose to use this time to talk directly to constituents in hopes of reelection, take positions that may curry favor with party leadership, and/or demonstrate a willingness to present themselves as an issue leader on domestic violence. These political maneuvers offer insight into lawmakers' comments on H.R. 4970 but only partly tell the story of representation. How legislators use their allotted time to substantively and/or descriptively represent women's issues is a demonstration of the lawmakers' priorities. These differences between Republicans and Democrats speech on the Reauthorization of the Violence Against Women Act indicate that protecting women is political. For example, Rep. Sandy Adams (R-FL) declared, "Mr. Conyers, I have sat quietly and tried to behave here, but I am offended when I hear that this does not protect victims. I am offended when I hear that we are politicizing something that was politicized." Indeed, representatives themselves viewed this debate as overly politicized, and accusations about this undue politicization were present on both sides of the aisle.

While this study is largely exploratory, we find that Republicans rhetorically offered little justification for why H.R. 4970 was a superior bill. The Democrats' rebuttal of the legislation included detailed facts about violence perpetrated against specific groups, letters opposing the bill from civic and religious organizations, and drew from previous iterations of the bill and similar bills that were successful in the past. Democrats were far more successful in presenting themselves as the party that is concerned with women's issues.

The quotes by Reps. Virginia Foxx (R-NC) are illustrative of the failures of inclusive language that only serves to marginalize groups who are already on the periphery of American society. The language of protecting "all women" only rhetorically addresses substantive issues. Instead, the Democrats move beyond rhetoric to provide specific examples of whom H.R. 4970 would harm—namely, Native American women, immigrant women, and members of the LGBTQ community. The sound bites or talking points of Republicans demonstrate that having greater female descriptive representation does not necessarily translate into substantive or symbolic representation for all women. Language that only acknowledges "all women" fails to recognize the material and real ways that only certain women can benefit from the proposed legislation. In the contemporary context, the debate around the utility of #BlackLivesMatter versus #AllLivesMatter similarly demonstrates that when proponents of culturally (or racially) specific solutions to identified problems fail to incorporate the perspectives of the privilege. The instance that privileged vantage points are including is how the oppressed are told how to articulate identity-specific issues only serves to center the experiences of the well off—not to improve the lives of the disenfranchised. The Republicans in this debate failed to recognize the plight of "all women" is redundant—as both parties agree that domestic violence is a bad thing. But only Democrats use identity in concrete ways to protect victims. The Democrats pointed out that the Republican bill did not go far enough to protect certain communities from domestic violence. What the Democrats are suggesting is that there is a specific set of problems that are occurring in immigrant, Native, and LGBTQ communities that are not being addressed in the current legislation. The phrase "all women" reduces the complexity in how groups of victims experience violence and seek protection.

The Republican-controlled Congress used their majority status to set the political agenda. The GOP framed the debates on the VAWA reauthorization in an attempt to connect with their political base. However, it is significant that Republicans appeared to be defensive in their articulation of the legislation. As the majority party, the GOP should have been able to use their numbers to dominate the debate. Instead, the Republicans used their allotted time to respond to Democrats' critique of the bill rather than speak to constituents, bolster claims about their party's responsiveness to women, or tout the benefits of the bill. By failing to offer substantive examples or detailed rationale for the bill's provisions, Republicans did not claim issue ownership of this subject.

Lastly, congresswomen on both sides of the aisle often used their gender identity as a proxy for representing women. They did not have to make explicit claims of being in touch with women's issues because their own identity provided that authority, unlike male lawmakers who often explicitly noted that they were advocates for women. Instead, both women and men legislators shared their professional experiences in combatting abuse and championing the rights of women. In this manner, the legislators used their narratives to connect to women voters. Lawmakers used different tactics to convey this point, some more successfully than others. Several members of Congress drew from personal stories of witnessing domestic violence, assisting victims, or prosecuting abusers. These personal narratives are helpful in connecting legislators to individuals; however, these narratives do not have policy implications. Democratic lawmakers, particularly women legislators, detailed how the Republican bill was shortsighted, and often tied their critique to an example based on a personal connection to a victim. Republican congresswomen, conversely, solely shared a narrative. As such, the GOP missed an opportunity to showcase their policy expertise on women's issues, as a way to connect with female voters.

The implications for this study are twofold. First, our study demonstrates that the C-SPAN Video Library is an excellent resource to examine congressional behavior. We are able to use the recordings of the hearings to see and hear how policy is debated, framed, and shaped. Second, we have illustrated that partisan talk is often mediated through gendered bodies as an attempt for political parties to reach certain constituencies. Having Rep. Sandy Adams author and present the Republican bill demonstrated that having a woman's face leading a women's issue bill has symbolic importance. While the GOP bill and its discussion offered more of a rhetorical commitment to representing women rather than substantively addressing the concerns of victims, it was a strategic move to have a woman introduce the bill. In a symbolic move, the Republicans placed a woman in the speaker's chair for the duration of the debate. Perhaps this symbolic gesture was an attempt to increase women's physical representation on the bill as a response to Democrats' accusation that the GOP was leading a war against women. However, by examining the content of the bill and lawmakers' articulation of the policy, we soon learn that descriptive representation does not necessarily lead to substantive representation. Scholars, practitioners, and policy makers must pay attention to what is being said and the language of the legislation, rather than assuming that women lawmakers are the best representatives for women's issues.

NOTES

1. The names of the authors appear in alphabetical order; this chapter is completely collaborative.

2. Two coders conducted this content analysis. All coders were trained together using floor debates not included in this analysis. Intercoder agreement was measured on a subsample of the speech segments used in this analysis, yielding an average agreement level of 90% (agreement ranged between 80% and 95%).

3. Throughout the analyses presented, the unit of analysis is the speaking segment (in other words, each separate time the representative took the floor to speak). However, analyses were run with the data aggregated to the representative level, and the substantive findings did not change.

4. Because of their relatively small numbers in Congress, we have collapsed minority men and women into one category. We readily recognize the differences among racial/ethnic men and women (as well as differences within each group). In order to isolate effects on identity-based representation we use linked fate as a theoretical explanation for why minority groups have a shared status that produces similar political behavior and preferences.

REFERENCES

Brown, N. E., & Gershon, S. A. (2016). Intersectional presentations: An exploratory study of minority congresswomen's website biographies. *Du Bois Review: Social Science Research on Race, 13*(01), 85–108.

Bystrom, D. G., Robertson, T., Banwart, M. C., & Kaid, L. L. (Eds.). (2005). *Gender and candidate communication: Videostyle, webstyle, newstyle.* New York, NY: Routledge.

Camastra, N. (2012). "War on Women" increasingly focused on women of color and immigrant women. *RH Reality Check.* Retrieved from http://rhrealitycheck .org/article/2012/06/12/%E2%80%9Cwar-on-women%E2%80%9D-increasing -focused-on-women-color-immigrant-women/

Canon, D. T. (1999). *Race, redistricting, and representation: The unintended consequences of the Black majority districts.* Chicago, IL: University of Chicago Press

Center for American Women and Politics (CAWP). (2015). Gender differences in voter turnout. Retrieved from http://www.cawp.rutgers.edu/sites/default/files /resources/genderdiff.pdf

Center for Reproductive Rights. (2013). *Under attack: Reproductive rights in the 112th Congress.* Retrieved from http://www.reproductiverights.org/sites/crr.civic actions.net/files/documents/crr_GR_wrapUp_3.13.pdf

C-SPAN (Producer). (2012, May 16). *House session* [online video]. Available from http://www.c-span.org/video/?306022-2/house-session

Darcy, R., Welch, S., & Clark, J. (1987). Women, elections, and representation. Lincoln, NE: University of Nebraska Press.

Dolan, J., &. Kropf, J. S. (2004). Credit claiming from the U.S. House: Gendered communication styles? *Harvard International Journal of Press Politics, 9*(1), 41–59.

Dolan, K. (2005). Do women candidates play to gender stereotypes? Do men play to women? Candidate sex and issue priorities on campaign websites. *Political Research Quarterly, 58*(1), 31–44.

Fenno, R. F., Jr. (1978). *Home style: House members in their districts.* New York, NY: Harper Collins.

Fox, R. L. (1997). *Gender dynamics in congressional elections* (Vol. 2). Thousand Oaks, CA: Sage.

Freeman, Jo. (1999). Gender gaps in presidential elections [Letter to the editor]. *PS: Political Science and Politics, 32*(2), 191–192.

Fridkin, K., & Woodall, G. (2005). Different portraits, different leaders? Gender differences in US Senators' presentation of self. In S. Thomas and C. Wilcox (Eds.), *Women and elective office: Past, present, and future* (2nd ed.) (pp. 81–93). New York, NY: Oxford University Press.

Gershon, S. A. (2008). Communicating female and minority interests online: A study of web site issue discussion among female, Latino, and African American members of Congress. *International Journal of Press/Politics, 13*(2), 120–140.

Grimmer, J. (2013). *Representational style in Congress: What legislators say and why it matters.* New York, NY: Cambridge University Press.

Gulati, G. J. (2004). First impressions: Congressional homepages and presentation of self on the WWW. *Harvard International Journal of Press Politics, 9(1)*, 22–40.

Herrnson, P. S., Celeste Lay, J., & Stokes, A. K. (2003). Women running "as women": Candidate gender, campaign issues, and voter-targeting strategies. *Journal of Politics, 65*(1), 244– 255.

Jones, J. (2012). Gender gap in 2012 vote is largest in Gallup's history. Retrieved from http://www.gallup.com/poll/158588/gender-gap-2012-vote-largest-gallup -history.aspx

Kahn, K. F. (1996). *The political consequences of being a woman: How stereotypes influence the conduct and consequences of political campaigns.* New York, NY: Columbia University Press.

Laney, G. P. (2010). Violence Against Women Act: History and federal funding. In D. Stickle (Ed.), *Women's issues: Economic, societal, and personal* (pp. 1–47). New York, NY: Nova Science.

Maltzman, F., & Sigelman, L. (1996). The politics of talk: Unconstrained floor time in the US House of Representatives. *Journal of Politics, 58*(3), 819–830.

Mansbridge, J. (1996). *In defense of "descriptive" representation.* Evanston, IL: Northwestern University, Center for Urban Affairs and Policy Research.

Mansbridge, J. (1999). Should blacks represent blacks and women represent women? A contingent "yes." *Journal of Politics, 61*(3):628–657.

Martinez, E. (1993). Beyond black/white: The racisms of our times. *Social Justice, 20*(1/2), 22–34.

Mayhew, D. R. (1974). *Congress: The electoral connection.* New Haven, CT: Yale University Press.

Miller, G. (2014). The shrinking sovereign: Tribal adjudicatory jurisdiction over non-members in civil cases. *Columbia Law Review, 114*(1825), 1825–1860.

Niven, D., & Zilber, J. (2001). Do women and men in Congress cultivate different images? Evidence from congressional websites. *Political Communication, 18*(4), 395–405.

Petrocik, J. R. (1996). Issue ownership in presidential elections, with a 1980 case study. *American Journal of Political Science, 40*(3), 825–850.

Rocca, M. S. (2007). Nonlegislative debate in the US House of Representatives. *American Politics Research, 35*(4), 489–505.

Schneider, M. C. (2014). Gender-based strategies on candidate websites. *Journal of Political Marketing, 13*(4), 264–290.

Sulkin, T., Moriarty, C. M., & Hefner, V. (2007). Congressional candidates' issue agendas on- and off-line. *Harvard International Journal of Press/Politics, 12*(2), 63–79.

Thomas, S. (1994). *How women legislate.* New York, NY: Oxford University Press.

Torregrosa, L. L. (2012, April 3). U.S. culture war with women at its center. *New York Times.* Retrieved from http://www.nytimes.com/2012/04/04/us/04iht-letter04.html?_r=0

Zilber, J., & Niven, D. (2000a). *Racialized coverage of Congress: The news in black and white.* Westport, CT: Praeger.

Zilber, J., & Niven, D. (2000b). Congress and the news media: Stereotypes in the news media coverage of African Americans in Congress. *Harvard International Journal of Press/Politics, 5*(1), 32–49.

APPENDIX A: REPRESENTATIVES INCLUDED IN ANALYSIS

NAME (PARTY ATTACHMENT)	STATE	DISTRICT
ANN MARIE BUERKLE (R)	NY	25
BEN RAY LUJAN (D)	NM	3
BETTY MCCOLLUM (D)	MN	4
BILL JOHNSON (R)	OH	6
BILL PASCRELL (D)	NJ	8
BOBBY SCOTT (D)	VA	3
CANDICE MILLER (R)	MI	10
CAROLYN MALONEY (D)	NY	14
CATHY MCMORRIS ROGERS (R)	WA	5
CORRINE BROWN (D)	FL	3
CYNTHIA LUMIS (R)	WY	1
DALE KILDEE (D)	MI	5
DEBBIE WASSERMAN-SCHULTZ (D)	FL	20
DENNIS KUCINICH (D)	OH	10
DIANE DEGETTE (D)	CO	1
DONNA CHRISTENSEN (D)	VIRGIN ISLANDS	1
DONNA EDWARDS (D)	MD	4
GWEN MOORE (D)	WI	4
HANK JOHNSON (D)	GA	4
JAMES SENSENBRENNER (R)	WI	5
JAN SCHAKOWSKY (D)	IL	9
JANICE HAHN (D)	CA	36
JARED POLIS (D)	CO	2
JEAN SCHMIDT (R)	OH	2
JERROLD NADLER (D)	NY	8
JIM COSTA (D)	CA	20
JO ANN EMERSON (D)	MO	8
JOE BACA (D)	CA	43
JOHN CONYERS (D)	MI	13
JUDY BIGGERT (R)	IL	13
JUDY CHU (D)	CA	32
KATHY ANN CASTOR (D)	FL	11
KRISTI LYNN NOEM (R)	SD	1

LAMAR SMITH (R)	TX	21
LAURA RICHARDSON (D)	CA	37
LINDA SANCHEZ (D)	CA	39
LLOYD DOGGETT (D)	TX	25
LOIS CAPPS (D)	CA	23
LUCILLE ROYBAL-ALLARD (R)	CA	34
LYNN JENKINS (R)	KS	2
LYNN WOOLSEY (D)	CA	6
MADELEINE BORDALLO (D)	GUAM	1
MARSHA BLACKBURN (R)	TN	7
MARTHA ROBY (R)	AL	2
MARY BONO MACK (R)	CA	45
MAXINE WATERS (D)	CA	35
MIKE QUIGLEY (D)	IL	5
NANCY PELOSI (D)	CA	8
RENEE ELMERS (R)	NC	2
RICHARD NUGENT (R)	FL	5
RICK LARSEN (D)	WA	2
ROSA DELAURO (D)	CT	3
RUBÉN HINOJOSA (D)	TX	15
RUSH HOLT (D)	NJ	12
SANDY ADAMS (R)	FL	24
SHEILA JACKSON LEE (D)	TX	18
SHELLY MOORE CAPITO (R)	WV	2
STENY HOYER (D)	MD	5
STEVE KING (R)	IA	5
SUE MYRICK (R)	NC	9
SUSAN DAVIS (D)	CA	53
SUZANNE BONAMICI (D)	OR	1
TOM COLE (R)	OK	4
TREY GOWDY (R)	SC	4
VICKY HARTZLER (R)	MO	4
VIRGINIA FOXX (R)	NC	5
XAVIER BECERRA (D)	CA	31
YVETTE CLARKE (D)	NY	11
ZOE LOFGREN (D)	CA	16

APPENDIX B: QUANTITATIVE CONTENT ANALYSIS CODE SHEET

1. NAME
2. DATE (OF SPEECH)
3. TIME (MINUTES SPEAKING)
4. POSITION TAKEN (0 = AGAINST HOUSE VERSION/FOR SENATE VERSION, 1 = FOR HOUSE VERSION/AGAINST SENATE VERSION, 2 = AGAINST REAUTHORIZATION OF ANY DOMESTIC VIOLENCE ACT, 3 = NO POSITION)
5. POSITION STATED (NUMBER OF TIMES POSITION IS STATED)
6. DEMOCRATS (NUMBER OF MENTIONS OF DEMOCRATIC PARTY)
7. REPUBLICANS (NUMBER OF MENTIONS OF THE REPUBLICAN PARTY)
8. BIPARTISANSHIP (NUMBER OF MENTIONS OF BIPARTISANSHIP)
9. DISTRICT MENTIONS (NUMBER OF MENTIONS OF DISTRICT OR STATE)
10. CREDIT CLAIMING (NUMBER AND CONTENT OF CREDIT CLAIMED)
11. EXPERTISE (NUMBER AND CONTENT OF EXPERTISE MENTIONED)
12. PRAISE (NUMBER AND CONTENT OF COMPLIMENTS)
13. CRITICISMS (NUMBER AND CONTENT OF CRITICISMS OF ACT)
14. GENDER (NUMBER OF MENTIONS)
15. RACE (NUMBER OF MENTIONS)
16. BLACK (NUMBER OF MENTIONS)
17. LATINOS (NUMBER OF MENTIONS)
18. ASIAN AMERICANS (NUMBER OF MENTIONS)
19. NATIVE AMERICANS (NUMBER OF MENTIONS)
20. SEXUAL ORIENTATION (NUMBER OF MENTIONS)
21. CHILDREN AND FAMILIES (NUMBER OF MENTIONS)
22. POVERTY (NUMBER OF MENTIONS)
23. AGE (NUMBER OF MENTIONS)
24. DISABLED (NUMBER OF MENTIONS)
25. UNDOCUMENTED IMMIGRANTS (NUMBER OF MENTIONS)
26. IMMIGRANTS (NUMBER OF MENTIONS)
27. GENDER IDENTITY (NUMBER OF MENTIONS)
28. RACIAL IDENTITY (NUMBER OF MENTIONS)
29. SEXUAL ORIENTATION IDENTITY (NUMBER OF MENTIONS)
30. PARENT IDENTITY (NUMBER OF MENTIONS)
31. SPOUSE IDENTITY (NUMBER OF MENTIONS)

CHAPTER **10**

"WORKING THE CROWD": HOW POLITICAL FIGURES USE INTRODUCTION STRUCTURES

Kurtis D. Miller

Politicians have always had a propensity for "working the crowd." Shaking hands, kissing babies, posing for pictures, and greeting supporters are all common to politicians. With the growth of media coverage of campaigns by television, we see more of these events. Even with security concerns, it is commonplace for candidates to step from the stage and mingle along the rope line following speeches and rallies. C-SPAN has also followed candidates working the crowd at fairs and walking down Main Street. These candidates are equipped with wireless mikes that allow C-SPAN cameras to pick up their interactions with the voters they meet. It is these interactions that are the data and the focus of this chapter.

This chapter examines the way that presidential candidates introduce themselves in these appearances as they interact with crowds during the early primary season in the United States. In order to study how these politicians use introduction sequences while working the crowd and how interactional dilemmas are navigated, data were drawn from the C-SPAN Video Library. Using a conversation analytic approach, this research extends current understandings of the structure and preferences for introduction behaviors and how these are adapted and sometimes co-opted by political candidates in the context of working the crowd. This activity is an example of a unique communicative situation that carries its own rules and norms of interaction, much as public speaking, interviewing, negotiating, and interrogating do. Nevertheless, there are no studies that examine this form of interaction, despite its prevalence in events of significant regional and national importance. These interactions are important to both focal and nonfocal persons, as crowd members are likely to share their experience of these rare and privileged encounters with focal persons, and are likely to share it far beyond the local context.

The communication dilemma for public figures, such as politicians, rock stars, or athletes, is that they are well known and recognized by members of a crowd, but generally speaking the individual members of the crowd are not known to them. Additionally, these public figures often have much to gain and lose by interacting with individual members of crowds. Working the crowd is an expected activity for many public figures, and the decision to avoid these crowd sessions are often seen negatively. Famous people are examples of what Sacks would call *storyable persons* (1984, p. 419). People who interact with storyable persons often recount these interactions, acting as opinion leaders with friends, family members, coworkers, and acquaintances. Effectively working the crowd directly influences both the number and quality of personal testimonies shared about the storyable person. Ineffectively working the crowd can result in serious public-relations gaffes. An Internet search for "refuses to sign autographs" reveals many examples of negative reactions that can occur.

This chapter grew from a pilot study, which used C-SPAN video of then–U.S. presidential candidate Joe Biden working the crowd at a campaign event in Iowa (C-SPAN, 2007). While watching Biden interact with the crowd, I noticed that he would often introduce himself to people at the event, even though it was an event organized for his campaign and attendees had come specifically to see him. Attendees were likely to know Biden by sight, or if not by sight, then through other cues such as his entourage and the behavior of members of the press and other crowd members. It should be apparent at a campaign event for Joe Biden that the older male being followed by a group of aides and media who others go out of their way to speak to is probably Joe Biden. Nevertheless, Biden continued to engage in self-introduction, even when this was not necessary. My own observation showed that Biden often leveraged the introduction sequence tactically by introducing people he was interacting with to others in the crowd after a short time. As a result, Biden was able to disengage from these conversations and continue the activity of working the crowd. To advance the fields of language and social interaction, political communication, and interpersonal communication research, this chapter builds on the pilot case study, applying the introduction sequence preference organization structures detailed by Pillet-Shore (2011) to working-the-crowd interactions. It extends existing knowledge about the structure of introduction sequences into new contexts, and identifies ways that candidates' uses of introduction sequences in these informal political interactions adhere to, and depart from, established norms for introduction sequences in everyday interaction.

BACKGROUND AND SIGNIFICANCE

Communication as a field has a long tradition of research involving interactions of individuals with crowds. The field traces its foundations to the ancient Greek sophists who focused on exactly these sorts of interactions in rhetoric and oratory (Craig, 1999). To this day, the vast majority of research involving interactions between individuals and crowds has been grounded in the rhetorical and public address traditions—two research traditions that share a lot of common ground. However, in addition to public address, there are many situations in life where a large number of people want to hear from, meet, talk to, or interact with a single focal person on an individual basis. From red-carpet events to political campaigns to book signings to kids asking for autographs after a baseball game, the interactions of focal persons with members of crowds on an individual basis is an important and unique form of interaction with its own rules and norms of interaction. This sort of situation can be handled in several ways, though two ways tend to dominate: queuing and working the crowd.

The queuing approach, where people stand in a line and await their turns to interact, is typical of events like book signings, graduations, or kids telling Santa what they want for Christmas. The focal person (or people) interacts with each person or small group of people individually. There are two main variations of the queuing approach. In the first, the line of people slowly moves past the focal person as those in the line await their turn to approach, such as in receiving lines. In the second, the focal person moves down a line of people who are generally standing still. These approaches are formal—rigidly controlled by social conventions if not by external authorities. The use of a line ensures that each person will have the opportunity to interact with the focal person individually as long as there is sufficient time and motivation for all parties concerned to devote. An example of this approach in action can be found in Figure 10.1.

Figure 10.1 President Bill Clinton and other officials in a receiving line at an official dinner for British Prime Minister Tony Blair.

Working the crowd is seen quite frequently at political events where a candidate purposefully shakes hands with as many people as possible in an informal, possibly haphazard, fashion. Likewise, a sports figure who approaches a section of fans to sign autographs also is working the crowd. Unlike cases where there is a line, interaction is not guaranteed for everyone attending the event, even if interaction with everyone is a goal of the focal person. An example of this approach can be seen in Figure 10.2.

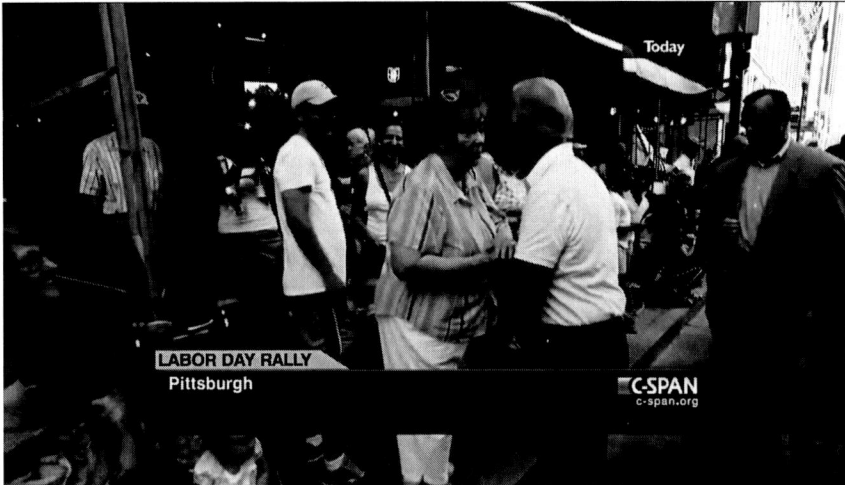

Figure 10.2 A man works the crowd haphazardly, along a street at a Labor Day rally in Pittsburgh.

In interactions among ordinary persons, either way of resolving this situation, perhaps even the situation itself, would be an example of what would best be called an "accountable action" (Heritage, 1984). If an ordinary person were to engage in the activities that normally constitute working the crowd, observers of this activity would generally consider it a violation of expected norms and would work to provide an account for the activity witnessed, perhaps by assuming that they merely do not recognize the individual, or by assuming that individual has a particular mental handicap. This suggests that working the crowd is an *accountable action* for ordinary persons (Heritage, 1984).

Political candidates who are working the crowd are engaging in a particular form of self-presentation. These candidates have multiple goals, which at times compete (O'Keefe, 1988; O'Keefe & Shepherd, 1989). Candidates often have the goal of appearing like an ordinary person, an activity Sacks (1984) called "doing 'being ordinary.'" Although all people engage in the activity of being ordinary, it is notable that those who are "storyable people . . . [that] stand as something different from [the rest of] us" (Sacks, 1984, p. 419), are among those working to do being ordinary. In addition to being ordinary, candidates have other goals, which may include managing an often-demanding schedule of campaign appearances, presenting themselves to both the audience in person and to additional audiences who will view the recorded interactions, persuading voters who may be on the fence, and motivating already committed voters to persuade others. This list is far from complete, as candidates may each be pursuing a number of additional, personal goals.

While working the crowd, it is possible, even likely, that all identifying information ordinarily conferred through personal introductions will be made available through other means. For example, in a political campaign environment, names may be locally available because the focal person is a candidate of whom other crowd members are already aware or have even come specifically to meet. Likewise, those who interact with the candidate sometimes wear name tags, making other identifying information explicit. Other introduction topics, such as personal connections, categorical relationships, and reasons for presence may also be inferable from context. Political candidates for national office generally campaign outside their home regions, and in most cases may assume that they share no personal connections with others in the crowd unless they are explicitly mentioned. Likewise, categorical relationships (potential supporter, protestor, candidate, volunteer, reporter, etc.) can often be inferred from local context, as can the reason for presence (to meet the candidate, to campaign for votes, to attend the fair, etc.).

INTRODUCTION SEQUENCES

People that we do not know are a cause of uncertainty, because they have not been defined (Goffman, 1966). Definition can be achieved, reducing this uncertainty, through introduction. People demonstrate a strong orientation toward nonintroduction when parties have been introduced before, and will perform interactional work to determine whether or not an introduction is necessary (Pillet-Shore, 2011). If the individuals have met previously, the introduction sequence will be skipped. Recent research suggests that humans on average can keep track of the social relationships within a group of approximately 150 people, and most can associate faces with names for around 2,000 people (Dunbar, 1993, 2003, 2004; Hill & Dunbar, 2003). Nevertheless,

Goffman (1966) theorized that once two individuals have become introduced to one another, they are each held responsible for remembering the other from that point forward (p. 120), and that failing to remember the other is *face-threatening* (that is, a source of embarrassment) for both the forgetter and the forgotten (Goffman, 2005), in spite of these cognitive limits.

In her 2011 monograph on introduction sequences, Pillet-Shore called for an extension of existing knowledge about the functions and processes of introduction beyond those that "occur in some private territory during occasions of sustained, focused interaction" (p. 90). This project fulfills that call by extending her work on introduction sequences into a very different context. Working the crowd is qualitatively different from private, sustained interaction; these interactions are necessarily public rather than private, and are characterized by transient rather than sustained interactions.

Introduction sequences may be described in terms of their composition, their *launch* (who initiates the introduction), and the directness of information seeking (Pillet-Shore, 2011). Everyday introduction sequences appear to consistently be composed of eight components:

1. gaze/body orientation-coordinating actions
2. person reference formulations
3. greetings
4. person reference formulation repeats
5. "howareyous"
6. claims of preexisting knowledge about introducible persons
7. introduction-specific assessments of "how it is to meet you"
8. touch/body contact (Pillet-Shore, 2011, pp. 77–78)

There are essentially two types of introduction launch in everyday introduction sequences: those where introduction is initiated by a mediating third party, and those where introduction is self-initiated by one of the two parties involved. According to Pillet-Shore, mediated introductions are preferred over self-introductions when a mutual acquaintance is present (2011).

Participants in everyday introduction sequences also generally prefer to offer implicit invitations for identifying information by offering self- or other-identifying information as opposed to requesting that others identify themselves (Pillet-Shore, 2011, p. 90). In addition to names, she also lists three essential pieces of information necessary for interactants to determine, which are often provided through introduction: connection and ownership ("Who do you know that I know?"); social category, identity, or categorical relationship ("Who are you categorically to the known in common?"); and account for presence ("What are you doing here?"). Interactants typically state information from these identifying categories explicitly when they determine that it is not inferable solely from the local context (Pillet-Shore, 2011, p. 84). For example, at social ceremonial gatherings such as funerals, guests are often asked only about the second of these three pieces of information. People typically can assume that they knew the deceased in common and that engaging in the ceremony itself is their reason for attending, but they may not know what relationship each had to the deceased. Similarly, at weddings the third piece of information can typically be assumed. Guests may be asked which of the two participants they know and how they are connected with that person.

RESEARCH QUESTIONS

Based on the pilot study and intuition, it seems clear that introductions are a key feature of working the crowd. However, considering that working the crowd has not been extensively studied in the communication field and that I will already be analyzing the relevant data, it is also important, as part of the key foundational research question (RQ) to determine what additional types of interactions are typical in this context :

RQ1: What types of interaction sequences are typical of working the crowd?

In addition, since there has been no prior research on working-the-crowd interactions, the first step is to establish whether introductions while working the crowd differ in meaningful ways from typical introductions in ordinary contexts. These descriptive features of introductions proposed by Pillet-Shore (2011, pp. 77–78; see list above in the section Introduction Sequences) suggest a series of three RQs based on comparing the preference structures for composition, launch, and information-seeking directness in ordinary interactions with the interactions observed with candidates working the crowd. (In this line of research, *composition* refers to the component building-blocks of the introduction sequence, launch refers to the manner in which introduction sequences are initiated, and *information-seeking directness* refers to how implicitly or explicitly introduction relevant information is pursued within the introduction sequence.) The three questions are:

RQ2: Do introduction sequences while working the crowd differ in composition from introduction sequences in ordinary interactions?

RQ3: Do preference structures for introduction launch while working the crowd differ from those in ordinary interactions?

RQ4: Do preference structures for information-seeking directness while working the crowd differ from those in ordinary interactions?

DATA AND METHODOLOGICAL APPROACH

In order to analyze candidate interactions with crowds, I used the C-SPAN Video Library to locate examples of candidates for similar positions working similar crowds during a narrow time frame. The C-SPAN Video Library is a fantastic resource for this type of research. In particular, it offers three key benefits: access, searchable and downloadable transcripts, and C-SPAN's neutral editing policy. C-SPAN has significant access to campaign events. Gathering these data independently involves both significant travel and challenges in obtaining consent from candidates and event attendees. Video files are watchable for free through the website, and are typically available as low-cost downloads in commonly used file formats. This last feature is particularly useful because the formats are compatible with all widely used transcription software that handles video. Additionally, the C-SPAN Video Library records and indexes transcripts of all C-SPAN video. For many of these videos, the transcripts are generated from uncorrected closed-captioning data. Because these transcripts are indexed and searchable, any researcher can identify phrases typical of highly scripted interaction sequences, such as introduction sequences, and search for program texts including these phrases. The closed-captioning data require only corrections and formatting/annotation additions to create a transcript that is in line with transcriptions typical of conversational analysis (CA) work, which records nonverbal aspects of speech that are not typically included in closed captioning (timing and rate of speech, locations of overlaps, pauses, etc.).

Finally, C-SPAN has demonstrated a long-standing commitment to presenting political events "without editing, commentary or analysis and with a balanced presentation of points of view" and to presenting political figures "without filtering or otherwise distorting their points of view." These are the first two tenets of C-SPAN's mission statement (Frantzich, 1996). Because C-SPAN engages in minimal editing (Taskiran & Delp, 2001), the records of these interactions between candidates and the public are typically presented without interruption, often within a single continuous shot. As a result, the records are defensible as records of entire, uninterrupted interactions with members of the public that have not been edited in a manner that could potentially bias the research. This benefit, in particular, is one that is not typically available through data obtained through any other broadcast outlet. C-SPAN also typically avoids the practice of reducing the volume of audio, or even eliminating audio, from unscripted interactions between political figures and the public in order to use these interactions as a visual backdrop for pundits, commentators, and network personalities engaging in analysis and commentary.

The C-SPAN Video Library contains many examples of political candidates working the crowd. A search of the C-SPAN Video Library for the phrase "with the crowd" revealed over 70 different interactions, 40 of which were in the *Road to the White House* series. The majority of these videos contained examples of candidates for office working the crowd before or after speeches at campaign events. A search of program text (uncorrected closed-captioning data) for the phrases "nice to meet you" and "how are you"—phrases typical of introduction sequences—combined with the key phrase "campaign event" resulted in nearly 100 programs, of which many included portions where the candidate works the crowd. I compiled a corpus of video recordings of 10 different candidates at events between July 18th and September 1st of 2015, identified using the earlier-described search criteria. Eight of the 10 candidates were recorded at the Iowa State Fair between August 13th and August 21st. The remaining two were recorded at a campaign event in Bedford, New Hampshire (John Kasich on September 1st) and at a town hall meeting in Carroll, Iowa (Scott Walker on July 18th). Recordings averaged just over 30 minutes (30:18.7), for a total duration of 5:03:07.0, or just over 300 minutes. This corpus contains over 700 unique spoken interactions involving candidates (an interaction is one or more turns of spoken conversation involving both the candidate and another person), most of which are introduction sequences, transactions, and/or expressions of encouragement. Further details about each video are available as a table in the Appendix to this chapter.

The existing partial transcripts, generated primarily from uncorrected closed-captioning data, were corrected with reference to the primary source videos. Additional reference to the primary source videos was used to add further detail to relevant portions of the transcripts using traditional CA symbols (Psathas, 1995; Sacks, Schegloff, & Jefferson, 1974; Sidnell, 2010). CA was codified as a methodology by Harvey Sacks, Emanuel Schegloff, and Gail Jefferson (1974). It uses highly detailed transcriptions of audio or video recordings of naturally occurring conversation to support data-driven analysis. This analysis is intended to identify patterns, systems, and components operating within interaction, with the intention of developing a model or set of rules that explain the patterns. In this chapter, I examine candidate interactions through existing understandings of introduction sequences in the CA tradition. Previously proposed rules and preference organizations (Pomerantz, 1984) for introduction sequences (Pillet-Shore, 2011) are compared with observed interactions in the context of the public, nonsustained interactions that characterize working the crowd.

FINDINGS

Typical Interaction Sequences When Working the Crowd (RQ1)

As one might expect, introductions occur frequently in the context of working the crowd. Working the crowd, or engaging in a connected series of public, nonsustained interactions, necessitates an atypically large number of introduction sequences compared to everyday interactions of ordinary persons. In fact, working the crowd seems to be characterized primarily by three broad types of interactions, which often overlap: introductions, transactions, and expressions of encouragement. Introductions typically occur when two parties meet one another for the first time. Transactions involve one or more parties obtaining a material object or service from or through the other. Expressions of encouragement involve nonfocal interactants praising the actions of, or expressing positive orientations to the success of, the focal interactant. These broad types of interactions often overlap in the working-the-crowd context. Excerpt 1 includes a series of interactions which demonstrate all three broad types of interaction:

Excerpt 1: Senator Ted Cruz Meet-and-Greet at the Iowa State Fair (C-SPAN, 2015i) (simplified)

		0:19:21.0
1	PP:	Oh. Ha ha. [Thank you.
2	H3:	[Alright, right here sir. (We
3		got a) picture right here.
4	BE:	↑Hi:↓:[::::.
5	TC:	[How are you doin'.
6	BE:	Goo:d, I am Beverly.
7	TC:	↑Hey Beverly. ((gaze directed at camera))
8	(2.4)	
9	H3:	There ya go. ((hands phone back to BE))
10	BE:	Thank ↓you.
11	TC:	Thank you for being here, (glad to meet
12		ya)
13	BE:	( ) ((hands an object to TC))
14	TC:	°Sure.°
15	H3:	Here. ((hands TC a pen))
16	BE:	Thank <u>you</u> for <u>you</u> bein' here and all you
17		do.
18	TC:	Well, than--thank you very much.
19	(2.2)	
20	82:	You're a Godsend. Thank you.
21	TC:	Thank you, sir. God bless you.
22	82:	Thank you for (everything)
23	TC:	Hey! What's your name.
24	83:	Carter.
25	TC:	Carter? How old are you?
26	83:	(Uh, I'm six)
27	TC:	Six! Good d--alright, fist bump.

28		Excellent. This is your brother?
29	83:	Umm hmm.
30	TC:	What's your name.
31	84:	Weston [(Pruitt)
32	TC:	[Weston. Well, it's good to see ya
33		and this is dad I'm guessin'.
34	85:	Ryan, nice to meet you. Thank you very
35		much.
36	TC:	Great--Great to see you. You guys havin'
37		fun at the state fair?
38	84:	Umm hmm.
39	TC:	Excellent. (.) Well thank you...
40	85:	Say good luck.
41	84:	(Good luck)
42	85:	Thank you.
43	TC:	Thank you very much.
		0:20:08.4

Excerpt 1 picks up with one of Senator Ted Cruz's aides (H3) directing the senator (TC) into a transactional encounter. The speech from PP on line 1 is overlapping speech from the closing of a prior interaction. TC greets the woman involved, Beverly (BE), who self-initiates an introduction sequence by voluntarily disclosing a person reference formulation on line 6. TC responds with a person reference formulation repeat, then directs his gaze to the camera. BE follows and they pose for a picture. H3 takes a photo, then hands a phone to BE. We do not see her give him the phone initially, but participants act as if he has used her phone to take the photo, then returned the phone to her. As H3 hands the phone back, both TC and BE thank one another at lines 10 and 11. Immediately afterward, BE hands TC an object, saying something which is inaudible, which TC treats as a request. H3 hands TC a pen, which he uses to autograph the object. As TC autographs the object, at lines 16–17 BE expresses thanks to TC again for both his presence and his actions generally. TC replies by thanking BE a second time, which all interactants treat as an interactional closing. In this single portion of the interaction, there have been two transactions, an expression of encouragement from BE ("thank you for…all you do"), and an extremely abbreviated introduction sequence. The next two interactions in Excerpt 1 are purer examples of expressions of encouragement and introduction sequences. TC walks a short distance in the crowd and bends over as if to greet a young boy (83). Before TC speaks, another man (82) greets him with an additional expression of encouragement at line 20, calling TC a "Godsend." TC expresses his appreciation, then turns back to 83. The senator then interacts with 83 and his family (84 and 85) by going through a relatively standard introduction sequence in lines 23–40.

Providing detailed analysis of preference organizations surrounding expressions of encouragement and transactions while working the crowd (as Pillet-Shore has done for introductions in ordinary interaction) is beyond the scope of this chapter, but this excerpt is an example of one of many ways that the three broad types of interaction observed in the context of working the crowd differ and yet often overlap.

Introduction/Greeting Sequence Structure (RQ2)

Introductions while working the crowd largely follow previously proposed rules and preference organizations proposed for private, sustained interactions, but there are also a number of interesting differences between these two interactions. Of the eight constitutive components listed by Pillet-Shore (2011, pp. 77–78; see list above in the section Introduction Sequences), many continue to occur while working the crowd. Gaze/body orientation-coordinating actions, greetings, introduction-specific assessments of "how it is to meet you," and touch/body contact (usually in the form of a handshake) are near-universally present. Candidates vary in their use of person reference formulation repeats and "howareyous." Person reference formulation repeats tended to be made only by the focal person and not by nonfocal interactants. Claims of preexisting knowledge about introducible persons occurred rarely, and were likewise nearly always made by nonfocal interactants in reference to the focal person. Expressions of gratitude are a unique feature of introduction sequences in this context and typically occurred at the end of introduction sequences, often being treated as closings (for example, see lines 15–16 in Excerpt 1). Examples of these tendencies are found in Excerpts 2 and 3.

Excerpt 2: Governor Scott Walker (R-WI) Meet and Greet (C-SPAN, 2015a) (simplified)

0:04:27.2

1	Man1:	This is Senator Kettering, he is a (former whip).
2	SW:	Good to see ya.=
3	SK:	=Nice to meet [you.
4	Man1:	[Now, Governor Walker.
5	SW:	[Yeah, thank you so much.
6	Man1:	He just retired from [politics.
7	SK:	[Yeah.
8	SW:	What do you do?
9	SK:	Yeah, (Brad) called, got me breakf[ast and
10	SW:	[It's hard
11	SK:	[said show up,] yeah.
12	SW:	[to turn down, right?]
13	SW:	( ) Thanks for coming.
14	SK:	Yeah.=
15	SW:	=We're gonna keep coming back.=
16	SK:	=Yeah.=
17	SW:	=We're doing the full grassroots,=
18	Man1:	=Yeah.=
19	SW:	=We're doing all 99 counties.
20	SK:	Ah perfect.
21	SW:	Yeah, we're going to have some fun.
22	SK:	Well, welcome to western Iowa anyway.
23	SW:	It's good to be back.
24	SK:	I'd love to have you.
25	SW:	Thank you.

0:04:52.4

In Excerpt 2, an unidentified man (Man1, interaction at line 9 suggests his name may be Brad) calls across the room to introduce Governor Scott Walker (SW) to former Senator Kettering (SK). During this stage, the parties establish mutual gaze and bodily coordination, and SW moves across the room to approach the introducible party. Man1 distributes person reference formulations at lines 1 and 4. The parties initially address each other by providing introduction-specific assessments of "how it is to meet you" at lines 2–3. During this time the parties engage in touch/body contact by shaking hands. Finally, SW expresses gratitude to SK at line 5, which all parties treat as a closing of the introduction sequence, but not the interaction. SK further initiates touch during the interaction by placing his hand on Man1's shoulder at line 9, and by placing his hand on SW's shoulder during the closing at lines 22–24. Missing from this interaction are greetings, person reference formulation repeats, "howareyous," and claims of preexisting knowledge about introducible persons.

Excerpt 3: Presidential Candidate Hillary Clinton Meet-and-Greet at the Iowa State Fair, Part 2 (C-SPAN, 2015f) (simplified)

0:00:43.5

1	Woman5:	Secretary Clinton!
2	HC:	How are ↑yo::u. ((Shakes hand))
3	Woman5:	I'm ↑goo::d! ↑How [are ↑yo:::::::::::u.=
4	HC:	[It's good to see you-
5		((Still shaking hand, Hillary tries to continue walking))
6	Woman6:	(To this side,) Lisa, turn! Turn! Lisa, turn!
7		((Man in hat taps Woman5 on the shoulder, then on the
8		hand until she ends handshake, then HC and Woman5
9		turn to pose for a photograph))
10	Woman5:	((Points to man in hat)) I used to work for this
11		guy.
12	HC:	Well, that's a good recomend↑a::tion!
13	Woman6:	Yaa::aa::y!
14		((photograph taken))
15	Woman5:	[↑Thank you so much! Nice to mee:t ↑you:!
16	Woman7:	[( ) ((shaking HC's hand))
17	HC:	°Thank you, thank you.°
18	Woman8:	Thanks for coming out ((shaking hand))
19	HC:	Hey, glad to be here. ((shaking hands))
20	HC:	↑Tha:::nk Yo:::u!
21	Fan:	(Would you like my fan?) ((shaking hands))

22		((Woman begins to fan Hillary))
23	HC:	I love it! I love it!
24	HC:	How are ya, sir? ((shakes hand)) Good ta see ya
25	Man2:	↓Thank you
26	Woman9:	We are glad to have [you here! ((Shakes hand))
27	HC:	[Oh! I love [your
28	Woman10:	[°Yes, we
29	HC:	["Keep Iowa Beautiful"
30	Woman10:	[are delighted to see: you!°
31	HC:	Great to see yo:↓u::
32		(2.2)
33	HC:	Thank you guys! ((walking away))
34		(6.9)
35		((Turns back to Woman8 & Woman9))
36	HC:	↑That is ↑so:: (good!)
37	Woman9:	We've got a whole (slew/crew) of (advisors) that
38		have em
39	Woman10:	((Indiscernible))
40	HC:	That's even ↓better!
41	Woman10:	↑Yeah?
42	HC:	That's even ↓better.
43		((Turns away))
	0:01:28.6

In Excerpt 3, former Secretary of State Hillary Clinton (HC) is walking down a pathway tightly lined with supporters while she greets a selection of people along the route. Those she greets seem primarily to be people who are in the front row and people who are not holding cameras. The excerpt starts with a woman (Woman5) who calls out to HC as HC approaches. HC orients to Woman5 and continues down the route, approaching Woman5. Both engage in touch/body contact with the handshake at line 2. HC and Woman5 exchange "howareyous" in lines 2–3, and HC provides an introduction specific assessment of "how it is to meet you" in line 4, which Woman5 does not yet return. Woman5 holds on to HC while continuing in conversation. At the same time Woman6 calls out the name "Lisa" at line 6, presumably addressing Woman5. With encouragement from an HC aide, Woman5 stops the handshake as both HC and Woman5 turn and pose for a photograph together. Conversation continues (lines 10–12), with Woman5 asserting a known-in-common individual while they hold the pose for the picture. After the picture, Woman5 expresses gratitude and returns her own introduction-specific assessment of "how it is to meet you," which both parties treat as a closing. Absent from this interaction are person reference formulations for the nonfocal interactant, person reference formulation repeats, and claims of preexisting knowledge about introducible persons. The thank-you delivered in line 15 does not appear to be an expression of encouragement.

As HC continues down the packed route, she engages in touch/body contact with a series of additional supporters. While shaking hands, HC consistently directs gaze/body orientation away from those she is speaking to, and toward those she is about to speak to. Woman8 thanks HC for her presence, and HC responds at line 19, offering a greeting and saying that she is "glad to be here"—a variant of the assessment "how it is to meet you," which is often used by the candidates. HC continues to offer expressions of gratitude. A woman in the crowd offers HC her hand-operated fan at line 21, and starts waving it intensely to cast a breeze on HC, who responds with an additional expression of gratitude at line 23, but does not take the fan. In these interactions, person reference formulations and person reference formulation repeats are both absent, as are "howareyous," and claims of preexisting knowledge about introducible persons.

HC continues by turning back slightly to shake the hand of Man2 at line 24, who reaches over those standing in the front row. This touch/body contact is accompanied by a "howareyou" and an assessment of "how it is to meet you." Instead of reciprocating, Man2 merely says "thank you." Turning back, HC is addressed by Woman9, who launches at line 26 with the same variant assessment of "how it is to meet you" used at line 19. HC engages in touch/body contact by shaking hands with Woman9 and Woman10, and expresses positive sentiment toward the brightly colored tee shirt that Woman9 and Woman10 are wearing, which displays the slogan "Keep Iowa Beautiful" (an antilitter campaign). There is a pause without conversation for 2.2 seconds, during which HC, Woman9, and Woman10 remain oriented toward each other. At this point HC volunteers an expression of gratitude at line 33, which all parties treat as an appropriate closing, and HC turns and walks away. HC turns back 6.9 seconds later to restate her appreciation of the shirts worn by Woman9 and Woman10 in lines 35 through 42 before continuing on her way. In these interactions, person reference formulations and person reference formulation repeats remain absent. Greetings also do not appear in these interactions.

Introduction Launches While Working the Crowd (RQ3)

As detailed earlier, two different types of introduction launch are typically observed in everyday introduction sequences: mediated and self-initiated. As in private, sustained interaction, mediated introductions seem to be preferred over self-initiated introductions, but only in certain contexts. Mediated introductions appear not to be preferred for ordinary nonfocal interactants when the potential mediator is affiliated with the campaign, as in Excerpt 3, line 10. However, regarding selected members of the crowd, the preference for mediated introduction remains. In some cases, as with the interaction starting at line 2 in Excerpt 1, candidates used an aide to mediate introductions or arrange for interactions between candidates and selected members of the crowd. An excellent example of aide-mediated introductions can be found in a recording of George Pataki at the Iowa State Fair, where Kevin McLaughlin (phonetic), an aide to Pataki, performs a number of these mediated introductions between Pataki and several VIPs (C-SPAN, 2015g). From 0:20:45.0 to 0:25:50 McLaughlin engages with a series of 12 interactants (primarily as individuals, though there are two couples and one group of four), including many who hold state or national office, prior to introducing them to Governor Pataki. A similar arrangement can be seen between Governor John Kasich and the host of a campaign event in New Hampshire in Excerpt 4:

Excerpt 4: Governor John Kasich Meet-and-Greet in Bedford, New Hampshire (C-SPAN, 2015j) (simplified)

0:02:31.5

1	Man2:	Paul ( )
2	Paul:	Hey Governor. Nice [to meet you. Welcome
3		to
4	JK:	[Paul, nice to see
5		you.

6	Paul:	New Hampshire. My [wife, Cathy.=
7	Cathy:	[Cathy
8	Man2:	=And his wife, Cathy
9	JK:	How are you?
10	Man2:	Great Americans, you look well
11	JK:	Good, [look at this.
12	Man2:	[A lot of people here.
13	JK:	Yeah.
14	Man2:	Uh, Rich will, uh, will introduce you
15		[(means) he's the host with the most.
16	RA:	[Yeah, thanks for sneaking by!
17	Man2:	I said hello to your (.) better half.
18	JK:	So let me grab you for two seconds
19	Man2:	Oh
20	RA:	You're gonna have a meeting before the
21		meeting
		0:02:53.0

In Excerpt 4, John Kasich (JK) is introduced to Paul and Cathy, by Man2, who then goes on to discuss how Rich (RA) will be responsible for introducing JK to everyone at the party (which RA proceeds to do throughout the rest of the event). In other cases, as with the interaction in Excerpt 2, another member of the crowd engages in mediated introduction. Members of the crowd typically do not engage in mediated introduction unless they have met the focal interactant before, though the timing of this previous meeting appears irrelevant. Nonfocal interactants typically mediate introduction after having a previous separate interaction with the candidate, even if that previous interaction was only moments ago, as illustrated in Excerpt 5:

Excerpt 5: Senator Ted Cruz Meet-and-Greet at the Iowa State Fair (C-SPAN, 2015i) (simplified)

		0:23:52.8
1	97:	Senator (Cruz). ( )
2	TC:	How you doin' (bud). ((no mutual gaze with
3		97))
4	TC:	Good to see ya. ((to 97))

5		((shake hands))
6	97:	Alright, could she get a picture with you,
7		sir?
8	TC:	Yeah, sure. What is your name.
9	CA:	Caitlin
10	TC:	Hey Caitlin, good to see you.
11	97:	( )
12		(2.6) ((97 takes picture))
13	97:	That's ama::zing. Thanks very much.
14	TC:	Yeah, sure. How you doin' sir.
15	98:	((in Spanish))
16	TC:	(Ecuamente)
17	H3:	Is that for me?
18	97:	My, uh:, my roommate.

Interactions from 0:24:10.2 to 0:25:07.0 omitted.

19	98:	Mi mama
20		((Indiscernible conversation))
21	TC:	(Quienes una foto)
22	101:	Si,[si, si.
23	98:	[Si, si. (La familia.)
24	102:	She got the donut. That is (0.6) skill.
25		Teach me how to eat a donut ( )
26	TC:	Hey, you want to hop in too?=We'll do all
27		of us.
28	102:	I can do the whole fam--just give me one
29		camera for the family
30	101:	Ah ha ha [ha.
31	102:	[Go ahead, hop in there. Get your
32		donut.
33	98:	((In Spanish))
34	TC:	Ah, qué bueno
35	102:	Alright, look at this camera then right
36		here, guys. A::[nd ( )

37	103:	[She's like, how do I get out.
38	102:	(Looks like something did). That was a
39		great shot. There you go.
40	98:	Gracias [( )
41	101:	[Gracias (0.4) ( ) día.
42	TC:	Y usted también.
		0:25:42.6

In Excerpt 5, Ted Cruz (TC) is interacting with the crowd when a young man (97) approaches to speak with him. TC does not initially respond to 97's attempt to gain attention and establish coordinating actions with TC at line 1, but does direct shift gaze to 97 at line 4. TC approaches 97, who has not interacted with TC prior to this interaction, and they shake hands. At line 6, 97 asks for a photograph on behalf of Caitlin (CA). TC agrees, but has to directly request a personal reference formulation in line 8. CA responds with her name only, and TC issues a greeting, a person reference formulation repeat, and an assessment of "how it is to meet you." TC and CA pose for a picture. They both orient toward the camera. TC places his arm around CA's shoulders and CA places her hand on TC's back. At line 12, 97 takes the picture then assesses the quality of the picture and expresses gratitude to TC for the photo. At line 14, TC acknowledges gratitude and addresses a different man (98), who walks up just as the interaction with 97 and CA ends and leans over and shakes hands with TC, speaking in Spanish. TC responds in Spanish, then 98 points at TC and nods in an affirming gesture. As TC continues to work the crowd, interacting with other groups of people over the course of a minute, 98 then walks away.

As TC is about to leave the area, he passes 98 again, who gains his attention. TC changes course to walk up to him, and 98 provides a person reference formulation for the woman standing next to him (101). TC asks if they want a photo at line 21, and both agree at lines 22–23. One of the cameramen traveling with TC (102) comments on how a female member of the family (who does not appear in the transcript since she doesn't speak) is operating a camera while holding a donut. TC invites the entire family into the photograph, and offers to take a photo for the family so everyone can be in it. After 102 asks for and receives a camera from the family to take the picture, 101 starts to laugh, and 102 reassures the original photo taker that she can keep her donut with her while they take the picture. TC and 98 engage in conversation until 102 indicates he is ready to take the picture. Then a different member of the family (103) speaks, 102 takes the picture with one hand while holding his own camera in the other hand, assesses that the picture is of good quality, and returns the camera to the family. Both 98 and 101 express their gratitude to TC.

Requests for Identifying Information (RQ4)

In the context of working the crowd, preferences for introduction sequences are different compared to ordinary everyday interactions. Introduction does not seem to be expected for the focal person in most cases. When the focal person is introduced, they are typically introduced to someone because that person is something more than an ordinary nonfocal interactant. In ordinary everyday interaction, there is a preference for introduction when meeting, whether that introduction is mediated or self-initiated. When interactants are not introduced and do not introduce themselves, others typically directly request person reference formulations. When candidates self-initiate introduction sequences with ordinary nonfocal interactants, it is often treated as an implicit request for identifying information. Candidates had different responses when the nonfocal person was not introduced. Some candidates directly requested identifying information, as TC does in lines 4 through 13 in Excerpt 5, and with 83 and each member of his family in lines 23 through 33 of Excerpt 1. Other candidates chose not to request identifying information, as HC did with Woman5, Woman7, Woman8, Fan, Woman9, Woman10, and Man2 throughout Excerpt 3.

Unlike in everyday introduction sequences, candidates almost never provided person reference formulations in interactions, and nonfocal interactants almost never disclosed person reference formulations unless directly asked. George Pataki and Martin O'Malley self-initiated disclosures of person reference formulations more frequently than other candidates. In the rare cases where nonfocal persons did provide person reference formulations, focal persons did not treat them as implicit requests for identifying information, in contrast to everyday introduction sequences. For example, at line 6 in Excerpt 1, BE provides TC with her name. TC clearly hears the name and replies with a person reference formulation repeat, but does not reciprocate by providing his own name.

DISCUSSION

In answering RQ1, working-the-crowd interactions where characterized by a number three primary types of interactions. These types of interactions were introductions, transactions, and expressions of encouragement. It is common for these types of interactions to overlap. For example, interactants may engage in an expression of encouragement during an introduction sequence, or an introduction may occur during a request for an autograph. Preference organizations surrounding both expressions of encouragement and transactions present an interesting opportunity for future research.

In answering RQ2, introductions seem to have many of the same component features in working-the-crowd situations as have been reported in private, sustained contexts. Many features left out of introductions while working the crowd can be inferred from the local situation. This is identical to the omission rule, which has been observed in private, sustained interactions. Component features of introductions are displayed both by nonfocal interactants and by focal persons. Introduction sequences while working the crowd differ from everyday introduction sequences regarding claims of preexisting knowledge about introducible persons, person reference formulation repeats, a lack of preference for implicit requests for identifying information, and the inclusion of expressions of gratitude. Additionally, working the crowd is characterized by asymmetry between interactants that manifests itself in how preferences for mediated introduction are resolved, and the likelihood of person reference formulation repeats.

Claims of preexisting knowledge about introducible persons are not displayed equally, being much more likely to be made by nonfocal interactants than by focal persons. This difference is to be expected given the specific nature of working-the-crowd interactions. Focal persons are more likely to be known to potential interactants; and a group of nonfocal interactants, who generally are less famous, are less likely to be known by the focal person. Focal persons are, therefore, less likely to have preexisting knowledge of the nonfocal interactants, so the lower incidence of these claims is unsurprising.

Person reference formulation repeats are also not displayed equally. Person reference formulations for the focal person were much less likely to be repeated than reference formulations for nonfocal persons. Since focal persons are generally already known to nonfocal interactants, it is not necessary for nonfocal interactants to display that they are "doing 'working to commit that name to memory'" (Pillet-Shore, 2011, p. 78). However, since focal persons are not expected to have prior familiarity with nonfocal interactants, demonstrating a commitment to remembering a name remains relevant (though considering the earlier-mentioned cognitive limits, the focal person is unlikely to remember many of these names).

In answering RQ3, mediated introductions do seem to be preferred generally, but the strength of the preference seems to be different for focal and nonfocal interactants. The preference for mediated introductions seems to be based on whether or not the introducible party is the candidate (focal person). When the introducible party is a nonfocal interactant, other nonfocal interactants have been observed to make an effort to introduce the introducible party. However, if the introducible party is a focal person, nonfocal interactants do not generally make an effort to introduce the introducible party. Focal interactants will go through work to avoid self-initiated introductions. Nonfocal interactants will avoid providing identifying information altogether rather than self-initiate. Examples of tactics used by focal persons to ease the burden of self-initiated introductions on nonfocal persons include soliciting this information early ("Hey, what's your name?"), and engaging aides to premeet and then introduce nonfocal interactants. Many candidates used aides who met nonfocal persons and then introduced the candidate to them.

Finally, in addressing RQ4, unlike in everyday interaction, there is no preference for making implicit requests for identifying information in the working-the-crowd context. Implicit requests for identifying information do not seem to be preferred over explicit requests. Focal persons may provide identifying information at times as an implicit request for information, but are more likely to make a direct request for identifying information from nonfocal interactants. In addition, when nonfocal interactants provide identifying information, this information is not likely to be interpreted by the focal person as an implicit request for identifying information. The fundamentally asymmetric nature of the context is a likely cause of this difference.

Overall, focal persons appear to have no obligation to provide person reference formulations. Nevertheless, the interactants display a preference for working through the introduction sequence, even when the exchange of person reference formulations is omitted. Both focal and nonfocal interactants frequently display the remaining components of the introduction sequence, such as exchanging "howareyous," providing introduction-specific assessments of "how it is to meet you," and touch/body contact. Interactants display unique modifications to the existing norms of everyday introduction sequences that are specific to the working-the-crowd context. Introduction sequences in the context of working the crowd differ from everyday examples of introduction sequences in their near-universal inclusion of expressions of gratitude as a component of the introduction sequence. Interactants also appear to apply different sets of norm expectations for introductions of focal persons than nonfocal persons. The consistent functioning of these preference organizations in different types of interaction, especially when no identifying information is conveyed, implies that there are deeper functions to the ritual of introduction than merely obtaining identifying information.

Limitations

It is probable that there are differing expectations and behaviors associated with the gender of candidates for any office . It is well established in communication and language literature that there are styles of speech and interaction that are perceived as typically feminine. An analysis based on gender is beyond the scope of this chapter, but Hillary Clinton did use a qualitatively different interaction style than her male colleagues. It is difficult to make extrapolations based on gender from the the sample of presidential nomination candidates used in this study, as Secretary Clinton is the only female candidate currently included. Video is available in the C-SPAN Video Library for a second female presidential candidate, Carly Fiorina, who was a Republican candidate. A further analysis of speech patterns in candidates' interpersonal interactions may prove fruitful, and an initial impression based on these limited data suggest that gendered language expectations may come into play.

Comparisons across focal persons are complicated by differing levels of support from their bases, and in some cases by the inclusion of stricter security protocols. While some candidates consistently encountered large crowds of enthusiastic supporters (e.g., Sanders, Clinton), other candidates had fewer supporters (e.g., O'Malley, Webb). Secretary Clinton's interactions were uniquely characterized by an element of crowd control and by the presence of individuals in plain clothes who appeared to be security personnel. As with an analysis of gender, an analysis of the effects of security on interpersonal interactions with crowd members could prove fruitful. The tactics that candidates and crowd members use to try to bridge the larger social gulf that can be a consequence of added security could prove interesting, and would be of particular interest to participants in these encounters.

This chapter focuses on analysis during a brief period of only a few weeks in one campaign cycle. In order to increase similarity across cases, the majority of campaign events happened in the span of a few days at the same location (the Iowa State Fair). Although Iowa is critically important to presidential campaigns for a number of reasons, the United States is a large and diverse country, and Iowa is not representative of that diversity. Initial impressions of this corpus suggest that the interpersonal interactions of political candidates while working the crowd are areas of interest for scholars interested in social justice generally. A further analysis by scholars whose work takes a critical or social justice perspective are likely to find these interactions to be fertile ground for a variety of issues, not the least is the issue of tokenism.

Finally, the Iowa State Fair is but one example drawn from a wide variety of situations in which political candidates work the crowd. In addition, working the crowd is an important mode of interaction for people from many different walks of life. Future research will need to extend this line of research beyond the political context into other contexts of working the crowd.

CONCLUSION

The appearance of introduction sequences in the working-the-crowd context provides additional confirmation of their importance as a feature of conversation that appears in a wide variety of contexts. Likewise, the appearance of previously observed components of introduction sequences in the working-the-crowd context adds to existing evidence that implies that these components apply universally to the construction of introduction sequences across all types of human interaction, though gaze/body orientation-coordinating actions, greetings, introduction-specific assessments of "how it is to meet you," and touch/body contact appear to be more consistently present than others.

Political candidates and their campaigns can also draw a number of conclusions from this study. Interactions with individual members of crowds are a unique form of interaction that is characterized by introductions, transactions, and expressions of encouragement. Introductions while working the crowd are not the same as introductions in other contexts. They are less likely to include the exchange and repetition of person reference formulations such as names and titles, questions about how people are ("howareyous"), and claims of preexisting knowledge about introducible persons. Successful candidates often use a "nice to see you" rather than "nice to meet you" construction, which saves face in the circumstance that they have met the other at some other event in the past but do not remember them.

Candidates engaging in working the crowd will often have to shift between interactions with general crowd members and interactions with key persons and donors. An understanding of how working-the-crowd introductions differ from ordinary interactions will serve the candidate well in choosing the right mode of interaction for each audience. Initial impressions from this research suggest that effectively working the crowd as a political candidate is a team effort. The ways that campaign staff and other figures effectively support working the crowd is an important area for future research.

Likewise, political candidates often have unique security considerations that can complicate interactions with crowds of people. The ways that candidates can effectively work the crowd while taking these security concerns into account may be useful both within campaigns and within the larger security community. Security professionals can be served by understanding what typical introduction sequences look like while working the crowd, in order to help them identify potential security threats.

This study of candidate interactions advances the larger field of communication research by examining a modality of face-to-face communication that has largely been overlooked in communication literature. Despite the importance and frequency of working the crowd, especially surrounding regionally and nationally important events, very little is known about working the crowd and how the rules and norms for this form of interaction vary from well-studied modes of communication. The present chapter has contributed to an improved understanding of the use of introduction sequences while working the crowd, but there is still much to learn. Other forms of public, nonsustained interaction are prime areas for further research in this area. Future research on working the crowd should examine the organization and structure of the expressions of encouragement and transactional elements associated with working the crowd.

REFERENCES

Craig, R. T. (1999). Communication theory as a field. *Communication Theory, 9*(2), 119–161. http://dx.doi.org/10.1111/j.1468-2885.1999.tb00355.x

C-SPAN (Producer). (2007, June 3). *Iowa Democratic Party event* [online video]. Retrieved from http://www.c-spanvideo.org/program/IowaDemocraticPartyE

C-SPAN (Producer). (2015a, July 18). *Governor Scott Walker (R-WI) meet and greet* [online video]. Retrieved from http://www.c-span.org/video/?327189-1/governor -scott-walker-rwi-meet-greet

C-SPAN (Producer). (2015b, August 13). *Former Governor Martin O'Malley meet-and-greet at the Iowa State Fair* [online video]. Retrieved from http://www.c-span.org /video/?327523-8/former-governor-martin-omalley-meetandgreet-iowa-state-fair

C-SPAN (Producer). (2015c, August 13). *Former Governor Mike Huckabee meet-and-greet at the Iowa State Fair* [online video]. Retrieved from http://www.c-span.org /video/?327523-6/former-governor-mike-huckabee-meetandgreet-iowa-state-fair

C-SPAN (Producer). (2015d, August 13). *Former Senator Jim Webb (D-VA) meet-and-greet at the Iowa State Fair* [online video]. Retrieved from http://www.c-span.org /video/?327523-7/former-senator-jim-webb-dva-meetandgreet-iowa-state-fair

C-SPAN (Producer). (2015e, August 15). *Presidential candidate Bernie Sanders meet-and-greet at the Iowa State Fair* [online video]. Retrieved from http://www.c-span .org/video/?327525-10/presidential-candidate-bernie-sanders-meetandgreet -iowa-state-fair

C-SPAN (Producer). (2015f, August 15) *Presidential candidate Hillary Clinton meet-and-greet at the Iowa State Fair, Part 2* [online video]. Retrieved from http://www .c-span.org/video/?327525-9/presidential-candidate-hillary-clinton-meetand greet-iowa-state-fair-part-2

C-SPAN (Producer). (2015g, August 16). *Former Governor George Pataki news conference at the Iowa State Fair* [online video]. Retrieved from http://www .c-span.org/video/?327573-5/former-governor-george-pataki-news-conference -iowa-state-fair

C-SPAN (Producer). (2015h, August 18). *Senator Marco Rubio meet-and-greet at the Iowa State Fair* [online video]. Retrieved from http://www.c-span.org /video/?327575-4/senator-marco-rubio-meetandgreet-iowa-state-fair

C-SPAN (Producer). (2015i, August 21). *Senator Ted Cruz meet-and-greet at the Iowa State Fair* [online video]. Retrieved from http://www.c-span.org/video/?327577-3 /senator-ted-cruz-meetandgreet-iowa-state-fair

C-SPAN (Producer). (2015j, September 1). *Governor John Kasich meet-and-greet in Bedford, New Hampshire* [online video]. Retrieved from http://www.c-span.org /video/?327900-2/governor-john-kasich-meetand-greet-bedford-new-hampshire

Dunbar, R. I. M. (1993). Coevolution of neocortical size, group size and language in humans. *Behavioral and Brain Sciences, 16*(4), 681–694. http://dx.doi.org/10.1017 /S0140525X00032325

Dunbar, R. I. M. (2003). The social brain: Mind, language, and society in evolutionary perspective. *Annual Review of Anthropology, 32*(1), 163–181. http://dx.doi .org/10.1146/annurev.anthro.32.061002.093158

Dunbar, R. I. M. (2004). Social cognition as a constraint on social interaction. *Journal of Cultural and Evolutionary Psychology, 2*(3–4), 181–194. http://dx.doi .org/10.1556/JCEP.2.2004.3-4.1

Frantzich, S. E. (1996). *The C-SPAN revolution.* Norman: University of Oklahoma Press.

Goffman, E. (1966). *Behavior in public places: Notes on the social organization of gatherings.* New York, NY: Free Press.

Goffman, E. (2005). *Interaction ritual: Essays in face-to-face behavior.* New Brunswick, NJ: Aldine Transaction.

Heritage, J. (1984). A change-of-state token and aspects of its sequential placement. In J. M. Atkinson & J. Heritage (Eds.), *Structures of social action: Studies in conversation analysis* (pp. 299–345).

Hill, R. A., & Dunbar, R. I. M. (2003). Social network size in humans. *Human Nature, 14*(1), 53–72. http://dx.doi.org/10.1007/s12110-003-1016-y

O'Keefe, B. J. (1988). The logic of message design: Individual differences in reasoning about communication. *Communication Monographs, 55*(1), 80.

O'Keefe, B. J., & Shepherd, G. J. (1989). The communication of identity during face-to-face persuasive interactions: Effects of perceiver's construct differentiation and target's message strategies. *Communication Research, 16*(3), 375–404. http:// dx.doi.org/10.1177/009365089016003004

Pillet-Shore, D. (2011). Doing introductions: The work involved in meeting someone new. *Communication Monographs, 78*(1), 73–95. http://dx.doi.org/10.1080 /03637751.2010.542767

Pomerantz, A. (1984). Agreeing and disagreeing with assessments: Some features of preferred/dispreferred turn shaped. In J. M. Atkinson & J. Heritage (Eds.), *Structures of social action: Studies in conversation analysis* (pp. 57–101). Cambridge, England: Cambridge University Press.

Psathas, G. (1995). *Conversation analysis: The study of talk-in-interaction.* Thousand Oaks, CA: Sage.

Sacks, H. (1984). On doing "being ordinary." In J. M. Atkinson & J. Heritage (Eds.), *Structures of social action: Studies in conversation analysis* (pp. 413–429). Cambridge, England: Cambridge University Press.

Sacks, H., Schegloff, E. A., & Jefferson, G. (1974). A simplest systematics for the organization of turn-taking for conversation. *Language, 50,* 696–735.

Sidnell, J. (2010). *Conversation analysis: An introduction.* Chichester, United Kingdom: Wiley-Blackwell.

Taskiran, C. M., & Delp, E. J., III. (2001). Distribution of shot lengths for video analysis. In M. M. Yeung, C. Li, & R. W. Lienhart (Eds.), *Proceedings of SPIE: Vol. 4676, Storage and Retrieval for Media Databases 2002* (pp. 276–284). http://dx.doi.org/10.1117/12.451098

APPENDIX

Party and Title	Candidate	Date	Length	Location	Video Title and Citation
R, Governor (WI)	Scott Walker	2015-07-18	59:18.0	Town Hall Carroll, IA	Governor Scott Walker (R-WI) Meet and Greet (C-SPAN, 2015a)
R, Former Governor (AR)	Mike Huckabee	2015-08-13	31:30.0	Iowa State Fair Des Moines, IA	Former Governor Mike Huckabee Meet-and-Greet at the Iowa State Fair (C-SPAN, 2015c)
D, Former Governor (MD)	Martin O'Malley	2015-08-14	26:54.0	Iowa State Fair Des Moines, IA	Former Governor Martin O'Malley Meet-and-Greet (C-SPAN, 2015b)
D, Former U.S. Senator (VA)	Jim Webb	2015-08-14	11:36.0	Iowa State Fair Des Moines, IA	Former Senator Jim Webb (D-VA) Meet-and-Greet at the Iowa State Fair (C-SPAN, 2015d)
D, Former U.S. Secretary of State	Hillary Clinton	2015-08-15	17:18.0	Iowa State Fair Des Moines, IA	Presidential Candidate Hillary Clinton Meet-and-Greet at the Iowa State Fair, Part 2 (C-SPAN, 2015f)
D, U.S. Senator (VT)	Bernie Sanders	2015-08-15	28:11.0	Iowa State Fair Des Moines, IA	Presidential Candidate Bernie Sanders Meet-and-Greet at the Iowa State Fair (C-SPAN, 2015e)
R, Former Governor (NY)	George Pataki	2015-08-16	28:53.0	Iowa State Fair Des Moines, IA	Former Governor George Pataki News Conference at the Iowa State Fair (C-SPAN, 2015g)
R, U.S. Senator (FL)	Marco Rubio	2015-08-18	33:16.0	Iowa State Fair Des Moines, IA	Senator Marco Rubio Meet-and-Greet at the Iowa State Fair (C-SPAN, 2015h)
R, U.S. Senator (TX)	Ted Cruz	2015-08-21	42:11.0	Iowa State Fair Des Moines, IA	Senator Ted Cruz Meet-and-Greet at the Iowa State Fair (C-SPAN, 2015i)
R, Governor (OH)	John Kasich	2015-09-01	24:00.0	Campaign Event Bedford, NH	Governor John Kasich Meet-and-Greet in Bedford, New Hampshire (C-SPAN, 2015j)

CHAPTER **11**

REPRESENTING OTHERS, PRESENTING SELF

Zoe M. Oxley

Albeit focusing on rather different topics, the previous two chapters well display the research potential of the C-SPAN Video Library. C-SPAN's coverage of both legislative activity in the U.S. Congress and campaigning for president is especially rich. Legislative politics scholars have many data sources at their disposal, of course, including roll call votes and transcripts of floor debates and committee hearings. C-SPAN video coverage of legislative floor debates captures the words spoken by representatives, but also the speakers' body language and interactions with other legislators. Analyzing the multiple dimensions that are contained in these videos can advance our understanding of representation, as demonstrated by Nadia Brown and Sarah Gershon's research. In particular, they provide insights into the representation of group interests during a debate on the U.S. House floor.

Candidate-voter interaction is the focus of Kurtis Miller's chapter. For him, analyzing C-SPAN videos was critical. The C-SPAN cameras continue to roll after formal candidate events, capturing presidential candidates as they informally greet audience members. This video footage documents interactions that are essentially unavailable elsewhere, making the C-SPAN campaign archive a veritable treasure trove for researchers of political communication, electoral campaigns, and leadership. As illustrated by Miller and in chapters earlier in this volume, examinations of unscripted political moments can yield interesting findings.

REPRESENTING OTHERS: DEBATING DOMESTIC VIOLENCE LEGISLATION

As Hannah Pitkin (1967) so eloquently articulated decades ago, representation is multifaceted. Representatives may stand for their constituents and groups in society, either symbolically or via descriptive resemblance, or they may act for others by substantively representing citizens' policy interests. Disentangling these types of representation has long interested scholars, especially those focused on the representation of women or racial and ethnic minorities. The title of Jane Mansbridge's 1999 article exemplifies this approach: "Should Blacks Represent Blacks and Women Represent Women? A Contingent 'Yes.'" Nadia Brown and Sarah Gershon's chapter fits squarely into this research tradition. Whether the descriptive and symbolic representation of women translates into substantive representation for women is contingent, they conclude, on partisanship.

Debate in the U.S. House over the reauthorization of the Violence Against Women Act in 2012 proved very good empirically for Brown and Gershon, largely because the majority of representatives who spoke on the floor were female. Using an intersectional approach, as well as quantitative and qualitative analyses, they explored whether the positions taken by representatives and the content of their comments varied by party, gender, or race/ethnicity of the lawmakers. Brown and Gershon's primary conclusion is that the contours of the debate were shaped most by party. Democratic women were more likely than Republican women to engage in substantive representation of women when debating this domestic violence legislation. In contrast, House Republicans deployed female legislators more symbolically (as bill sponsor, floor speakers, and presiding officer) than as substantive advocates for domestic violence victims. Brown and Gershon's analyses contribute to a growing body of work demonstrating the role of party in influencing women's representation (e.g., Osborn & Kreitzer, 2014; Swers, 2014). By virtue of using C-SPAN videos, however, and by examining racial/ethnic identity alongside party and gender, Brown and Gershon present a more nuanced picture of representation than is typically found in the literature.

PRESENTING SELF: PRESIDENTIAL CANDIDATES WORK THE CROWD

What do political candidates say and do when they work the crowd after a campaign event? More specifically, do these brief encounters resemble the introductory exchanges we engage in when first meeting someone during our day-to-day lives? These questions guide Kurtis Miller's research. Much is known about introduction sequences during everyday conversation. Drawing upon this work, most notably that of communication scholar Danielle Pillet-Shore (2011), Miller analyzes meet-and-greet sessions of presidential candidates at the Iowa State Fair and other venues during the summer of 2015. These interactions between candidates and voters do contain many familiar elements. The two conversants orient their bodies toward each other. Body contact, typically in the form of a handshake, occurs. Greetings are sometimes exchanged. "How are you" inquiries do happen, although less commonly than during typical day-to-day introductions.

Perhaps not surprisingly, introductory exchanges between candidates and the public do depart from everyday situations. As Miller notes, many of these disparities reflect the status differential between the candidate and the person the candidate is meeting. People in the crowd sometimes share their names with the candidates, while candidates rarely use their names during introduction sequences. Little speaking time is devoted to preexisting knowledge claims, or exploring what the two might already know about each other. Very often, candidates and voters thank each other, such as the woman who told Ted Cruz, "Thank you for you bein' here and all you do" followed by Cruz's "thank you very much." Expressions of gratitude rarely crop up in other introduction scenarios. Finally, although Miller's main contribution is in demonstrating whether candidate-voter introductory sequences resemble those we encounter in everyday contexts, he does uncover some interesting differences among candidates. Two candidates, Martin O'Malley and George Pataki, did introduce themselves by using their names whereas the other eight candidates tended not to. Furthermore, the pattern of Hillary Clinton's exchanges was rather different than the other candidates. Miller reasonably suggests that this might be due to societal expectations of how female candidates should act as well as the fact that Clinton travels with a security detail.

AVENUES FOR FUTURE RESEARCH

A few weeks before the 2016 New Hampshire primary, I spent some time in that state to observe presidential campaign politics up close. As an audience member at many campaign events, I couldn't help but notice that some candidates were much better at interacting with the crowd than others. At one extreme was the candidate who engaged well with voters not only after his formal town-hall event, but also throughout. While taking questions from the audience, he queried his questioners, seeming genuinely interested in trying to get to know them and their concerns better. At the other extreme was the candidate who took very few questions after a long speech. When working the crowd, he came to me and I asked whether I could take a picture of him with two 18-year-old women who would be voting for the first time in 2016. His response was essentially, "Make it quick, I need to move on to my next engagement."

As a political scientist, I couldn't help but wonder whether any of this matters. Some candidates are more personable and more like "one of us" than other candidates are, but do these interpersonal traits have broader consequences? Miller's chapter demonstrates the potential of using videos from the C-SPAN library to analyze candidates working the crowd. Building from this, further research could explore if candidates who interact with voters most effectively are viewed more favorably overall and perhaps even are more successful at the ballot box. Furthermore, Miller's analysis of introduction sequences could be expanded, such as by trying to account for individual differences in candidates' interactions. Communication scholars might wish to examine other features of interpersonal communication, whereas psychologists could explore topics such as the candidates' self-presentation styles. As mentioned previously, C-SPAN videos are well suited for this type of scholarship. They present unedited interactions between candidates and voters, in unscripted encounters, and in an easily accessible manner for researchers.

C-SPAN's collection of congressional videos also offers many opportunities to advance scholarship on representation. Building on Brown and Gershon's analyses, scholars could test whether their findings regarding the representation of women apply to other types of bills, such as those less explicitly focused on women than is domestic violence legislation. Representational style in other congressional venues, including committee hearings or investigations, could also be easily explored using material from the C-SPAN Video Library. Finally, C-SPAN video footage could be used to analyze another feature of congressional activity: interpersonal interaction among representatives. During the give-and-take of hearings and floor debates, do lawmakers treat each other with respect and deference equally? Are interruptions and hostile body language more likely to be directed toward certain representatives versus others? Videos of hearings and debates capture real-time interactions, allowing for questions such as these to be analyzed. If some representatives (those in the minority party, women, racial and ethnic minorities, etc.) are indeed more likely to be treated less well than their peers, successfully representing their constituents and the substantive interests of specific groups could be ever more challenging tasks.

REFERENCES

Mansbridge, J. (1999). Should blacks represent blacks and women represent women? A contingent "yes." *Journal of Politics*, 61, 628–657.

Osborn, T., & Kreitzer, R. (2014). Women state legislators: Women's issues in partisan environments. In S. Thomas & C. Wilcox (Eds.), *Women and elective office: Past, present, and future*. Oxford, England: Oxford University Press.

Pillet-Shore, D. 2011. Doing introductions: The work involved in meeting someone new. *Communication Monographs*, 78, 73–95.

Pitkin, H. F. 1967. *The concept of representation*. Berkeley: University of California Press.

Swers, M. L. 2014. Representing women's interests in a polarized Congress. In S. Thomas & C. Wilcox (Eds.), *Women and elective office: Past, present, and future*. Oxford, England: Oxford University Press.

CONCLUSION

The chapters in this book clearly show the range and depth of the research that is possible using the C-SPAN Video Library. The approaches are cross-disciplinary, but collectively advance our knowledge of politics and communication. With such a diverse group of topics and approaches, it is difficult to strike a common theme and conclusion.

Morris and Joy, Castor, and Brown and Gershon examine Congress and congressional policymaking. Morris and Joy address a perplexing question about Congress. For years, political scientists have pondered why individual members of Congress are so popular, but the institution itself has the lowest rating of any of our branches of government. Members of Congress run against the institution—asserting that they are not like all the others. Underlying Morris and Joy's work is the unanswered question: What impact has television had on the institution's popularity? Stated another way, could television be responsible for the low popularity?

The legislative process is not pretty, and that is what Morris and Joy try to test. Some have argued that it is the partisanship that people do not like; while others suggest it is the complexity of the legislative process. Procedural aspects, that are difficult to understand, cause people to be turned off. This is the question that our authors address. Through experimental research, they find that procedural aspects, more than partisanship, is responsible for negative views about Congress. Partisanship suggests action and resolution of conflict. The results show that procedural aspects are less interesting to viewers.

In an era of polarization, perhaps one can take solace that partisanship does not turn off viewers. There is a bit of irony there in that while partisanship is not viewed negatively, gridlock is. Gridlock is the result of partisanship. It will take further research to sort out this difference. Partisan conflict in itself is not viewed negatively, but when the end result is no action, that can result in a negative view of Congress.

The Castor chapter and also the Brown and Gershon chapters look at specific policies enacted by Congress, but their approaches are very different. Castor takes a deconstructive approach, while Brown and Gershon use a more traditional content analysis method. One common theme in these two approaches is the emphasis on language. Castor describes vocabularies that are used to describe the Great Lakes water issues. A fear of diversion of the water dominates the debate. Proponents used an economic vocabulary and arguments, while the opponents used arguments about the public trust.

Both of these congressional chapters use the Video Library to account for all the speakers in the debate. The Great Lakes debate is dominated by regional representatives. The Violence against Women Act debate is dominated by women speakers from both parties. The Democrats tend to attack the bill for ignoring categories of women such as immigrants and Native Americans. Republican women are more defensive in their speeches. This descriptive representation of having women speakers and even women presiding over the session fail to substitute for substantive representation where the substance of the bill matters more. These two chapters are models for others who seek to analyze congressional policymaking. With all the bills debated each year, there is no shortage of congressional policy analysis that can follow either of these approaches.

The two conversational analyses should be of interest to communication scholars. These studies also suggest that the Video Library is full of examples that can be used for conversational analysis. One takes Clinton's grand jury testimony in 1998. The other uses informal candidate meet-and-greet sessions. These are very different events, but the conversational approach relies on the informal communication styles. In the Clinton case, Garcia documents the evasive manner and techniques that he uses to answer and not answer questions. The Miller chapter demonstrates that the informal responses of candidates in this situation are very different from more formal interactions.

There are two chapters that look at debates. Both are ambitious. The Kropf and Grassett paper deals with a large number of campaign debates and continues a line of research represented well by Banwart. Do women and men use different language in these debates? With the large number of female candidates currently running for office and the Hillary Clinton senatorial and presidential candidacies, this is undoubtedly a very important topic. Kropf and Grassett do not find the results that they expect. Men are more inclusive in their debate language. The research method of using the software called Linguistic Inquiry and Word Count employed with computerized text analysis presents an approach that others will want to emulate with the C-SPAN Video Library collection.

In another debate analysis Stewart and Hall build on a long tradition of assessing nonverbal communication started by the Dartmouth Group in the 1980s. Each of the volumes in this series has a paper on facial traits in video analysis. The C-SPAN Video Library is a treasure trove for this type of analysis. With presidential debates there are also split-screen recordings that provide even more opportunities for coding nonverbal reactions. This approach is now well established and the chapters by Kowal (2014) and Bucy and Gong (2015) and now Stewart and Hall (2016) provide a corpus of guidance to future researchers.

The final chapter discussed here is very different in its approach. Kerr examines the Video Library to understand how liberals and conservatives present themselves. He calls this branding. This approach is one of using the search engine of the Video Library to examine video and textual references. It is a common method that we have seen in other papers that use the Video Library. Kerr's research is part of a larger question about whether the conservatives have been more successful in getting their message out and their message established than liberals have been.

This third volume in the research using the C-SPAN Archives series presents depth and diversity. These chapters are not meant to be the last word in research, but a starting point for those seeking to understand the possible. It is hoped that they will encourage others to follow the path of these pioneering studies and advance both their technique and their substantive findings. It is only then that the full potential of the C-SPAN Video Library collection will be realized.

CONTRIBUTORS

Nadia E. Brown is an associate professor of political science and African American studies at Purdue University. Professor Brown received her PhD in political science in 2010 from Rutgers University, with major fields in women and politics and in American politics. She also holds a graduate certificate in women's and gender studies. Dr. Brown's research interests lie broadly in identity politics, legislative studies, and Black women's studies. While trained as a political scientist, her scholarship on intersectionality seeks to push beyond disciplinary constraints to think more holistically about the politics of identity. Brown's *Sisters in the Statehouse: Black Women and Legislative Decision Making* (Oxford University Press, 2014) has been awarded the National Conference of Black Political Scientists' 2015 W.E.B. DuBois Distinguished Book Award from the National Conference of Black Political Scientists; the Research in Excellence Award from the Center for Research on Diversity and Inclusion at Purdue University; and the 2015 Anna Julia

Cooper Best Publication Award from the Association for the Study of Black Women in Politics. She is the author of numerous peer-reviewed articles, book chapters, and book reviews that focus on identity politics in general and Black women's politics more specifically. Dr. Brown and Dr. Gershon (of this volume) recently published a coedited volume *Distinct Identities: Minority Women in U.S. Politics* (Routledge, 2016). Her current research projects address the politics of appearance for Black women candidates and lawmakers.

Robert X. Browning (PhD, University of Wisconsin) is a professor of political science and communication at Purdue University. In 1987 he founded the C-SPAN Archives where he serves as Executive Director. He is the author of *Politics and Social Welfare Policy in the United States*, and the editor of *The C-SPAN Archives: An Interdisciplinary Resource for Discovery, Learning, and Engagement* and *Exploring the C-SPAN Archives: Advancing the Research Agenda*. Awarded the George Foster Peabody Award for its online Video Library in 2010, the C-SPAN Archives is housed in the Purdue Research Park and offers a window into American life.

Theresa R. Castor (PhD, University of Washington) is an associate professor of communication and department chair at the University of Wisconsin–Parkside. She conducts research in the areas of organizational communication, language and social interaction, and social construction. Her current research involves the analysis of how risk and organizational crises are discursively constructed and the intersections of discourse, materiality, and agency, with specific attention to projecting/anticipating future risks, climate- and weather-related problems, and freshwater governance. Her work has been published in *Management Communication Quarterly*, *Communication Yearbook*, *Discourse Studies*, *Journal of Business Communication*, the *Electronic Journal of Communication*, and the *International Journal of Public Participation*.

Angela Cora Garcia is an associate professor in the Department of Sociology at Bentley University, with a secondary appointment in the Department of Global Studies. Her research focuses on conversation analytic studies of talk in institutional settings such as mediation hearings, emergency phone calls, and computer-mediated communication. She is the author of the textbook on conversation analysis *An Introduction to Interaction: Understanding Talk in Formal and Informal Settings* (Bloomsbury Press, 2013). She also conducts qualitative research using semistructured interviews and autoethnographic methods to study the sociology of sports and leisure.

Sarah Allen Gershon is associate professor of political science at Georgia State University. She received her PhD from Arizona State University in 2008. Dr. Gershon's research interests include media and politics, gender politics, and race and ethnicity. Her research has been published in several academic journals, including *Political Communication*; *Political Research Quarterly*; *Politics and Religion*, the *Journal of Women, Politics, and Policy*; *Social Science Quarterly*; and the *Journal of Politics*. She recently published a coedited volume (with Nadia Brown) entitled *Distinct Identities: Minority Women in U.S. Politics* (Routledge, 2016).

Emily Grassett graduated summa cum laude and with honors in political science from the University of North Carolina at Charlotte in May 2016. Her research interests include U.S. Senate elections, rebel groups, and international politics. Her political science honors thesis focused on the funding of rebel groups and how this affects their ability to engage in elections postconflict. She will be working for a political consulting firm in Washington, D.C., and plans to attend law school in the future.

Tim Groeling is a professor and the former chair of UCLA's Department of Communication Studies. He is the author of numerous articles and two books: *War Stories: The Causes and Consequences of Public Views of War* (with Matthew A. Baum; Princeton University Press, 2009), and *When Politicians Attack: Party Cohesion in the Media* (Cambridge University Press, 2010). He has been the recipient of numerous honors, grants, and awards, including the Goldsmith Book Prize and the Bruce E. Gronbeck Political Communication Research Award, funding from the National Science Foundation, and a Copenhaver Award for effective teaching with technology. He is currently leading an effort to digitize and preserve UCLA's massive Communication Studies News Archive.

Spencer C. Hall is currently a graduate student at Vanderbilt University, pursuing the study of American politics, with specific interest in campaign effects and voter decision making.

Michael W. Joy is a graduate of East Carolina University, with a BS in political science and BA in economics. Joy has been recognized by Phi Beta Kappa for academic excellence and has been involved with such diverse groups as the Chancellor's Student Leadership Academy, National Residence Hall Honorary, Pi Sigma Alpha Political Science Honor Society, and the Dean's Student Leadership Council. Joy currently lives in Jeongeup, South Korea, where he teaches English.

Robert L. Kerr, PhD, teaches media law and history and is a professor in journalism and mass communication at the University of Oklahoma. His books include *The Corporate Free-Speech Movement: Cognitive Feudalism and the Endangered Marketplace of Ideas* (2008) and *How Postmodernism Explains Football and Football Explains Postmodernism* (2015). He has twice been named the top teacher in his College, and is a past recipient of the Franklin S. Haiman Award for Distinguished Scholarship in Freedom of Expression. He received his doctorate from the University of North Carolina at Chapel Hill.

Martha E. Kropf is professor of political science and director of the Public Policy PhD Program at the University of North Carolina at Charlotte. Kropf is an expert on election administration and political participation. She is the author of two books: *Institutions and the Right to Vote in America* (in press, 2016) and *Helping America Vote: The Limits of Election Reform* (with David C. Kimball; 2012). Kropf has published her research in journals such as *Public Opinion Quarterly* and the *Journal of Politics*.

Kurtis D. Miller is an assistant professor of communication at Tusculum College. His research focuses on extending interpersonal and organizational communication theories into under-studied contexts, such as uncertainty management for new members of changing organizations and interactions between famous people and members of crowds. His birth and early childhood in Iowa probably had no influence on his interest in presidential campaigning, but it sure makes a good story at a cocktail party.

Jonathan S. Morris (PhD, Purdue University) is a professor of political science at East Carolina University. His research focuses on the media and politics, especially political humor and cable news. He is coauthor of *Politics is a Joke! How TV Comedians are Remaking Political Life*, and has published in several journals, including *Political Research Quarterly*, *Public Opinion Quarterly*, *Legislative Studies Quarterly*, and *Political Behavior*.

Zoe M. Oxley (PhD, Ohio State University) is professor of political science at Union College. Her research interests include the effects of the media on public opinion, gender and public opinion, women in electoral politics, and political psychology. She is the coauthor of *Public Opinion: Democratic Ideals, Democratic Practice* from CQ Press, and she has published articles in several journals, including the *American Political Science Review*, *Journal of Politics*, *Political Research Quarterly*, and *Politics & Gender*.

Joshua M. Scacco (PhD, University of Texas at Austin) is an assistant professor of media theory and politics in the Brian Lamb School of Communication and courtesy faculty in the Department of Political Science at Purdue University. He also serves as a faculty research associate with the Engaging News Project. His research is focused on how emerging communication technologies influence established agents in American political life, including news organizations and the presidency. His research has appeared in journals such as the *Journal of Computer-Mediated Communication*, *New Media & Society*, and the *International Journal of Press/Politics*.

Patrick A Stewart (MA, University of Central Florida; PhD, Northern Illinois University) teaches in the Department of Political Science at the University of Arkansas, Fayetteville. He is a certified Facial Action Coding System (FACS) coder whose research concentrates on the emotional response of followers to leaders. In addition to his book *Debatable Humor: Laughing Matters on the 2008 Presidential Primary Campaign* (2012), he has published research concerning nonverbal communication by politicians in the journals *Presidential Studies Quarterly*, *Political Psychology*, *Motivation and Emotion*, *International Journal of Humor Research*, *PS—Political Science & Politics*, and *Politics and the Life Sciences*. His work on nonverbal communication by political leaders has been published by the *New York Times* and the *Washington Post*, and covered by CNN, NPR, *U.S. News and World Report*, *Wired*, *Forbes*, *New York Magazine*, the *National Review*, the *Huffington Post*, among others.

INDEX

Page numbers in italics refer to figures.

W